KU-262-996

BRITISH

THE ILLUSTRATED HISTORY OF

STEAM

THE LEGACY OF THE STEAM LOCOMOTIVE

RAILWAYS

BRITISH
THE ILLUSTRATED HISTORY OF
STEAM
THE LEGACY OF THE STEAM LOCOMOTIVE
RAILWAYS

DAVID ROSS

Bath • New York • Singapore • Hong Kong • Cologne • Delhi
Melbourne • Amsterdam • Johannesburg • Auckland • Shenzhen

This edition published by Parragon in 2011

Parragon
Queen Street House
4 Queen Street
Bath BA1 1HE, UK

Editorial and design by Amber Books Ltd.

ISBN: 978-1-4454-3506-0

Printed in China

Contents

Introduction

Railway timetables from the age of steam still hold great fascination for many people. But when they were used on a daily basis, they were vital documents. *Bradshaw's Railway Guide* was far from being a slim volume: in 1922 it had 911 pages of timetables. Often these pages were turned with great anxiety, and much licking of thumbs, to aid in cross-referral from one timetable to another. To plan a cross-country journey could be quite a challenge. Here are just two examples from the *Bradshaw* of July 1922. The village of Reedsmouth, in remote Northumberland, was a junction of rural lines on the North British

BELOW A 1990s replica version of the Stephenson 'Planet' 2-2-0 type of 1830, in steam with replica passenger vehicles of the same era. This was the first locomotive which could be said to form a distinct class.

system. To go from there to the metropolis of Newcastle, was it better to take the line eastwards to Morpeth, and change to the North Eastern main line; or to take the line south to Hexham, and meet the North Eastern (former Newcastle & Carlisle Railway) there? Three trains a day went via Morpeth, and the earliest, the 8.00, offered a through carriage to Newcastle. At Scotsgap, another through carriage, from the Rothbury branch, was added; and both carriages, during a fourteen-minute stop at Morpeth, were duly attached to a Berwick–Newcastle train, and went on to reach Newcastle Central at 9.51, with a single intermediate stop at Manors East. On the other hand, the Hexham route, also with three trains a day, offered a through train from Hawick to Newcastle, via Riccarton Junction, which called at Reedsmouth at 7.44, and reached Newcastle at 9.07.

ABOVE Nineteenth-century industrial buildings at the Manchester Museum of Science and Technology rise up behind the replica *Planet*.

CROSS-COUNTRY JOURNEYS

To travel from Newcastle Emlyn, at the end of a Great Western Railway branch in far Carmarthenshire, to Shrewsbury, there were again two options. One could take the branch train to the tiny junction of Pencader, and go southwards to Carmarthen Town station. Here there was a connection with the London & North Western Railway's line through the hills of central Wales to Craven Arms, and on from there to Shrewsbury. Or one could change at Pencader to go north to Aberystwyth and there catch a Cambrian Railways train that wound its way via Machynlleth, Moat Lane and Welshpool to Whitchurch in Shropshire. Neither offered a wholly convenient set of connections. Leaving Newcastle Emlyn at 6.08, reaching Pencader at 6.30, there was a wait of two hours and twenty minutes before a Carmarthen train arrived.

LEFT Former North British 4-4-0 *Dugald Dalgetty*, as BR Class D30 No. 62423, at Reedsmouth with a train for Hexham. The high-level signal-box was typical of this part of the country. The line closed in October 1956.

London, Midland and Scottish Railway
Joint Railways
London and North Eastern Railway
Great Western Railway
Southern Railway
PRINCIPAL LINES OF THE 'BIG FOUR'
Wick
Lybster
Helmsdale
Tain
Dingwall
Porres
Elgin
Banff
Fraserburgh
Keith
Peterhead
Inverness
Kyle of Lochalsh
Boat of Garten
Fort Augustus
Aviemore
Aberdeen
Mallaig
Ballater
Fort William
Kinnaber
Stanley
Arbroath
Killin
Oban
Dundee
Crianlarich
Perth
Stirling
Greenock
Glasgow
Edinburgh
Paisley
Berwick
Ardrossan
Galashiels
Carstairs
Peebles
St. Boswells
Ayr
Moffat
Beattock
Portrush
Coleraine
Morpeth
Londonderry
Larne
Dumfries
Stranraer
Hexham
Newcastle
Silloth
Carlisle
Sunderland
Durham
Cookstown
Belfast
Penrith
Hartlepool
Darlington
Middlesbrough
Whitehaven
Tebay junc.
Stockton
Newry
Scarborough
Hawes junc.
Northallerton
Dundalk
Barrow
Greenore
Settle
Lancaster
York
Fleetwood
Leeds
Selby
Preston
Blackburn
Grimsby
Liverpool
Manchester
Doncaster
Birkenhead
Louth
Sheffield
Holyhead
Lincoln
Stockport
Chester
Newark
Wells
Cromer
Crewe
Ruabon
Derby
Pwllheli
Nottingham
Gobowen
Stafford
Trent junc.
Spalding
Kings Lynn
Great Yarmouth
Barmouth
Leicester
Shrewsbury
Birmingham
Peterborough
Norwich
Moat Lane junc.
Aberystwyth
Rugby
Ely
Worcester
Northampton
Cambridge
Cardigan
Ipswich
Hereford
Bedford
Fishguard
Banbury
Carmarthen
Harwich
Talyllyn junc.
Hitchin
Gloucester
Oxford
Pembroke
Newport
Swindon
Swansea
Didcot
Southend
Reading
Cardiff
London
Queenborough
Bristol
Bath
Basingstoke
Ilfracombe
Canterbury
Tonbridge
Andover
Minehead
Redhill
Dover
Barnstaple
Winchester
Ashford
Salisbury
Folkestone
Taunton
Brighton
Lewes
Bude
Southampton
Hastings
Portsmouth
Newhaven
Eastbourne
Exeter
Padstow
Bournemouth
Weymouth
Bodmin
Truro
Plymouth
Kingswear
Penzance
Falmouth

LEFT The single-platform terminus at Newcastle Emlyn in the 1950s, with evidence of road-rail co-operation. An 0-4-2T waits at the head of a train to Pencader.

After that, things improved. It reached Carmarthen at 9.35. A train on the London & North Western line to Llandilo left at 10.10, and arrived at 10.54. A Swansea (Victoria)–Shrewsbury train stopped at Llandilo at 11.10, and reached Shrewsbury at 14.07. Using the Aberystwyth route, one could get up later, catching the 10.10 to Pencader, arriving at 10.40. The Aberystwyth train arrived at 11.00 and reached that terminus at 12.50, allowing ample time for lunch and a stroll by the sea before the Cambrian Railways' Whitchurch train left at 15.05. This train got to Welshpool at 18.03, and the Shrewsbury connection left there at 18.25, finally bringing the traveller, by way of Yockleton and Cruckmeole Junction, to the General Station at Shrewsbury at 19.25.

Basic Facilities

Journeys could be much more complicated than those. But it is many years since it was possible to travel by train from Reedsmouth, or Newcastle Emlyn. The same applies to the more than two thousand other places which have lost their railway stations, and usually also their railway lines, since the 1960s, if not even earlier. But in 1922, for most people, the train was the only possible means of medium- or long-distance travel. It is impressive, studying the close-packed pages of *Bradshaw*, to see how many through carriages and cross-country services were offered by the railway companies. Usually they were slow, and often involved long, rather mysterious periods of standing still at rustic junctions where fields stretched away on either side. Often they had no buffet or restaurant car, and passengers had to rely on their own supplies, or purchase luncheon baskets or hasty meals at stations that had refreshment rooms. *Bradshaw* advertised such travellers' friends as Brand's Meat

BELOW Beyer, Peacock Ltd of Manchester built this 2-4-0 express engine of 1864 for the London Brighton & South Coast Railway.

Lozenges, 'sustaining and invigorating'. Main line trains were more likely to have catering facilities. Those that did had their services noted in bold type, sometimes adjusted to the time of day. The London & North Western's 8.30 express from Manchester to London, for example, had a Breakfast and Luncheon Car. The London Brighton & South Coast's 21.35 from Brighton to Victoria had a First-Class Pullman Supper Car.

Though Richard Trevithick's original locomotive ran in 1804, the steam railway era in Britain really began with the opening of the Stockton & Darlington Railway in 1825, and lasted 143 years, until the last few steam-hauled trains of British Railways in December 1968. That period, of almost a century and a half, saw greater change across the country than in any comparable period before it. The railways themselves displayed a prime aspect of this, but

BELOW 'Cauliflower' 0-6-0 No. 28484 crosses the girder bridge over the Glenderamackin River, at Threlkeld, on the Cockermouth, Keswick and Penrith line, with a passenger service in the 1940s.

they also were the agents and drivers of change in a tremendous variety of ways.

This book traces many of these developments, and shows how the railways formed the supply and distribution system to support a quadrupling of the population and a vast growth in industrial productivity. From an early stage, the technological marvel of self-propelled power was taken for granted. People became accustomed to the benefits brought by the railway and to the increasing range of technical aids in daily life. For most of the second half of the nineteenth century, the railways did not have a very good public reputation. It was felt – with some justice – that they could be faster, and safer, and pay more attention to their passengers' needs. Information systems were inadequate; delays were often unexplained and hardly ever were the subject of apology. Towards the end of the century, things began to improve, and the first fifteen years of the twentieth century were in some ways the finest era of the steam railway in Britain. Locomotives, still painted in bright colours, became larger, more powerful, and more capable of sustained high speed with a heavy train. Passenger carriages reached heights of opulence not attempted before or since – even Third Class had cushions, and arm rests for passengers in long distance trains. It was still the age of the passenger compartment rather than the open saloon, as favoured on US railroads: this last vestige of the old stage coaches persisted in Great Britain for as long as steam traction. After 1914, though railways long remained the prime transport system, the effects of war, industrial depression and road competition all inflicted a succession of blows on the railway companies, preventing or reducing the opportunities for maintenance and improvement.

The Illustrated History of British Steam Railways has been written, and its pictures specially selected, to provide a wide-ranging survey of Britain's steam railways, how they evolved, how they were run and their effect on life and society in both town and country.

ABOVE *Evening Star*, the last steam locomotive built by British Railways, at Swindon in 1960, was the only 'Standard' 9F 2-10-0 to carry a name, with lettering in the old Great Western style.

LEFT When Axminster was the junction for Lyme Regis: on 11 June 1935, an ex-LSWR Adams 4-4-2 tank, No. 3125, is waiting to detach through carriages for the branch line from a west-bound train.

1 • The Pioneering Years

A few short decades will see the railways grow into a major industry dominated by speculators and managers. But in the early days it is the engineers – among them George and Robert Stephenson, Isambard Kingdom Brunel and Joseph Locke – who are at the heart of the steam railway.

LEFT Stephenson's *Invicta*, the first locomotive to run in Kent, was shipped from Newcastle to Whitstable in 1830. Not a particularly successful engine, it was unable to cope with the gradients on the line. A failed attempt to sell it nine years later led to its storage and subsequent preservation.

OPPOSITE The restored Furness Railway 0-4-0 No. 20 is Britain's oldest working locomotive, built in 1863. In 1870, it was sold to the local steelworks and converted to a saddle tank, working in this form until 1960. The Furness Railway Trust restored it to its original appearance, and it has been in steam again since January 1999.

By the year 1804, the steam engine had already been a well-known and accepted fact of industrial life for several decades. A few inventive pioneers had succeeded in driving ships with it. But on land, it had always been fixed in one place, driving pumps or other machinery. No self-propelling steam engine had ever run on land. Then, in February 1804, the owner of Penydarren Ironworks, in South Wales, made a hefty bet with a local rival. He wagered the sum of 500 guineas that a steam-powered 'travelling engine', set up on his mining tramroad by the Cornish engineer Richard Trevithick, would pull a load of 10 tons (10.16 tonnes) from Penydarren to Abercynon, a distance of just under 10 miles (16km). The bet was taken. The locomotive, first in the world to run on rails, made the journey in 4 hours 5 minutes, with 70 men clinging on to the wagons, which were loaded with pig iron. The brittle, flanged cast-iron track was broken and cracked by the engine's wheels, however, and

LEFT *Puffing Billy*, built by William Hedley and Christopher Blackett for the Wylam Colliery in Northumberland in 1813, had a rocking-beam drive, transmitting power via cog-wheels to the four driving wheels, and was among the first engines to have exhaust steam directed through the long chimney.

Penydarren went back to pony-hauling for 30 years. But that day, on a bleak Welsh plateau, the steam railway was born.

Twenty-one years later, it came of age. On 27 September 1825, the Stockton & Darlington Railway opened for business, the first public steam-powered railway in the world. In 1830, it was followed by the Liverpool & Manchester. With its great embankment across Chat Moss and the imposing Sankey Viaduct, this line showed how railways would slice through the landscape. Linking two fast-growing industrial cities, it also showed how railways would bring

BELOW In July 1925, the centenary of the world's first public railway, the Stockton & Darlington, was celebrated by a number of events mounted by the ever publicity-conscious LNER, including this re-enactment of the first train, drawn by a replica of *Locomotion*.

a revolutionary change to inland transport. Although its opening was marred by the death of the politician William Huskisson – ironically, an enthusiastic supporter of railways and the first victim of a railway accident – the progress of railways was unstoppable.

0-4-0 LOCOMOTION S&D 1825

Tractive effort: 1900lb (862kg)
Axle load: 4704lb (2.13 tonnes)
Cylinders: two 9½x24in (241x609mm)
Driving wheels: 48in (122cm)
Heating surface: 60sq ft (5.6m^2)
Superheater: n/a
Steam pressure: 50psi (3.5kg/cm^2)
Grate area: 8sq ft (0.74m^2)
Fuel: Coke – 2200lb (1 tonne)
Water: 400gall (480 US) (1.8m^3)
Total weight: 15,232lb (6.9 tonnes)
Overall length: 10ft 4in (3.15m)

EXPERIENCE, THE BEST TEACHER

There was a great deal to learn, and no one to teach it. The first generation of railwaymen had to make up the rule book, and the technical handbooks, as they went along. One of the reasons the first railway engineers avoided all but the gentlest of gradients was that no one knew how effective the adhesion of an iron driving wheel, on an iron rail, would be on a rising grade. Locomotive building was still in its infancy. Before the Liverpool & Manchester opened, a set of trials was held at Rainhill in October 1829 to determine the type of engine that would be used on the line. A prize of £500 was offered for the one which best satisfied the conditions laid down. Timothy Hackworth, engineer of the Stockton & Darlington, entered his *Sans Pareil*, and two other designers also competed. The competition was won with ease by George Stephenson's locomotive *Rocket*, which was in fact the only competitor to stay the course.

By this time, a number of technical problems had been solved. Trevithick had developed the flanged wheel, to run on a flat rail, in 1805. George Stephenson (father of Robert), whose engine-building business began in 1814, improved on the blast system that drew steam through the boiler; with his colleague Henry Booth he also devised the multi-tube boiler.

Rocket had amazed and alarmed spectators by reaching 29mph, but it was soon eclipsed by a new model from the same designer. This engine, *Planet*, further developed in *Patentee* of 1837, showed the shape of things to come; indeed, its basic design remained that of all British

ABOVE *Locomotion*, built by George Stephenson, was the first engine to operate on a public railway – between Stockton and Darlington – on 25 September 1825. It was also the first to have its wheels linked by coupling rods, but was soon to be superseded by more powerful and less fragile types.

LEFT A replica of *Rocket*, built in 1980, steams on the Kent & East Sussex line at Tenterden. The paint scheme is the original livery of the Liverpool & Manchester Railway. Despite *Rocket*'s triumph at Rainhill, it, too, was very soon made obsolete by further developments.

RIGHT George Stephenson (1781–1848), born near Wylam, Northumberland, was the man chiefly responsible for giving the steam locomotive the form which it kept throughout its existence. A self-taught engineer, he also surveyed lines, designed bridges and laid the tracks – a true father of the steam railway. Portrait by John Lucas, engraved by T.S. Atkinson.

steam locomotives for more than a hundred years. Unlike all previous engines, whose cylinders drove the pistons from above or behind, *Planet*'s cylinders were in front, tucked beneath the smoke-box and inside the frame.

A minor but very public attribute of each locomotive was its name. In these early years, a 'class' of engines was hardly thought of; each was an individual, with improvements on its predecessor, and a name was deemed to be the best identifier. The tradition of naming engines, which goes back to their very beginning, would be continued by most British lines.

In its first year, the Liverpool & Manchester Railway carried 460,000 passengers. This was more than four times the previous number of travellers between the two cities. For both business and pleasure, the railway opened up new opportunities. From the first, animals were carried, as well as people and freight. Just as the first railway carriages simply reproduced the form of the road coach, so goods wagons copied the side-loading farm cart – as also did the cheapest passenger vehicles, which

0-2-2 ROCKET L&MR 1829

Tractive effort: 2405lb (1089kg)
Axle load: 5600lb (2.54 tonnes)
Cylinders: two 8x17in (203x432mm)
Driving wheels: 56½in (143.5cm)
Heating surface: 117.75sq ft (10.9m^2)
Superheater: n/a
Steam pressure: 50psi (3.52kg/cm^2)
Grate area: 8sq ft (0.74m^2)
Fuel: Coke – 2200lb (1 tonne)
Water: 400gall (480 US) (1.8m^3)
Total weight: 9520lb (4.32 tonnes)
Overall length: 7ft 2in (2.18m)

possessed neither roof nor seats. Luggage was carried stagecoach-style, on the roofs of carriages.

The success of these Northern lines was noted in the South. Even in 1824, a line had been planned between Canterbury and Whitstable, in Kent, replacing a plan for a canal. It was opened in 1830 and its first engine, *Invicta*, was sent down from Newcastle by sea. The Leicester & Swannington, in the Midlands, was opened in 1832. Another early line was in Cornwall, Trevithick's home county, between Bodmin and Wadebridge in 1834. Other short lines opened elsewhere, sometimes to be incorporated into main trunk lines later on. But for the engineers – and for investors, who were beginning to get interested in the money-making potential of railway companies – the great prize was London, the biggest city in the world. The capital's first railway was the London & Greenwich, with its terminus at London Bridge. The tracks were carried all the way on a brick viaduct, which set the pattern for other South London lines. The heyday of the commuter line was still some way off, and the promoters' eyes – in this first, relatively mild outburst of 'Railway Mania' – were mainly on trunk routes from the capital.

Giants of the Early Days

The great men of the early railway were not in fact the promoters or managers, but the engineers. Among these were the towering figures of George Stephenson and his son Robert. George had begun as a working man in the collieries of the North East. An interest in engines, and his own drive and energy, made him into first a mechanic, then an engineer. The intelligence, common sense and determination of George Stephenson underlay the success of the Liverpool & Manchester Railway. The design both of its bold permanent way and of its

BELOW *Northumbrian*, which was built by Stephenson in 1830, less than a year after *Rocket*, embodied many improvements, including a smoke-box, horizontal cylinders and a boiler incorporating water-space around the firebox – all fundamentals of locomotive design. It also had what was probably the first true tender.

PLANET
38
F
RA5

2-2-0 PLANET L&MR 1830

Tractive effort: 1371lb (622kg)
Axle load: 6720lb (3 tonnes)
Cylinders: two 11x16in (279x406mm)
Driving wheels: 60in (152.5cm)
Heating surface: not known
Superheater: n/a
Steam pressure: 50psi (3.52kg/cm^2)
Grate area: 8sq ft (0.74m^2)
Fuel: Coke – 2200lb (1 tonne)
Water: not known
Total weight: 17,920lb (8 tonnes)
Overall length: 9ft 6in (2.9m)

locomotives set the pattern that others would follow. Robert Stephenson inherited his father's gifts as both a civil and a mechanical engineer. As new railway schemes were proposed, the developers would inevitably come to the Stephensons, or to one of the engineers whom they had trained. It was not only their expertise that was wanted; their very names spelt success to potential investors. It would be George Stephenson's immense personal authority, as much as anything else, that later won the so-called 'Battle of the Gauges'.

The first of the great trunk lines was the one which linked London to Birmingham, Manchester and Liverpool. It began in the North with the Grand Junction Railway, running from Birmingham to join the Liverpool–Manchester line at Warrington. Its engineer was Joseph Locke, another of the giants of the early railway age. He had been trained by George Stephenson, though later he and the Stephensons became rivals, with no love lost between them. At this time there was no great distinction between the branches of engineering – the same man might design and lay out the line and also design the locomotives which ran on it (sometimes with unfortunate results). Locke, however, stuck to the civil engineering side, and he employed locomotive engineers. A vital contribution from him was the development of a heavier, 'double-headed' rail in 1835, allowing for heavier trains and a greater axle-loading on the engines. The engineering contractor for the Grand Junction line was another notable figure, Thomas Brassey, who was

OPPOSITE A modern replica of the first of the 2-2-2 'Planet' class, shown here at Loughborough on the Great Central Railway in 1993. The wood-lined boiler can clearly be seen. The cylinders are set under the smoke-box, inside the frames, a practice which would continue to be common in British locomotive design.

BELOW The elevated Blackfriars Station, looking north across the Thames in 1863. The link via Blackfriars to the Great Northern at King's Cross had a strategic potential that remained undeveloped beyond suburban services.

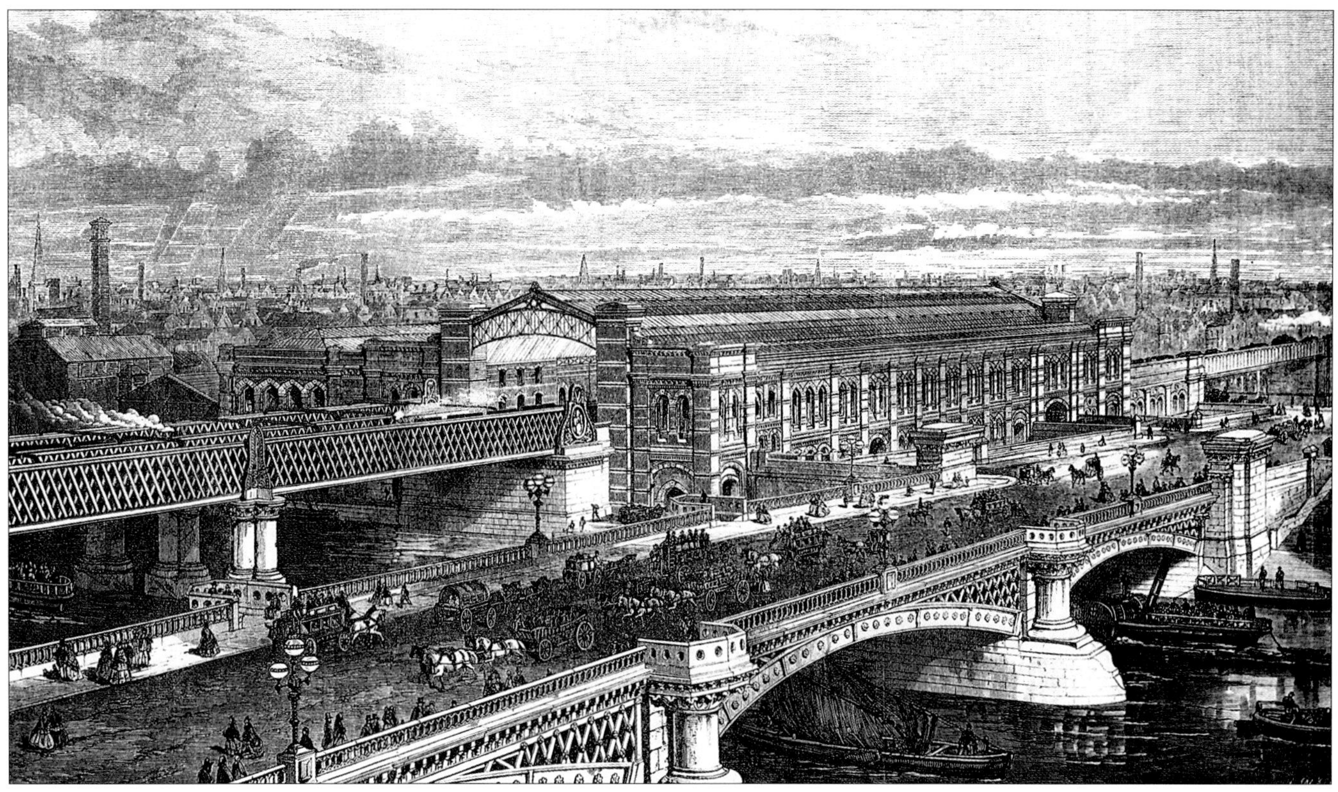

to become the greatest railway contractor in the world, laying tracks as far away as Russia, and often managing the lines he built. In Britain alone, Brassey's company laid 1700 miles (2736km) of railway.

South of Birmingham, the London & Birmingham line was engineered by Robert Stephenson. The Grand Junction opened on 4 July 1837, and the London & Birmingham followed on 9 April 1838. Its opening had been delayed by the digging of Kilsby Tunnel, 2400yds (2.19km) long, just south of Rugby, where unexpected underground springs had caused massive problems. Its eventual cost was more than three times the estimate of £99,000. The line's London terminus was at Euston Square. Trains made a refreshment pause at Wolverton, where later a locomotive and carriage works would be set up.

With these long lines, and the cuttings and embankments they needed, emerged the nomadic army of navvies (the name, from 'navigators', shows how they began as canal diggers). Part of Brassey's genius was in the management of these strong and frequently unruly men (a day's work for one of them was reckoned as the equivalent of hoisting 20 tons (20,321kg) of earth to a height of 6ft/1.83m). The shanty towns where they lived attracted all kinds of merchants, con men and entertainers of various sorts.

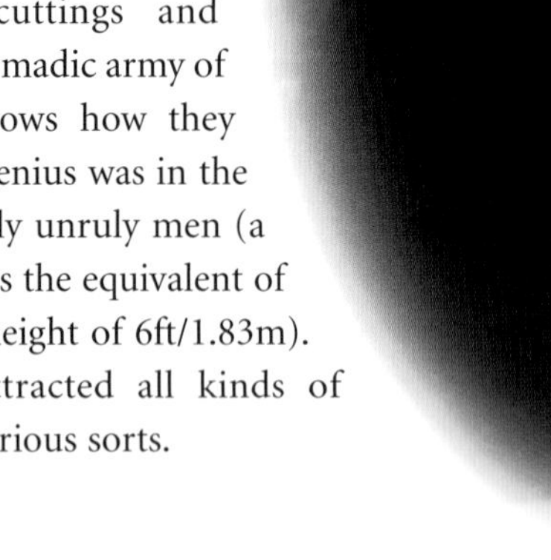

ABOVE Isambard Kingdom Brunel (1806–59) was an engineer of genius who liked to operate on the grand scale. It was he who decreed the broad gauge to which the original Great Western Railway was built. His vision was of a London–New York service, in which passengers would transfer at Bristol from magnificent trains on to magnificent steamships – all of his own design.

BRUNEL, MAN OF VISION

The trunk-route map of 1838 looked like a wobbly T with a narrow top bar, but already its shape was changing. As early as 1832, a group of Bristol merchants put forward a plan for a London-to-Bristol line. They employed a 27-year-old engineer, Isambard Kingdom Brunel, son of an immigrant French engineer, who already had experience of tunnelling beneath the Thames and was known in Bristol for his design of the Clifton Suspension Bridge over the River Avon. The board's plan had been to appoint the man who

LEFT The coats of arms of the Cities of London and Bristol are linked in the arms of the Great Western Railway, reminders of the Committees in each place which together founded the company.

gave the lowest estimate, but Brunel roundly told them that this would be a disaster and that he would withdraw his application if they maintained this policy. The board caved in, and he was appointed. From then on, Brunel was the moving spirit of the railway.

His concept for the line, already known as the Great Western Railway, was on the grand scale. Its gauge was to be, not Stephenson's 4ft 8½in (1.435m), which was based on the old colliery tramways, but 7ft ¼in (2.14m). Instead of being laid on transverse sleepers, it was laid on long baulks placed underneath the rails. In a few weeks of hectic activity, the line was surveyed. A 1.8-mile (2.9km) tunnel was planned to cut through the limestone ridge at Box, east of Bath. Because this was to be built on a grade of one in 100, regarded by many as impossible to climb, there was a great public outcry, whipped up by such vocal opponents of the railway as Dr Dionysus Lardner, who also claimed that, if the brakes failed going downhill, the train would come out of the tunnel at 120mph (193km/h). It took until 1835 to get Parliamentary approval to build the line, and the works were not completed until 30 June 1841.

By this time, a line from Bristol to Exeter was also under construction further west. As on the Birmingham line, a central spot was chosen for a refreshment stop and engine-changing. This was Swindon. Engine-changing proved unnecessary, but the refreshment stop was traditional for decades. It was a profit source to the company, which received a high rent from caterers, who in turn charged inflated prices for indifferent fare. Brunel wrote: 'I have long ceased to make complaints about Swindon. I avoid taking anything there when I can help it.'

Brunel had original ideas about everything, but not all of them worked in practice. The locomotive designs for the new railway proved hopelessly inefficient and unreliable.

ABOVE A distinguished veteran, this well-tank 2-4-0T was designed by Joseph Beattie for the London & South Western Railway in 1863 and built in 1874. With two companions, it survived on the Bodmin–Wadebridge line in Cornwall into the 1950s, although it acquired a new boiler more than once during its long life.

LEFT A distinctive feature of the Newcastle–Carlisle line is its lofty, jettied signal boxes, which give the signalman an especially good view of approaching trains. This one is at Haltwhistle.

OPPOSITE A Bristol-bound local train drawn by a Great Western tank locomotive approaches Box Tunnel, once described by an opponent of railways as 'monstrous, extraordinary, most dangerous and impractible'.

Fortunately he had hired a young mechanical engineer trained by the Stephensons, Daniel Gooch. The 20-year-old Gooch had a nightmare task in getting Brunel's huge-wheeled and underpowered machines to work, but eventually his own designs would make the Great Western the fastest and most punctual of all the early lines.

The next port to be joined to London was Southampton, via the London & Southampton Railway (renamed London and South Western Railway from 1839). Engineered by Joseph Locke, it cut through the downs in steep cuttings, with minimal tunnelling, and crossed valleys on lofty embankments. It was opened in stages and completed on 11 May 1840. At that time Southampton was not a major seaport, and it was perhaps surprising that Portsmouth, the country's chief naval base, was not selected as a terminus. But the British government, unlike those of some other countries, took no part in planning the rail network. Instead, new schemes were promoted by the businessmen and industrialists of individual towns. It was the railway which made Southampton into a major transatlantic seaport. Later, too, the LSWR would be an efficient carrier of large numbers, but its first effort – to take racegoers to the Derby at Epsom in 1838 – caused a riot when far too many people tried to board the race-day specials at its Nine Elms terminus (Waterloo would not become the London terminus for another 10 years).

BELOW The GWR's first Great Western, Daniel Gooch's 4-2-2 design of 1846, embodied most of the features of his broad-gauge engines to come. In size, power and performance, it outclassed any locomotive then in existence.

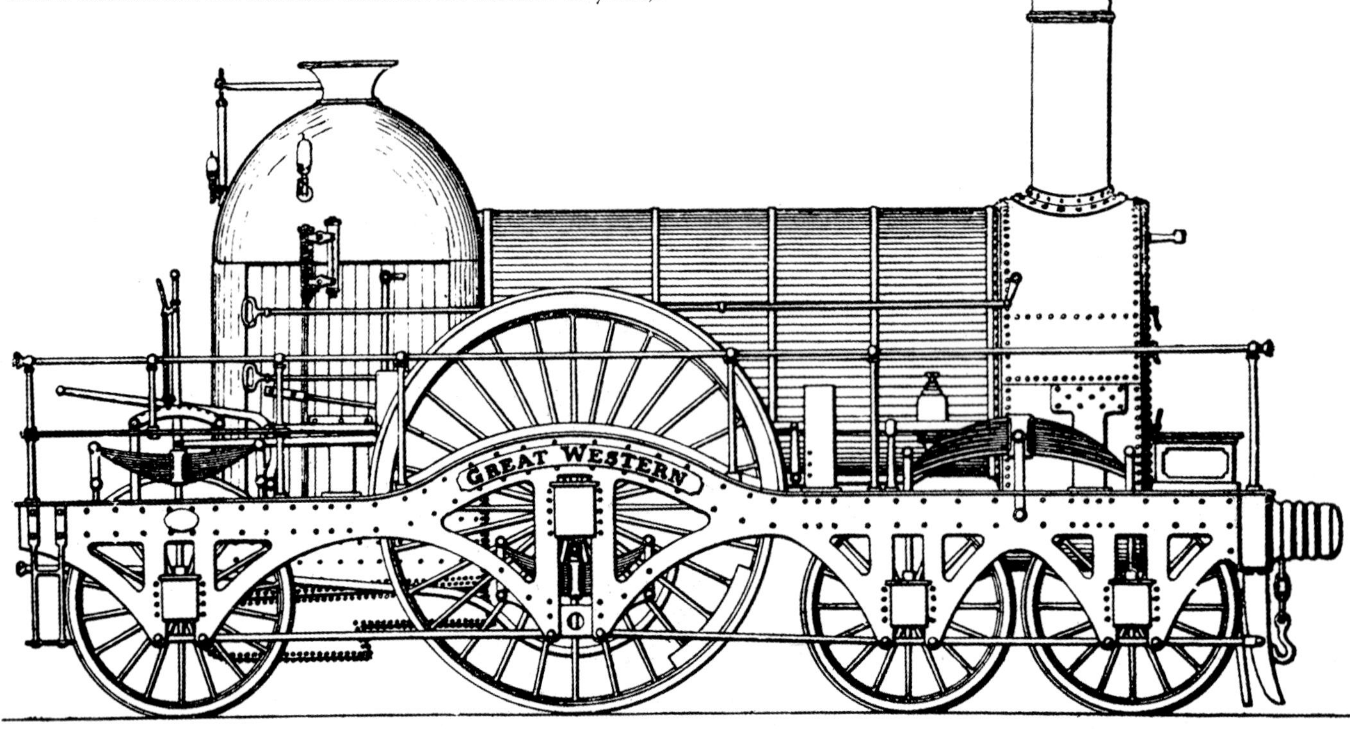

ABOVE Track-laying was a labour-intensive activity, as this 1930s painting by Stanhope Forbes, R.A., shows. Each section of track was maintained by a separate 'gang', but bigger teams combined for the heavy work of laying new track-lengths. Rail weights more than doubled between the 1830s and 1870s.

By 1839, the first east–west cross-country line was completed, the Newcastle & Carlisle. With its main purpose being to transport iron ore from Cumberland to the Tyne, it made a regular and handsome profit. It was on this line that a ticket clerk, Thomas Edmondson, invented the ticket-printing machine, which remained standard on all lines for many decades and made him a rich man.

Control under the Board of Trade

In 1844, with schemes for new railways arising all over the country, the government made an effort to control the development of railways and to regulate existing companies. The Board of Trade, led by its president, William Ewart Gladstone, aimed to bring some strategic vision into the piecemeal and competitive proposals for new railway lines. This was fiercely resisted by the companies, which were among the first to employ what today would be known as PR consultants. The main result was the 'Parliamentary train': every company had to run at least one daily train conveying third-class passengers, 'in carriages provided with seats and protected from the weather', at a speed not less than 12mph (19.3km/h) and at a fare of a penny a mile for adults. This compulsory service was often provided grudgingly and at extremely unsociable hours. The railway companies were interested in the 'carriage trade', first- and second-class passengers, who paid the full fare. The Board of Trade remained the government body responsible for railways, but it played no part in determining their progress.

In the early 1840s, many people felt that the country by now had all the railway lines it really needed. In fact, a huge expansion of railway planning and building was about to take place. This was the 'Railway Mania', which raged in 1845–46. It had several causes. One was the failure of the government to achieve control over railway development. Others were the increasing reliability of rail technology and the growth of public acceptance of the new transport medium.

But the chief cause of the mania was greed, which operated at various levels of the social scale. At one end, it brought in rich men such as George Hudson, a former Lord Mayor of York, who saw opportunities in railway management to get much richer. At the other end, many ordinary individuals borrowed money to buy shares in new companies, which they then immediately sold at a profit, in order to

ABOVE The LNWR co-opted Britannia and her lion onto its coat of arms. The companies liked florid heraldry, and their emblems could be found on every kind of equipment, from cast-iron platform seats to crockery in the restaurant cars, as well as locomotives (see next page).

LEFT The preserved Furness Railway 0-4-0 No. 3, *Coppernob*, a goods engine designed by William Bury and built in 1846, is a more substantial machine than the lightweight types built by Bury for the London & Birmingham Railway. It shows his typical bar-frame construction (frames inside the wheels).

buy even more shares in other companies. To secure shares, only a 10 per cent deposit was necessary, with the balance to be called up later. When the companies came to call up this balance, the shareholders were often unable to pay. In the middle, many well-off people invested heavily in what their financial advisers assured them was a bonanza.

As more and more new companies were formed, the existing ones tried to fight them off by building new lines, often with no other intention than to block rivals' plans. Railway shares, selling at completely unrealistic prices, were the equivalent of the dot.com shares of the first years of the twenty-first century. In 1845–46, 6710 miles (10,798km) of new railway were authorized, including extensive mileage in Scotland and Wales. More than 1200 new companies put forward schemes, at an estimated total cost of more than £500,000,000 – a colossal sum even for a fast-growing industrial economy.

The crash was inevitable. Much of the promised capital investment was non-existent. Many companies collapsed even before their schemes were approved. Others got approval, but had no money to proceed. Thousands of people were ruined, and a

BELOW The fine paintwork of the 1890s is shown off in this detail of a class T3 express engine of the London & South Western Railway.

special body had to be set up to deal with the problems of lines which had Parliamentary approval, but no funds to complete, or sometimes even to begin, the work.

There were sound business reasons for getting an Act of Parliament to promote a railway. Most importantly, it gave the company compulsory purchase powers to get the necessary ground, albeit at a fair price. While towns were glad to get railways, rich landowners often strongly resisted. The London & Birmingham Railway avoided the important town of Northampton, despite the town's enthusiasm to be on the line, mainly because the owners of the land around the town created so many difficulties. A loop eventually linked Northampton to the main line in 1875.

OPPOSITE The elegant left-hand driver of F.W. Webb's celebrated 1874 'Precedent' class 2-4-0 Hardwicke, built by the LNWR at Crewe, and one of the participants in the great Race to the North of 1895. The opening in the wheel-splasher is not just for aesthetics: it provides a space via which the inside axle-box can be lubricated.

Formation of the Great Companies

For those railway companies which survived the mania, the worst effect was to make them jealous and mistrustful of one another. The growing complexity of the system had already made it necessary, in 1842, to establish the Railway Clearing House, a central office which recorded all movement of goods and passengers through the system from company to company, allocating the routes taken and the correct share of the carriage cost to each one. Membership was voluntary, and it was not until 1865 that the majority were linked in. Beginning with a staff of six clerks, it would have almost 3000 employees by 1910. Its annual handbook was an indispensable volume for anyone in the transport business. The Clearing House was almost the sole example of cooperation, other than when the companies banded together to resist any new efforts at government 'interference'.

Through the troubled years of the mania and the more cautious time that followed, the main arteries of the rail system became clear. The great companies that would gradually dominate the scene were being formed. In October 1848, the London & Birmingham, Grand Junction and Liverpool & Manchester amalgamated to form the London & North Western Railway, which would proudly call itself the 'Premier Line'. The Midland Railway was formed in May 1844 out of a cluster of lines between Birmingham and Derby. After overcoming intense opposition from the Midland and the London & Birmingham, the Great Northern Railway was established in May 1846, running in a direct line from London to York. With the Great Western and the London & South Western, these lines held the central ground. In between, and to east and west, were dozens of other companies, most destined to be swallowed up eventually by one of the titans. Only in the South East of England were there lines which remained outside their net.

The most prominent railway figure at this time was George Hudson, nicknamed the Railway King, the first non-engineer to achieve national fame through the railways. Hudson was involved with a great number of lines, mostly between the Midlands and York and in the North East, but also with the Eastern Counties Railway, which ran from London to East

Anglia and had hopes of extending northwards to York and so providing an East Coast London–Edinburgh service. Hudson, through his involvement with the Midland Railway and the Eastern Counties, and also with the York–Newcastle–Berwick line, coordinated virulent opposition to the Great Northern's plans for a direct London–York line. Then, in 1848, Hudson, who controlled the little York & North Midland line, made a deal with the Great Northern, allowing GN trains to use his line from Burton Salmon, just north of Doncaster, into York, rather than make its own line (at this time the GN was extremely short of money). Although a director of the Midland and the Eastern Counties Railways, Hudson had made a private arrangement with an 'enemy' line for his own benefit. Up to then, there had been subdued murmurs against his business practices, but now critics became more vocal. Committees of board members and shareholders began to examine the accounts of Hudson-managed companies and found all kinds of evidence of illegal share-dealing and manipulation of the accounts. By 1849, the former Railway King had fallen into disgrace.

In 1848, it became possible to travel by train from London to Glasgow following the completion of the Lancaster & Carlisle Railway and the Caledonian main line through the Clyde and Annan valleys. These lines, in British terms at least, were mountain ones, topping summits of almost 1000ft (304m) at Shap and 1014ft (309m) at Beattock. At Beattock and Tebay stations, banking engines were kept into the 1960s to help push heavy trains up the grades. The establishment of the West Coast route into Scotland spurred on the East Coast interests. They had no

ABOVE A portrait of George Hudson (1800–71) in his prime. Something comes through of the truculence and confidence, as well as the self-importance, of the great railway promoter. In his hand, no doubt, is another prospectus for a line which cannot fail to make its shareholders' fortunes.

LEFT Few people in history have built themselves such a memorial as I.K. Brunel's Saltash Bridge over the Tamar, finished just before his death in 1859 and completing the mainline connection from Paddington to Penzance. The main tubular/suspension spans are each 455ft (138m) long.

mountains, but two water gaps over the Tyne and the Tweed, bridged by Robert Stephenson's High Level Tyne Bridge in 1850 and the Royal Border Bridge at Berwick-upon-Tweed in 1849, the year in which through services from London to Edinburgh began. A more formidable gap was bridged in 1850 by Robert Stephenson's Britannia tubular iron bridge across the Menai Strait, completing the Irish Mail route between London and Holyhead. In 1859, a further spectacular bridge was completed, Brunel's last great achievement, the Royal Albert Bridge over the Tamar estuary at Saltash. He died soon after it was finished.

The up-and-over technique of the West Coast line was less feasible with trans-Pennine routes. Lengthy tunnels were dug to link the manufacturing districts to east and west of the backbone of England. In 1845, the Woodhead Tunnel, between Manchester and Sheffield, was opened, the

ABOVE Robert Stephenson's Royal Border Bridge of 1849 displays the quality of the best Victorian engineering. More than a hundred years later, in 1954, LNER class A4 4-6-2 *Golden Plover* takes a northbound express off the bridge and into the station at Berwick-upon-Tweed.

longest in the world at 3 miles and 22 yards (4.85km); in 1850, it was pipped by the Standedge Tunnel, just 35 yards (32m) longer.

ABOVE Deliberately imitating the great arches at the ends of Roman roads, the London & Birmingham Railway's classical-style gateway to Euston Station. Designed by Philip Hardwick, it was intended to reassure anxious passengers. It was pulled down in 1966 prior to the building of the new Euston.

Station Design on a Grand Scale

By mid-century, some of the great stations were established in a form still recognizable today, such as Newcastle Central, built in 1850–51, and York. Brunel's original building at Bristol Temple Meads still stands, though reduced to being a car park. In London, several great terminal stations were established by 1854, including Euston, Paddington (rebuilt by Brunel and Wyatt in 1854), King's Cross, Liverpool Street and London Bridge. Engineer-architects created these buildings; one of them, Lewis Cubitt, designer of King's Cross (first much criticized and later much admired for its 'plainness'), had also laid out the Great Northern line.

Railway architecture was often designed to reassure the inexperienced and anxious traveller. The great Doric arch at the entrance to Euston deliberately recalled the triumphal arch at the end of a great Roman road. Every style of architecture was used in station building. Some were grand – Hereford had a sort of Tudor mansion, while Kidderminster an imitation half-timbered Elizabethan house – but many lines, such as the South Eastern, could only afford 'temporary' wooden sheds, which often lasted a very long time. Builders had to resolve new problems, such as the ventilation of engine sheds. The first roundhouse was built at Derby in 1840. Much use was made of new material such as wrought and cast iron. Vast, curving aisled halls such as that of York Station were completely new in architecture. In 25 years from the opening of the Stockton & Darlington, the railways had come to express a proud confidence in the newly invented business of mass transport of goods and people.

This confidence was based on considerable improvements in the power and reliability of that

OPPOSITE The original train shed at Temple Meads Station, Bristol, designed by I.K. Brunel and built in 1841. The central tracks of termini such as this were used as carriage sidings, until traffic expansion required additional platforms.

LEFT The original Britannia bridge across the Menai Strait, designed by Robert Stephenson and William Fairbairn, built in 1850 and completing the Irish Mail route from Euston to Holyhead. After a fire in 1970, it was rebuilt on steel arches, reopening in 1972.

most vital feature, the locomotive. By 1850, the engines of the early years were obsolete, and the survival of even a handful is remarkable. The Planet type had established the basic layout and components, but many improvements of detail were made, and there was a steady increase in size, weight and tractive effort. Some lines designed their own engines from the start. The Liverpool & Manchester benefited from Robert Stephenson's, while the young Great Western suffered from Brunel's.

BELOW A modern view of York Station, designed by Thomas Prosser and built in 1877. The curving nave was without precedent in conventional architecture.

Locomotive works were already established to build engines for collieries. They built to each designer's specification or supplied their own models, as required. Bury, Curtis and Kennedy supplied the engines for the London & Birmingham line and were notorious for their lack of innovation. Their answer to demands for greater power was simply to supply more of their little 2-2-0 four-wheeler engines, of which as many as four might be attached to a single train. Eventually their contract was terminated. More enterprising builders included Robert Stephenson's own company, also E.B. Wilson of Leeds, and Sharp, Roberts of Manchester, though there was still a degree of trial-and-error in design and construction.

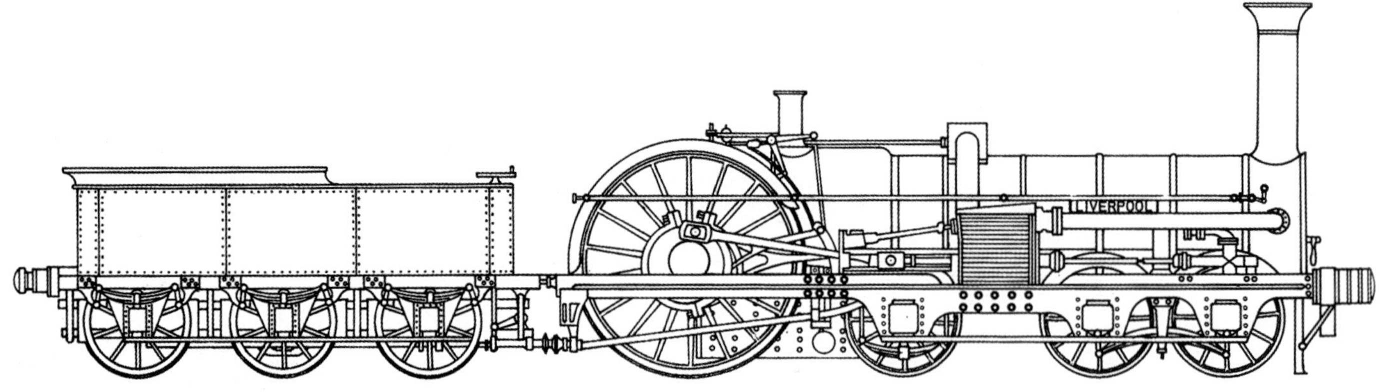

6-2-0 LIVERPOOL LNWR 1848

Tractive effort: 5700lb (2585kg)
Axle load: 26,208lb (11.9 tonnes)
Cylinders: two 18x20in (457x508mm)
Driving wheels: 96in (243.8cm)
Heating surface: 1529sq ft (142m^2)
Superheater: n/a
Steam pressure: 100psi (7.05kg/cm^2)
Grate area: 16sq ft (1.48 m^2)
Fuel: Coke
Water: 1600gall (1921 US) (7.3m^3)
Total weight: 57,344lb (26 tonnes)
Overall length: 18ft 6in (5.6m)

Each railway company had to set up workshops for maintenance and repair, and soon also for building. The Grand Junction moved its works from Edge Hill in Liverpool to the greenfield site of Crewe in 1843. The Great Western started the growth of Swindon in the same way in 1840. Doncaster became the home of the Great Northern's 'Plant' in 1853, more than doubling its population. These places were company towns where everything was owned by the railway. Even the vicar of Crewe was appointed by the head of the locomotive works (Francis Webb just happened to appoint his own brother).

ABOVE Thomas Russell Crampton (1816–88) patented his rear-drive locomotive in 1843.

BELOW On the completion of the East Coast main line between London and Edinburgh in 1850, the Great Northern Railway elaborated its already gaudy heraldic design by including the Scottish thistle and English rose – united by railway.

Small is Beautiful

British steam locomotives have always been considered relatively small compared to those of other countries. The main reason is the tight loading gauge, self-imposed by the first builders – Brunel excepted – for operating reasons. The first engines were built to run on tightly curving tracks in the narrow confines of collieries and factory yards. Later, when overbridges and tunnels were necessary, the smaller the required height and width, the cheaper the construction. Designers had to excel in getting the maximum amount of steam from a boiler which, even in the twentieth century, could be hardly more than 6ft (1.83m) in diameter.

The first trains were very lightweight, especially the passenger trains. For these, the single-driver 2-2-2 engine was the most common motive power. For freight, the 2-4-0 and the longer-lasting 0-6-0 (with smaller driving wheels, but more of them) were the rule. The frame – the basic body structure supporting the boiler and resting on the axles – could be inside or outside the wheels; usually, except on the Great Western, it was inside. According to the designer's choice, the cylinders might be inside the frame, invisibly driving a crank axle, or outside, with connecting rods exposed. From early on, there was a preference for inside cylinders and the apparently effortless effect of movement they made. A Scottish engineer, Patrick Stirling, scornfully likened an outside-cylinder engine to 'a laddie running with his breeks down'.

Incidentally, these early locomotives were not great polluters. Most burned coke and made little smoke. Each main depot had coking ovens, to convert the coal into coke before it was used to fire the engines. The locomotives themselves were brightly painted in the company's livery and usually embellished with copper domes and fittings. They were kept in a state of high polish. Often the engine driver ran his machine under contract to the company, himself paying the fireman and cleaners.

Influential Engineers

Through the 1840s and 1850s, the job of mechanical engineer became steadily more specialized, and, with the work of construction of the line largely done, he became the company's most important non-administrative officer and very often a law unto himself. Significant design improvements were made, such as William Fernihough's use of balancing

BELOW In 1863, the world's first underground railway, the Metropolitan, opened in London. Cut-and-cover tunnelling was the method used, seen here in an engraving of 1868, showing navvies hard at work digging out the junction at Baker Street for the Uxbridge line.

ABOVE In 1863, Archibald Sturrock designed a steam-tender 0-6-0 for the GNR, with an auxiliary engine driving the six tender wheels. It was unpopular with the crews and was removed when his successor rebuilt the engines, as seen here.

BELOW The GWR 4-2-2 *Iron Duke*, built in 1847, represents Daniel Gooch's standard express type. This would remain the basic traction of GW mainline services until the abolition of the broad gauge in 1892.

weights on the driving wheels to counterbalance the cranks. This innovation, on the Eastern Counties line, soon became universal. Engines began to be more substantially built and they lasted longer. Some of Daniel Gooch's single-drivers of 1840 lasted until the 1870s, though they acquired new boilers in the 1850s. (The process of cannibalization began early, whereby an apparently new locomotive might contain much of various predecessors. Rebuilds were frequent, and sometimes fictional, all designed to avoid incurring the capital cost of a completely new machine.)

Gooch was probably the most influential locomotive man of the mid-century. His achievement was based on providing engines with ample boilers, with steam pressure at 100psi (7.05kg/cm^2), which was standard for the time. Their performance was outstanding. His *Great Western* 2-2-2 of 1846 ran from Paddington to Swindon at almost a mile a minute with a 100-ton (101.6-tonne) train in June of that year. Gooch also introduced scientific testing of locomotives, using a dynamometer car the equipment of which could measure the speed and power output. It was thought that such achievements were only possible on the broad gauge until one of Gooch's trainees, Archibald Sturrock, brought what he had learned to the Great Northern.

Sturrock, a Scot, was keen to speed up the East Coast route, and in 1853 he built a 4-2-2 express engine. Unlike previous British express types, the front four wheels were a bogie – prior to this, most engines had been on a rigid wheelbase with no pivoting wheels. But this 4-2-2 was

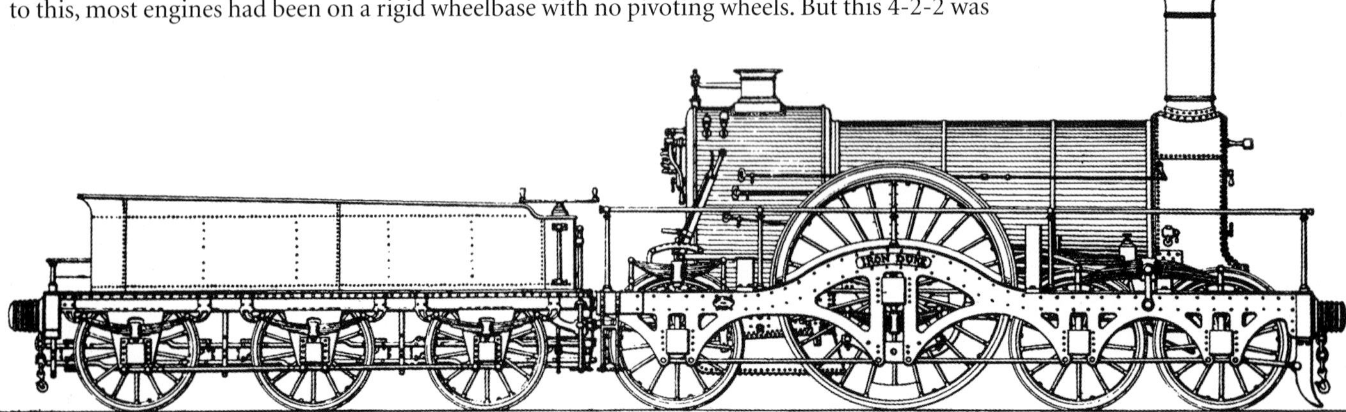

a one-off: the time for racing to the North was not yet come, and Sturrock's other express engines were 2-4-0s and 2-2-2s, though with the very high boiler pressure of 150lb (68kg) and with fireboxes twice the size of anything that had gone before on the 'standard' gauge. Sturrock also designed a steam tender for his 0-6-0 freight engines, with steam piped to auxiliary cylinders which drove the tender wheels.

Another able designer, John Gray, was the inspiration behind the highly successful 'Jenny Lind' 2-2-2 type, built by E.B. Wilson's Railway Foundry at Leeds, which ran first on the London Brighton & South Coast line in 1847. Gray demonstrated that boilers could be mounted high above the wheels without making the engines prone to capsize. Among other major developments of the 1850s was that by Charles Markham on the Midland

ABOVE No broad-gauge locomotive has been preserved, but this view of a replica of *Iron Duke*, under steam, gives an indication of their imposing appearance. Even as mid-century approached, and speeds of up to 60mph (96km/h) became common, the enginemen were denied a cab.

LEFT The 2-2-2 'Bloomer'-type locomotive, designed by J.E. McConnell in 1851, ran the trains on the London-Birmingham stretch of the LNWR. Eventually they came in three sizes: small, big and extra-large (1861). Here, 'Big Bloomer' No. 851 *Apollo* stands at Coventry in 1879.

2-2-2 BLOOMER LNWR 1851

Tractive effort: 8500lb (3854lb)
Axle load: 27,664lb (12.5 tonnes)
Cylinders: two 16x22in (406x558mm)
Driving wheels: 84in (213cm)
Heating surface: 1448.5sq ft (106.6m^2)
Superheater: n/a
Steam pressure: 150psi (10.57kg/cm^2)
Grate area: not known
Fuel: Coke/coal
Water: 1600gall (1,921 US) (7.3m^3)
Total weight: 66,080lb (29.9 tonnes)
Overall length: 18ft 10in (5.74m)

Railway: a big firebox which efficiently burned bituminous coal was achieved by building an arch of firebrick across the leading end. The coke ovens speedily disappeared.

Up to 1861, the LNWR built locomotives at both Crewe and Wolverton, for its northern and southern sections, as if the Grand Junction and London & Birmingham were still separate companies. The chief at Wolverton from 1849–61 was J.E. McConnell, famous for his 'Big Bloomers' introduced in 1851 (their nickname coming from Mrs Amelia Bloomer, a pioneer of ladies' trousering). Still with 2-2-2 wheel arrangement, the Bloomers followed Gray's example in having a high-set boiler, with the then very high pressure of 150psi (10.57kg/cm^2). McConnell also designed the basic form of six-wheeled tender used by most other engine designers to replace the original, inadequate four-wheeled water-cart type. At Crewe, Francis Trevithick (son of locomotive pioneer Richard) was in charge when its first locomotive, the 2-2-2 *Columbine*, appeared in 1845. Many designers, notably Joseph Beattie on the London & South Western, tried their hand at improvements, often with an eye on royalties from patents, but the most successful engines were invariably those least festooned with such gadgets as feedwater heaters or double fire-boxes (which burned coke in front and coal behind).

BELOW William Dean's GWR standard-gauge successors to the 'Iron Duke' class are represented here by the handsome 4-2-2 *Great Britain*, built (as a 2-2-2) in 1892. The massive domes were protected by sacking while the locomotives were on shed: appearance on the road had to be pristine.

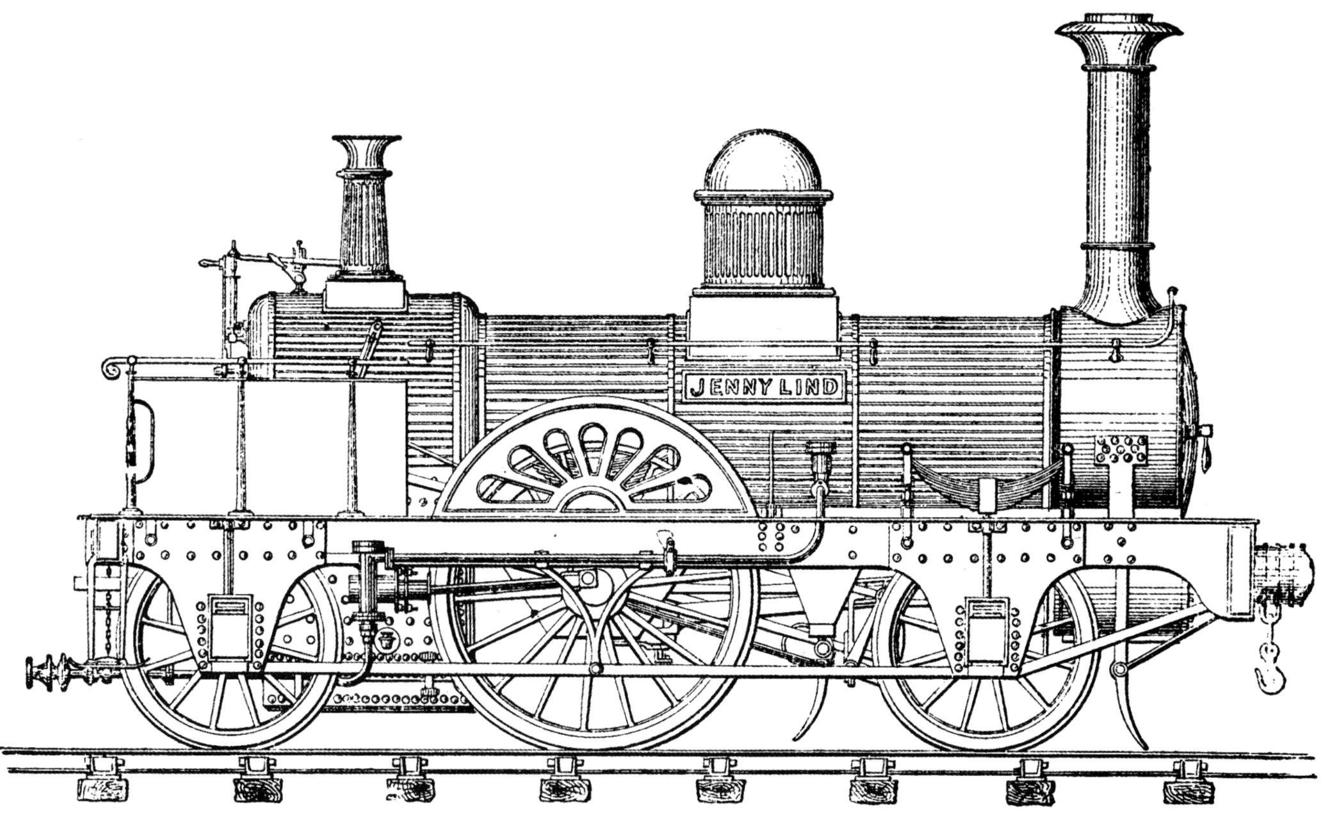

0-2-2 JENNY LIND 1847

Tractive effort: 6300lb (2857kg)
Axle load: 22,400lb (10.15 tonnes)
Cylinders: two 15x20in (381x508mm)
Driving wheels: 72in (183cm)
Heating surface: 800sq ft (74.3m^2)
Superheater: n/a
Steam pressure: 120psi (8.46kg/cm^2)
Grate area: not known
Fuel: Coke
Water: 1600gall (1921 US) (7.3m^3)
Total weight: 53,760lb (24.4 tonnes)
Overall length: 13ft 6in (4.12m)

ABOVE Named after Jenny Lind, a Swedish singer popular with mid-nineteenth century British audiences, and designed in 1847 by David Joy, this neat 2-2-2 was built as a works venture by the Leeds Engine Foundry and sold to the London Brighton & South Coast Railway. Many were also exported.

Surprisingly perhaps, the first 25 years of railway operation saw the introduction of many aspects which are more familiar from later years. The Grand Junction had a 'bed-carriage' which anticipated the sleeping car. The first Travelling Post Office was introduced on the same line in 1838, using a converted horsebox as a sorting carrriage, and in the same year the automatic pick-up of mail bags from the lineside was introduced. Organized excursion traffic began in 1841 with Thomas Cook's temperance picnic outing from Leicester to Loughborough – the first venture in what became an international business – and received a powerful boost from the Great Exhibition of 1851. Great improvement was made to the rails themselves and to the permanent way. Brunel's baulk road, rigidly fixed into the ground by log piles, had to be unfixed and given the same elasticity as lines laid on transverse sleepers.

BATTLE OF THE GAUGES

Despite some flirtations in East Anglia and Scotland with a 5ft (1.52m) or 5ft 6in (1.68m) gauge, the great majority of new schemes utilized the 4ft 8½in (1.43m) gauge established by George Stephenson. The only exceptions were schemes originated or supported by the Great Western, which insisted on Brunel's gauge being used. The advantages and disadvantages of

LEFT Although intended to show the chaotic nature of the change-of-gauge at Gloucester, this engraving of 1853 in fact also shows how the railway companies provided elements to make it as efficient as possible: the platform at truck level and the derricks.

BELOW The curves and gradients of the Axminster–Lyme Regis branch of the LSWR led to to the retention of these 4-4-2 tank engines, designed by William Adams for the LSWR in 1882, into the 1960s.

ABOVE John Ramsbottom's 2-2-2 'Problem' class for the LNWR was a very successful type, despite its name. These locomotives were capable of hauling lightweight trains at high speed. During the 1860s, their regular duties were Liverpool and Manchester expresses and the Irish Mail. By now reduced to secondary services, No. 803 *Tornado* stands at Carlisle in 1899.

'broad' or 'narrow' were widely argued. In 1844, Gloucester became the storm centre of the 'Battle of the Gauges'. Here the broad-gauge Bristol & Gloucester, allied to the Great Western, met the standard-gauge Birmingham & Gloucester. Every passenger and goods item travelling between Bristol and Birmingham had to be transferred to another train at Gloucester, with consequent delays. The GWR's proposed solution was to widen the track all the way to Birmingham, and talks on amalgamation were held in January 1845 with the Birmingham & Gloucester. Satisfactory financial terms were not reached, however, and the Midland Railway, in the person of its deputy chairman John Ellis, leapt into the gap. A deal was struck between the Midland and the two Gloucester companies, which resulted in the Midland leasing the lines of both and thus acquiring mainline access to Bristol. Not only was this a blow to the Great Western's expansion plans, it was a death blow to further development of the broad gauge.

At the end of 1844, broad-gauge mileage was just under 10 per cent of the total, then 2236 miles (3598km). But the broad gauge had the reputation of being faster, safer and more reliable. There were many railways still to be built, and the use of the narrower gauge did not seem inevitable. In one of its less hesitant forays into railway affairs, the government appointed a Gauge Commission in 1845. Despite acknowledging a far superior performance by broad-gauge engines, the Commissioners reported in early 1846 in favour of the narrower gauge. Parliament duly made it a requirement of all new railways to be of Stephenson's gauge, except when they were built as extensions to the broad-gauge lines already existing in the West Country, South Wales and the West Midlands.

SOUTHERN
1556
CONSTRUCTED AT
ASHFORD WORKS

2 • The Old Companies

Now part of the fabric of national life, the railway network spreads across the country in an ever more complex system, run by over a hundred companies. Often, they are competing for the same limited number of passengers, and the inevitable result is rivalry and hostility. Each one proudly maintains its individuality.

LEFT 'Flying Dutchman' was a famous racehorse of 1849, and the GWR named its morning mail train between London and Bristol as the *Dutchman*. Here, the down service passes Worle Junction behind a Gooch 4-2-2 on Brunel's original 'baulk road' track.

OPPOSITE A late Southern Railway style of lettering is shown on this South Eastern & Chatham P-class 0-6-0, designed under the charge of Harry Wainwright in 1910, built at Ashford Works, and originally intended for push-pull passenger service. The station is Tenterden, on the Kent & East Sussex Railway.

Between 1850 and 1860, the pioneering and early phases came to an end. The railways were now part of national life and playing a vital role within the industrial and financial economy. By 1856, they were carrying double the amount of freight sent by canal. From its initial half-hearted efforts to exercise control, the government had backed off, and railway companies were in a state of free competition. The effects of this were more obvious in some areas than in others. Kent, with its commuter towns, farm traffic and lucrative cross-Channel routes, was served only by the South Eastern Railway until 1858. This monopoly was broken by the advent of the East Kent Railway (later renamed London Chatham & Dover). Every significant town in Kent, apart from Folkestone, was eventually served by both railways. The duplication was in most cases unnecessary and financially wasteful. The revenues were not great enough to make both companies profitable. As a result, the services offered by both were poor, the stations mean and the trains slow and dirty. The other side of competition was shown by the occasional flaring-up of price wars between the northern companies, which brought fares down for a short time at least.

The great men of the first generation had been the constructor-engineers. By the 1850s, with the trunk-route network largely established, the main railway companies had become large and complex businesses. The great men were now the general managers, such as Charles Saunders of the Great Western, John Ellis of the Midland and Edmund Denison of the Great Northern. Mostly these were men of vision and action, as well as of honesty, sagacity and common sense. Mostly, but not all. The first general manager of the London & North Western, Captain Mark Huish, has been described as 'perhaps the most ambitious figure which even Victorian industry can show'. Unlike George Hudson, Huish's pursuit of power was not motivated by money; he wanted power for its own sake. His ambitions were for the LNWR to dominate totally all other railways, and for himself to be the dictator of the LNWR. Seeing the independence and growing strength of the Great Northern as the main impediment to his

BELOW Patrick Stirling designed this 4-2-2 class in 1870 for the Great Northern Railway, and No. 1 has been preserved. Although considered by many to be one of the most beautiful of locomotives, and the favourite of Stirling himself, its outside cylinders and other visible means of traction were something of which he normally disapproved.

ABOVE As suburban services became busier, longer trains and larger engines were needed. This imposing 4-6-4T was built by R.H. Whitelegg in 1922 for the Glasgow & South Western Railway. The same designer had produced a very similar engine for the London Tilbury & Southend line in 1913. Unusually, the GSW engines could be driven from either side of the cab.

goals, he set up an alliance known as the Euston Confederacy, drawing in the Midland, the Manchester Sheffield & Lincoln, the Lancashire & Yorkshire, and even the Eastern Counties and North British railways to hem in and obstruct the GNR.

Unscrupulous Tactics

An ex-army man, Huish was combative and quarrelsome by nature. He was also a slippery negotiator whose word could not be trusted. Newspapers of the time called it 'the Battle of the Railways' when, in January 1856, the Great Northern and the London & North Western (the latter with its allies in the Confederacy) failed to renew an agreement on level-pegging fares and charges between London and towns in Yorkshire and Lincolnshire served by both lines. The Euston party were first to reduce fares. King's Cross followed suit, then Euston reduced the fares again, with further reductions following from the East Coast. Passenger traffic soared, but at no profit. 'If this goes on,' said Edmund Denison, chairman of the GN, 'I should think the great majority of my West Riding constituents, washed and unwashed, will visit London in the course of next week.' (Like several other railway chiefs, including Daniel Gooch and George Hudson, he was a member of Parliament.)

Something more akin to a war happened in 1850 on the less remunerative routes between Birkenhead and Birmingham, one operated by the Shrewsbury & Birmingham and Shrewsbury & Chester companies, the other by the Shropshire Union company, whose track was leased by the North Western. At the orders of Huish, the North Western applied illegal strong-arm tactics

against the smaller companies and attempted to destroy their trade by charging ultra-low fares between Shrewsbury and Wolverhampton on his less direct route via Stafford. An army of North Western navvies forcibly prevented the Shrewsbury & Birmingham from getting a siding laid to the Birmingham Canal; troops had to be called out to halt the ensuing battle. Huish then attempted to hijack the Shrewsbury & Birmingham by buying shares in it and passing them to his employees. In this way, a so-called shareholders' meeting illegally elected a new board of directors, who attempted to force through an alliance with the North Western. In the end, Huish was outmanoeuvred, and the Shrewsbury companies amalgamated with the Great Western, securing routes for the latter from London and South Wales to Birkenhead on Merseyside.

By the later 1850s, time was running out for Captain Huish. His battles to increase the LNW empire had

BELOW A publicity notice advertises the features offered by the East Coast Joint Service in the mid-1890s.

CORRIDOR LAVATORY CARRIAGES OF THE MOST IMPROVED
DESCRIPTION ARE ATTACHED TO ALL THROUGH TRAINS.
SLEEPING CARS ARE RUN ON ALL NIGHT TRAINS.
CORRIDOR DINING CAR TRAINS RUN ON WEEK-DAYS BETWEEN
EDINBURGH (WAVERLEY) AND LONDON (KING'S CROSS).
FULL PARTICULARS OF TRAIN SERVICE ETC. CAN BE HAD
ON APPLICATION TO THE SUPERINTENDENT.
EAST COAST RAILWAYS, 32 WEST GEORGE STREET, GLASGOW.

ultimately cost the company both profits and reputation. His frequent efforts to promote 'amalgamation' – for which read takeover – with the Great Western, the Midland and the Manchester Sheffield & Lincoln regularly came to nothing. He had broken agreements so often, and made so many enemies, that his confederacy fell apart. With heavy hints of his impending dismissal in the air, Huish submitted his resignation in September 1858 and disappeared from the railway scene.

OPPOSITE The invention of steam-powered sanding gear extended the life of the slippage-prone 'single driver'. Samuel Johnson's 4-2-2 'Spinner' class was built for the Midland Railway in 1897. It was the last and most powerful single, with some surviving into the 1920s. No. 119, in immaculate condition, is seen here at Bedford in 1901.

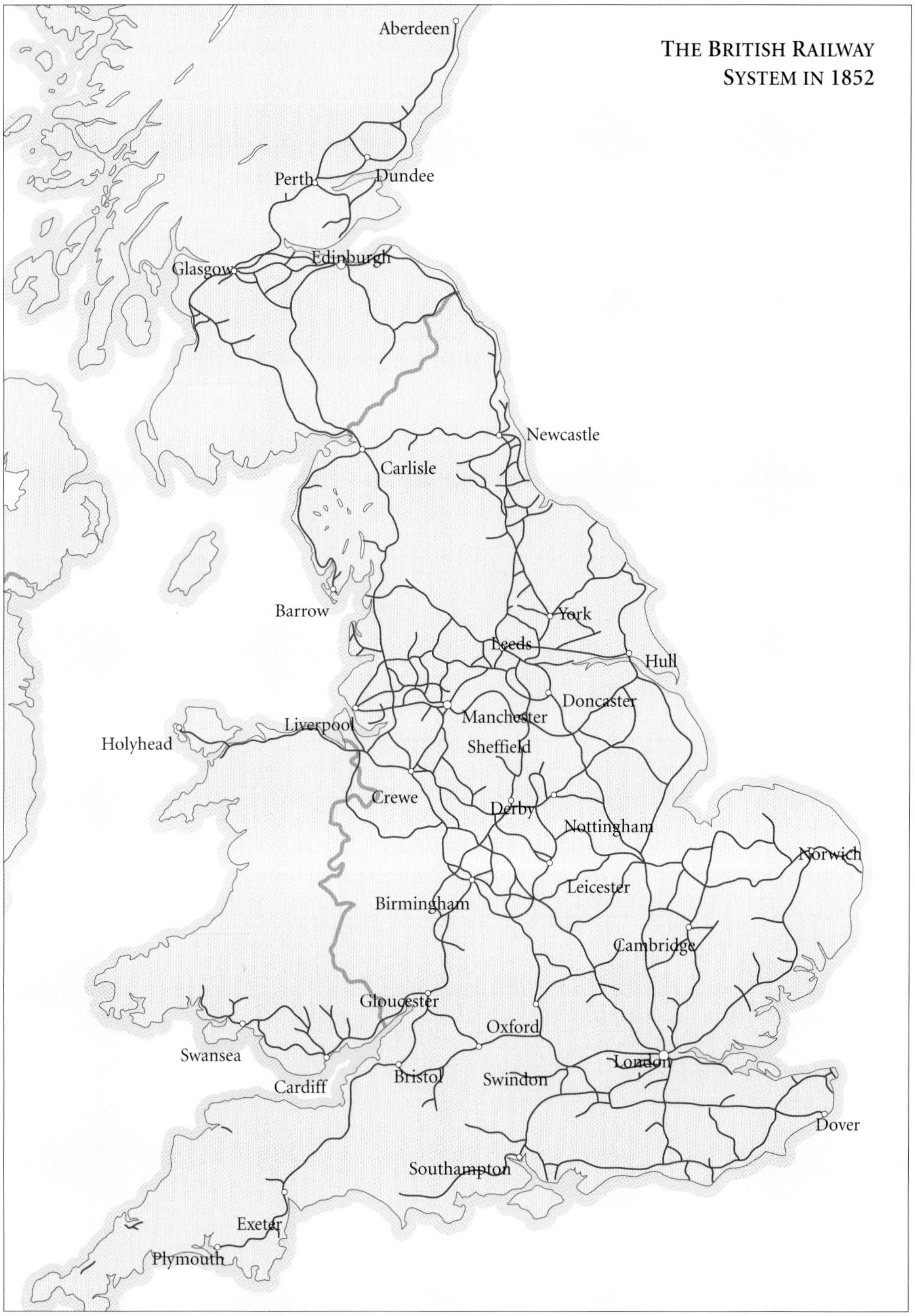

THE BRITISH RAILWAY SYSTEM IN 1852

Aberdeen
Perth
Dundee
Glasgow
Edinburgh
Newcastle
Carlisle
Barrow
York
Leeds
Hull
Doncaster
Holyhead
Liverpool
Manchester
Sheffield
Crewe
Derby
Nottingham
Norwich
Leicester
Birmingham
Cambridge
Gloucester
Oxford
Swansea
Cardiff
Bristol
Swindon
London
Dover
Southampton
Exeter
Plymouth

ABOVE Samuel Johnson's meticulous approach to design is shown in the symmetry of this Midland 2-4-0 Class 101 passenger engine.

In Search of Easy Money

Far more of an out-and-out villain was John Parson, who presided over the affairs of the Oxford, Worcester & Wolverhampton Railway from 1851 to 1856. At least Huish was out to serve the interests of his company; Parson was one of those who saw the railway as a means of getting rich by chicanery. The OWW had been conceived as part of the Great Western's broad-gauge network, but its funds ran out before any building was done. Parson, failing to prise extra cash from the GWR, turned to its LNWR rivals and made a deal to build the line on standard gauge, though its enabling Act clearly specified broad gauge. For several years, Parson wriggled out of the Great Western's demands to have broad gauge laid. Largely to spite his rivals at Paddington, Huish sent his Euston–Wolverhampton trains via Bletchley to Oxford and thence over the OWW. Parson's only aim was to sell the company to the GWR – or anyone – for a handsome profit. In the end, the 'Old Worse and Worse' amalgamated with the Worcester & Hereford and Newport Abergavenny & Hereford railways, the combined line taking the name of West Midland Railway from 1860. In September 1861, the West Midland was amalgamated with the Great Western. Parson was briefly a GW director and was last heard of when he

OPPOSITE A diminutive 'Terrier' 0-6-0T, No. 55, leaves Sheffield Park station on a Bluebell line train. This was class A1, designed by William Stroudley in 1872, for the London Brighton & South Coast Railway.

ABOVE Former Southern Railway locomotives on shed at Reading in the mid-1950s: two Maunsell N-class fast goods 2-6-0s and one of the long-lived D1 4-4-0s.

resigned from the board of the Hammersmith & City line in London. Knowing that particular land would be required by the company, he had bought it at £820 an acre (0.4ha) and attempted to sell it to the company at £10,000 an acre.

The great majority of railway chairmen and officials, who were honest men, had also to be tough and suspicious-minded, as there were many people who saw railways as a way to easy money. Even under the eagle eye of Denison, the GNR was able to be swindled out of £220,000 between 1848 and 1856 by a relatively minor official, Leopold Redpath, head of the share registration department.

Autocrats at the Helm

By training and custom, the men who ran the railways were autocrats. Sir Richard Moon, who ran the LNWR for 30 years from 1861, was the director chiefly responsible for speeding Huish on his way in 1858. He also fired the easy-going Francis Trevithick as chief mechanical engineer (CME) and replaced him with the far tougher John Ramsbottom. He terrified his directors as much as he did the staff. One very senior official, arriving one day at Euston at 9 a.m., was curtly informed: 'Sir, the North Western starts work at eight.' Probably the greatest railway administrator of them all, Moon ran the company with iron rectitude. His officials were informed that 'a North Western officer keeps his promises. But he will be careful what he promises in the first place'.

Some general managers were more open-minded than others, and progress often tended to come from those who had experience of other systems than the British. James

BELOW The architecture of some country stations could at times verge on the sumptuous, as Chathill in Northumberland shows.

LEFT Conversation piece at York: framed by wrought-iron columns and girders, two preserved veteran engines rest at the platform in a scene that replicates the steam age of the 1890s.

Allport, who had begun as one of Hudson's lieutenants, went to the USA before returning and ultimately taking charge of the Midland Railway. Apart from astute if sometimes devious management to enlarge his company – which he extended from central England to become the third Anglo-Scottish main line – he studied the tastes and needs of all its customers, actual and potential. In 1872, the Midland put third-class carriages on all of its trains. Other lines continued with first and second only, third still being relegated to the Parliamentary train or to inconvenient hours. Two years later, Allport went further and abolished second class – in effect turning third into second by replacing the wooden seats with cushions. Other companies were outraged at such pandering to the public, but all had to follow the Midland's lead (some took a very long time). At the top end of the price scale, Allport was also responsible for introducing Pullman cars from the USA to Great Britain. They did not form whole trains, but were attached to the Anglo-Scottish expresses.

BELOW In the heart of the Grampians, at the highest point reached by British mainline railways (1484ft/ 452m), a Jones 'Big Goods' 4-6-0 of the Highland Railway shows it has steam to spare as it hauls a Perth–Inverness goods through the Pass of Drumochter.

LEFT The Midland Railway's monogram in tilework, from the station at Shackerstone, Leicestershire. Although the era of brands was yet to come, all the railway companies set great store by public recognition. Conscious of being among the country's biggest businesses, they were proud of their identity.

Another managerial figure with a visionary streak was Sir Edward Watkin, who trained in the school of Huish, but ended as a baronet and elder statesman. Watkin was the planner of the new Great Central route from the Midlands to London, but long before that his grand scheme was a Channel tunnel, which would be the Paris branch of his South Eastern and Manchester Sheffield & Lincoln companies (he was also chairman of the Metropolitan Railway). Preliminary diggings were made in 1871, but the plan was stopped by opposition from the War Office (still with a Napoleonic Wars mentality), prompted, it was alleged, by James Staats Forbes, wily chairman of the London Chatham & Dover, who did not want to lose his lucrative boat-train traffic. Also, Watkin was chairman of the South Eastern, and both companies, from the chairmen down, were at war with each other over the Kentish and Continental traffic.

Under the chairman or general manager was a hierarchy of senior officers. The locomotive superintendent was one, but it was now managers rather than engineers who ran the business. The traffic manager, who was responsible for timetabling, providing services and charges, was perhaps the key official. The locomotive department was there to provide the necessary power,

BELOW The few controls and spartan layout of the enginemen's cab are seen in this unusual shot of the Great Northern Railway's 4-2-2 No. 1, waiting in line outside King's Cross Station to be attached to its train. The driver is on the right.

at carefully controlled cost. There was still ample room for invention and development in railway matters. John Ramsbottom, chief mechanical engineer of the LNWR, laid the first-ever locomotive water troughs at Mochdre, on the Chester–Holyhead line, in 1860. The choice of this line was no whim. Over it ran the Irish Mail, at this time the only fast train on the LNWR. The lucrative Post Office mail contract specified tight timing, and the company had no intention of losing the contract. A gifted engineer, Ramsbottom also devised a new and much improved safety valve, although he is chiefly remembered for his reorganization of Crewe Works into a highly efficient factory, which was a true predecessor of the twentieth-century production line.

0-4-2 D1 TANK LBSCR 1873

Tractive effort: 12,500lb (5,670kg)
Axle load: 30,240lb (13.7 tonnes)
Cylinders: two 17x24in (416x609mm)
Driving wheels: 66in (167cm)
Heating surface: 1020sq ft (94.75m^2)
Superheater: n/a
Steam pressure: 140psi (9.9kg/cm^2)
Grate area: 15sq ft (1.4m^2)
Fuel: Coal – 1120lb (0.5 tonne)
Water: 860gall (1037 US) (3.9m^3)
Total weight: 86,240lb (39.1 tonnes)
Overall length: 15ft (4.57m)

Timely Changes

As the steam railway spread across the country, it introduced for the first time a national standard of time. For centuries, country towns had set their own clocks without a care as to what time it was elsewhere. Now, with the introduction of timetables and a requirement to maintain punctuality, time became important and stations had to conform. The process was aided by the use of the electric telegraph. The lineside poles and wires became a familiar feature of the steam railway. Later, the telephone became a vital instrument. At one time, indeed, it seemed that the railway stations might act as telegraph offices for the towns they served, but the monopoly on telecommunications was eventually given to the Post Office. The process of standardizing time was slow and uneven, and it was not until 1880 that Greenwich Mean Time became the official and legal standard throughout Great Britain. Among the innumerable side effects of the railway was a boom in the clock-making business.

ABOVE William Stroudley's D1 0-4-2T first appeared in 1875, and it was a highly successful and long-lived class. This one, No. 2226 of the Southern Railway, was at Stewarts Lane depot in 1936.

Even when times were standardized, commercial hostility and the resultant lack of liaison meant that railway companies were slow to provide the benefits of a system of interconnections.

H.R 103

Traffic managers preferred to seek running powers over neighbouring lines in order to convey passengers in their own trains all the way. At this period, it would also have been very difficult to achieve the necessary precision of timing. But some companies, such as the Great North of Scotland, became notorious for deliberately obstructing the possibility of connections. Their northbound trains were despatched from their Aberdeen terminus even if there were passengers from the Caledonian station hammering on the gate.

One aspect of railway operation which left much to be desired throughout the 1860s and 1870s was that of safety. Crucial to safe travel were three things: effective signalling, block working and automatic braking. The lack of the first two of these was brought home by the Clayton Tunnel crash on the LBSCR on 25 August 1861. Trains were still despatched on the time-interval system: when a stationmaster judged that enough time had elapsed since the previous train's departure, he let the next one go. Signals, where in use, were often unreliable. The signal controlling access to the Clayton Tunnel was worked by the train, turning to 'danger' as the train went by. On this occasion, however, it failed to do so. Alerted by the signalman, who had noticed this, the driver of the next train came to a stop in the tunnel. A third train, despatched from Brighton after too short an interval, also passed the defective signal as well as the signalman and ran into the stationary train, causing 11 deaths.

STEP BY STEP TO SAFETY

The ensuing Board of Trade enquiry pressed for the imposition of block working. This, of course, required a fully signalled line, so that trains could maintain one 'block' of track free between them. Not unaware of the cost of this, the railway companies preferred to put the onus

OPPOSITE The first British 4-6-0, No. 103 of the Highland Railway, built in 1894 and now preserved, is seen on a special mixed-train run on the Dingwall–Skye line, skirting Loch Carron between Plockton and Strome Ferry, with the Skye Cuillin in the background.

BELOW When continental travel was for the privileged few: the London Chatham & Dover's paddle steamer *Maid of Kent*, launched in 1861, meets the waiting LC&D boat train, with four 4-wheel carriages, at the Admiralty Pier, Dover, some time during the 1860s.

on the engine crew to keep a lookout ahead. In its defence, the Brighton company pointed out that reliance on mechanical aids was a main cause of the Clayton smash.

In 1856, the first interlocking frame, combining points and signals, was installed at the busy Bricklayer's Arms junction in South London. A fully interlocking frame was set up at Kentish Town, North London, in 1860. The signals could not show a clear road unless the points were correctly set. Single-line working was governed by clear rules; however, when these were ignored, nasty accidents could happen. One was at Thorpe, Norwich, on the GER on 10 September 1874, when up and down expresses were allowed to collide on a single-line section. By this time, block working was practised on about half the main lines of the country. But many lines were wholly or partly single-tracked, and it was not until 1878, when Edward Tyer patented the electric tablet instrument, which allowed access to a particular stretch of line to only one train at a time, that single-line working became – almost – foolproof. A chapter of minor errors led to a head-on collision on the single-track Cambrian line between Abermule and Newtown, in January 1921, causing 17 deaths.

The third essential, an automatic braking system, was unknown on British railways in the

BELOW Locomotives might suffer misadventures, but usually could be repaired. This Southern C2x class 0-6-0, designed by R.B. Billinton for the London Brighton & South Coast Railway, fell into a stream bed while hauling a local goods train near Midhurst in November 1951, but was back on the rails in 1952.

LEFT An example of the handsome H-class Atlantics designed by D. Earle Marsh for the London Brighton & South Coast Railway between 1905 and 1911. He was an ex-GNR man, and his locomotives have a distinct Doncaster look.

1860s. Most trains relied on a combination of the engine's brakes and a hand-operated brake in the guard's van. Continuous brakes throughout the train were rare. Some lines, including the LNWR and the North London Railway, used chain brakes, operated from the brake van or two or three other brake vans fitted into a long train, but most lines had none at all. On 23 August 1858, 17 people were killed in a smash on the Oxford, Worcester & Wolverhampton Railway, when a train comprising 30 carriages parted and 18 ran backwards downhill to collide with a following train.

Little progress on braking was made over the next 15 years until, following a number of bad accidents, a Royal Commission on Railway Accidents was set up in 1875; in June of that year the Midland organized a series of brake trials on its Nottingham–Newark branch. Several companies sent trains, fitted with different systems. The most effective was the American Westinghouse automatic air brake, favoured by the Midland itself. Another American system,

BELOW GWR 'Castle' class 4-6-0 No. 5032 *Usk Castle* emerges from the Severn Tunnel, Britain's longest at 4 miles 628 yds (7km), with a South Wales–Paddington express. The crew are at pains to minimize smoke output, despite the adverse gradient as the line rises to ground level.

LEFT GWR 4-6-0 No. 1027, of the post-war 'County' class. A powerful mixed-traffic type, this engine is from the 1947 production batch and was built, like the great majority of GWR locomotives, at Swindon. A double chimney was provided for all the 'Counties' in 1955.

Smith's non-automatic vacuum brake, was taken up by some companies, including the Manchester Sheffield & Lincolnshire. Its fatal disadvantage was that if the train parted in two, the brake immediately became ineffective. A crash at Penistone on the MSL on 16 July 1884 demonstrated this at the cost of 24 lives. It was only in 1889, following a serious accident at Armagh in Ireland, that government action compelled the companies to install effective continuous automatic brakes on passenger trains. Although the technology had been available for nearly 15 years, little had been done. Reluctance to spend money on installing

BELOW The preserved GWR 'City'-class 4-4-0 *City of Truro* was the first British locomotive to be recorded as exceeding 100mph (160km/h) on 9 May 1904, on an 'Ocean Mail' special descending Wellington Bank between Plymouth and Bristol.

ABOVE This slightly ungainly-looking 4-4-2, *President*, represents G.J. Churchward's close interest in the work of Alfred De Glehn, of the Nord railway in France. Constructed in 1905, above the waist it looks impeccably Great Western; below, it is a French four-cylinder compound.

efficient systems and perhaps a xenophobic dislike of American technology were the only hold-ups. It was a discreditable episode.

Declining Appeal

During the 1860s to 1880s generally, the railways did not enjoy great public esteem. Safety concerns were only one reason for this. The economic depression of the mid-century had reduced business expansion, and many companies were short of money. Apart from a few lines, such as the coal-carrying Taff Vale, the railways themselves were not in any case as profitable as had once been hoped: this was partly because they ran so many duplicated or loss-

LEFT Filling tenders with coal was a necessary task in preparing a locomotive for service. This hopper-and-chute method, from a raised coaling track, helped to speed up the process. The engine is GWR 4-4-0 No. 3702 *Halifax*, a 'City' class rebuilt from the 'Atbara' class in 1908.

making services, started up to fend off or challenge a rival company. Investors were not seeing a very good return for their money.

Rail travel was a spartan affair, especially in cold weather. Most carriages were still uncomfortable and unheated. Although experiments were being made with gas lighting, most carriages were lit by sooty oil-burning pot-lamps. Foot warmers were available for first-class passengers only. Corridor stock with toilets was a rare luxury, even in first. Some very old rolling-stock was still in use. Trains were usually very slow. This was partly because of the deficient brakes and absence of signals; partly because the permanent way was often unable to cope with high speeds; and not least because going faster was more expensive for the railway company. The travelling public had long ago become used to the novelty of rail travel; what they wanted now was a safe and comfortable service. The public could also see that many railway services were unnecessarily slow, and the entrenched hostility among the companies irritated most people.

Railway managements were often chiefly inspired by the need to economize, led in this respect by Sir Richard Moon on the Premier Line. 'It is so much easier to get over a difficulty by increasing the quantity by a large outlay of money than to arrange for properly using what we have got,' wrote Moon in a memorandum on the subject of tarpaulin covers for goods wagons. No item was too small for him to take account of.

The heroic age was past, it seemed. Yet one or two undertakings on a heroic scale were still to be noted. One was the Severn Tunnel, opened for goods traffic in September 1886 after 14 years of struggle against underground springs and seawater incursions. Daniel Gooch, who

OPPOSITE TOP Divers at work in late December 1879 at the site of the Tay Bridge collapse. The engine that fell, North British Railway 4-4-0 No. 229, was hoisted up, repaired and ran for many years. It was known to staff as 'The Diver', and no driver would take it over the new Tay Bridge.

OPPOSITE BOTTOM The opulence of first class: a padded door leads into a thickly carpeted compartment with panelled wood interior in this preserved six-wheeled carriage of the South Eastern & Chatham Railway.

LEFT The massive scale of the Forth Bridge (opened in 1890) is captured in this shot of an LNER A4 Pacific passing through the girders of one of the three great cantilever sections.

had left the Great Western in 1864 and was invited back to become its chairman in 1866, was the first man through when the headings met on 27 October 1884. At 4 miles 682 yards (7.06km), it was the longest railway tunnel in the country.

Then there was the Tay Bridge. North of Edinburgh, the wide firths of Forth and Tay compelled all northbound rail traffic to go round via Stirling and Perth. The world's first train ferry, *Leviathan*, was put in service across the Firth of Forth, for goods wagons and deck passengers only, in February 1850. A similar craft was built for the Firth of Tay. Their designer was a versatile engineer, Thomas Bouch, who had also designed the high iron viaducts on the Stockton & Darlington line between Darlington and Kirkby Stephen. When the decision was taken to bridge the easier Firth of Tay in 1870, it was Bouch to whom John Stirling of Kippendavie, the North British chairman, turned. In 1873, Bouch was also appointed as engineer of a bridge to be built over the Firth of Forth. The single-track Tay Bridge, longest in the world at 3884yds (4247m) was passed for service in February 1878, and on 20 June Queen Victoria crossed it on the way from Balmoral to Windsor. On the evening of 28 December 1879, the bridge collapsed in a gale, taking with it a train. About 80 people were killed. The subsequent enquiry found the bridge to have been incompetently designed, built and maintained. Bouch succumbed to death soon afterwards, and his design for a great suspension bridge over the Forth was consigned to oblivion.

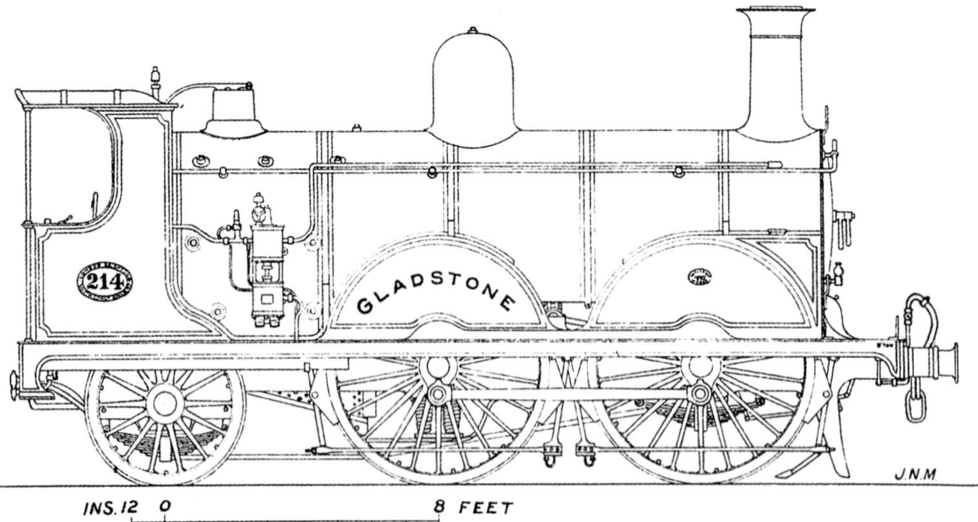

LEFT William Stroudley's 0-4-2 'Gladstone' type was built for the London Brighton & South Coast Railway from 1885. Its lack of truck or bogie wheels in front of the drivers was unusual in a fast passenger locomotive, but it proved highly successful in service.

Bridge and Reputation Rebuilt

Kippendavie nevertheless pressed on to have the Tay Bridge rebuilt, and a new design was commissioned for the Forth Bridge. This time there were no corners cut. The new double-track Tay Bridge was opened on 13 June 1887. Then, 4 March 1890 saw the opening of the Forth Bridge, with its triple cantilever towers the mightiest monument to Victorian engineering, completing the direct East Coast route between London and Aberdeen. As such a structure was beyond the resources of the North British Railway alone, the Forth Bridge Railway was a joint venture of all the East Coast companies.

The railway companies had battled for their independence from government control, if not entirely from regulation. In the process, they perhaps invented the PR man, in the person of Sir Henry Cole, who was retained by the London & North Western in 1846 to 'create a public opinion' against the broad gauge. But they could not entirely be laws unto themselves. Competition with rivals – and, increasingly, the power of public opinion – had to be taken into

BELOW Originally built in 1879 as a 2-2-2T, this Highland Railway tank engine was rebuilt by David Jones as a 4-4-0T and served as a shunter at Inverness into the 1940s. Its front end design perpetuates the Allan 'Crewe' type, although the louvred chimney was a Jones speciality.

ABOVE 'Gladstone' 0-4-2 *Allen Sarle* at Oxted, LBSCR, 1901. Like all Stroudley's engines, it is painted in his very bright 'Improved Engine Green'. Behind the tender is a fine example of a ducketed brake van, the extended windows of which allowed the guard a fore-and-aft view of the train.

0-4-2 GLADSTONE LBSCR 1882

Tractive effort: 13,200lb (5986kg)
Axle load: 32,480lb (14.7 tonnes)
Cylinders: two 18¼x26in (463x660mm)
Driving wheels: 78in (198cm)
Heating surface: 1485.4sq ft (138m^2)
Superheater: n/a
Steam pressure: 140psi (9.9kg/cm^2)
Grate area: 20.65sq ft (1.9m^2)
Fuel: Coal – 8960lb (4 tonnes)
Water: 3000gall (3603 US) (13.6m^3)
Total weight: 86,800lb (39.3 tonnes)
Overall length: 15ft 7in (4.75m)

account. Public opinion went all the way up to Queen Victoria, who had strong views on railways, chiefly to do with speed (the pace of the Royal train was always a decorous one).

In the early years, the companies had treated passengers with a degree of suspicion and disdain: suspicion because they might injure themselves and demand compensation (this was based on the income of the sufferer, to the alarm of the Great Northern when a bishop and the Lord Mayor of London were involved in a collision in 1853); disdain because the companies felt they had a safe monopoly, and, anyway, passengers got in the way of efficient working. Late in the century, the Great North of Scotland Railway (which enjoyed a monopoly in its area) would still unlock the compartment doors one by one at Aberdeen, ensuring that each was full before the next was opened. More typical was Edmund Denison, exhorting his staff in 1850: 'Formerly when the London & Birmingham and the Midland lines were opened, people were almost obliged to go down on their knees to be allowed to enter a carriage. Now directors and managers have to make a most civil and respectful bow to parties to coax them to go.' The campaign for good manners on the Great Northern brought it more custom at a time when the North Western tolerated or encouraged the old arrogance. Even so, passengers were often victims of intercompany feuds.

ABOVE Excursion and special traffic was a lucrative extra revenue-earner for the railways, utilizing plant at weekends and holiday times. The Great Northern was a leader in this sort of traffic.

Regional Dominance

In 1860, although there were by now more than a hundred companies, the pattern of regional dominance was clear. In the South, the territories radiated from London. The London Chatham & Dover and the South Eastern were still locked in a somewhat sluggish battle for Kent. The London Brighton & South Coast served the towns of Sussex. The London & South Western ran through Surrey, dividing into main lines to Southampton and west to Basingstoke, Salisbury and Exeter. The Great Western's narrow corridor from Paddington opened out into the broad fan of Wessex, Devon and Wales. Most of it was still broad gauge, although some frontier lines were mixed gauge. The London & North Western ran to the Midlands and beyond to Liverpool and Manchester. The Great Northern's domain stretched up to York, extending east and west between Sheffield and Lincoln. The Great Eastern ran north-east to Colchester, Ipswich and Norwich. Further north, the map includes the great enclave of the Midland around Nottingham, Leicester, Derby and Birmingham. Further still, the Lancashire & Yorkshire spread across the Pennines between those two counties. The North Eastern controlled most of the lines north of York. Beyond the border, two large companies, the Caledonian and the North British, controlled most Scottish lines, apart from the south-west corner, occupied by the Glasgow & South Western Railway.

It was not a static picture, however. The biggest, and still growing, industrial cities – Manchester, Birmingham, Leeds, Sheffield – were magnets to all companies with a hope of reaching them, whether by building a new line or by obtaining running powers on an existing railway. Intertwined with the LNWR, Midland and GNR, the Manchester Sheffield & Lincoln, managed with suave aggressiveness by Edward Watkin, survived by constantly playing off one of the larger companies against the others. Many small companies owned some of the lines used by the giants: in due course they would be absorbed by one or another. The proprietors of the short Trent Valley Railway, which provided a bypass to the east side of Birmingham, through Lichfield, did extremely well out of its sale to the LNWR in 1845.

Other small companies managed to preserve their independence. Some, such as the North Staffordshire, did so by a kind of symbiosis with a mighty neighbour, in this case the North Western. Other running systems wriggled across several of the giants' preserves, but with routes no one was in a hurry to snatch. These usually ended up as jointly owned. Among them

BELOW It was Samuel Johnson who developed the deep crimson lake colour which distinguished Midland, and later LMS, express engines from 1873 until 1939. Here, it is set off to great effect by the polished brasswork of this 4-2-2, a 7ft 6in (2.28m) bogie single of 1889.

were the Midland and Great Northern Joint, a collection of local East Anglian lines embracing King's Lynn and Norwich, with later outliers to Yarmouth and Cromer. They formed the Eastern & Midlands Railway in 1882 and were bought up jointly by the Midland and the Great Northern in 1893. Its headquarters remained at King's Lynn, and it had its own works at Melton Constable, maintaining and sometimes building its own yellow-liveried engines. In Wessex, there was the Somerset & Dorset, jointly run by the Midland and the South Western, cutting right across Great Western territory between Bath and Bournemouth with distinctive blue-painted engines. In the North West was the largest and busiest joint operation, the Cheshire Lines Committee, with a network of lines between Chester and Manchester. Formed

ABOVE A Great Western broad-gauge train travelling on dual-gauge track. The engine is scarcely wider than the track (compare page 307). If the GWR had taken full advantage of the potential of the broad gauge, British locomotives may have dwarfed even those of Russia.

LEFT GWR 'Duke'-class 4-4-0 *Comet* at Swindon: Swindon's 4-4-0s had a look very much of their own, with outside axle-boxes on the bogie wheels, inside cylinders and cranks set outside the frames.

LEFT With cranks flying around outside the frame, a GWR 'Bulldog' 4-4-0, No. 3410 *Columbia*, speeds a semi-fast train from Birmingham Snow Hill to Worcester and Hereford, along the former 'Old Worse and Worse' line, in 1934.

OPPOSITE The west side of Waverley Station, Edinburgh, in the 1950s. The station pilot, an ex-North British J83 0-6-0T, draws out a train of empty stock, while a Gresley Pacific waits for the off with a northbound express. The North British station hotel looms above the platforms.

in 1867 by a partnership between the Midland, the Manchester Sheffield & Lincoln and the Great Northern, it used its owners' engines, but had its own carriages and wagons, and continued to do so until November 1948.

A small independent survivor was the Midland & South Western Junction, tracing a path through the Cotswolds and the Downs from Andoversford, near Cheltenham, to Andover on the South Western main line to Salisbury. In 1891, the year of its inception, it went into receivership, but the man put in by the receivers to run the line, Sam Fay, re-energized the company, made it pay and set up exemplary cross-country connections from Southampton (LSWR) to points as remote as Bradford and Liverpool. Few managers had the drive and ability of Fay, who later became general manager of the very much larger LSWR and ultimately of the Great Central.

BELOW The Midland Railway coat of arms was proudly displayed in stations and on the side of every locomotive.

FILLING THE GAPS

Although the building of new railways continued right through the nineteenth century and into the twentieth, it was largely a matter of filling gaps (real or imagined) and, in several cases, shortening city-to-city routes – as with the Midland's Chinley cut-off via the long Totley Tunnel between Manchester and Sheffield, completed in 1893; the Great Western cut-offs, of which the most notable were the South Wales & Bristol Direct, bypassing Bristol to the north; and the Castle Cary–Langport line, completing an alternative main line between Reading and Taunton and at last enabling the GWR, long sneered at as the 'Great Way Round', to rival the timings of London–Exeter trains via Salisbury on the LSWR. Both of these were completed early in the twentieth century.

ABOVE Placed in service in 1889, and now preserved, L&Y No. 1008 was the first locomotive to be built at the new Horwich Works, and leader of a very numerous class. It has radial axles at each end and water pick-up apparatus for running both forward and backward.

2-4-2T L&YR 1889

Tractive effort: 16,900lb (7,664kg)
Axle load: 35,448lb (16 tonnes)
Cylinders: two (i) 18x26in (457x660mm)
Driving wheels: 67¾in (172cm)
Heating surface: 1,216.4sq ft (113m²)
Superheater: n/a
Steam pressure: 160psi (11.3kg/cm²)
Grate area: 18.75sq ft (1.7m²)
Fuel: Coal – 5,600lb (2.5 tonnes)
Water: 1,340gall (1,609 US) (6m³)
Total weight: 125,328lb (56.8 tonnes)
Overall length: 24ft 4in (7.42m)

In remoter parts of the country, however, several major lines had not been built by 1860. In the central Highlands, the Perth & Dunkeld line was linked in 1864 to the Inverness & Aberdeen at Forres by a long railway rising to 1484ft (452m) in the Druimuachdar Pass, the highest point to be reached by a British mainline railway. In 1865, this, as the Inverness & Perth Junction, became part of the newly formed Highland Railway, with its headquarters and works at Inverness. The Highland gradually extended itself north to Thurso, on the Pentland Firth, although the mainline terminus was Wick, reached in 1874. At the same time, the Callander & Oban extension of the Caledonian was being built, although Oban was not finally reached until 1880.

The 1860s also saw railway development in central Wales, with the Oswestry & Newtown Railway, open by 1861, linking up with the already built but isolated Llanidloes & Newtown. By early 1863, the Newtown & Machynlleth was open. Aberystwyth was reached in 1865, and the northward line via the Mawddach Viaduct to Pwllheli was completed in October 1867. In the far South West of England, the LSWR had endured somewhat restricted access to Plymouth from its Lydford branch by way of the GWR Yelverton branch. In 1890, it leased the new Plymouth Devonport & South Western Junction Railway, down the Tamar Valley to its own station at Plymouth Friary. With its London–Salisbury–Exeter main line, opened in July

OPPOSITE Richard Maunsell's South Eastern & Chatham Railway L-class 4-4-0s were known as 'Germans', as the first 11 of the type were built by Borsig of Berlin in 1914. Still on mainline service in the 1950s, the L and its development, the L1, were often 'clocked' by enthusiasts at speeds of more than 70mph (112km/h).

LEFT The Cambrian Railway's viaduct across the Mawddach at Barmouth, built in 1867, is the longest wooden structure of its kind in Britain. At the northern end, a metal bowstring-girder section was built as a swing bridge to enable coastal vessels to sail up the estuary. A Shrewsbury–Pwllheli train is crossing.

1860, the LSWR picked off the South Devon seaside towns east of the Exe. By careful and delicate stages, it extended itself through North Devon and into Cornwall by what appeared to be a succession of branch lines, but which by 1899, when it reached its westernmost point at Padstow, made a sort of main line for holiday traffic (the proudly named Atlantic Coast Express would operate from 1926), as well as for a respectable amount of fish traffic.

ABOVE On a Bristol–Birmingham service in 1921, Midland 4-4-0 No. 525, a rebuild by R.M. Deeley of Johnson's '60' class (1898), breasts the Lickey Incline at Blackwell, with a banking engine at the rear of the train. The station equipment, including the oil lamp, is of interest.

To Carlisle in Comfort

Some of these lines would be barely profitable, but their social value in opening up remote or mountain country was indisputable. The need for the Midland Railway to construct a new main line from the West Riding of Yorkshire to Carlisle was less obvious, especially to the LNWR, which, with the Caledonian, had enjoyed a monopoly on the West Coast route to Glasgow from the very beginning. Since 1858, the Midland had found a way into London by agreeing running powers with the Great Northern from Hitchin into King's Cross. The GN line was heavily congested, and, by the early 1860s, the Midland was building its own line south from Bedford towards a new terminus at St Pancras.

The thought of a London–Scotland Midland service was immensely appealing to a number of companies. At Carlisle, two potential allies eagerly awaited the Midland traffic: the Glasgow & South Western Railway, with its line to Glasgow via Dumfries, and the NBR with its new (1862) Border Union line linking Edinburgh and Carlisle via Hawick. A further ally was the Lancashire & Yorkshire, which was also irked by the LNWR monopoly. When at one point the Midland lost confidence and sought to abandon the project, the L&Y and the Scottish companies forced it back on the rails. Rising to 1151ft (351m) at Ais Gill summit, the line had heavy engineering works, including two long tunnels and the Ribblehead Viaduct, and, although it received Parliamentary assent in 1866, it was not finished until 1875, when freight traffic began. Passenger traffic began on 1 May 1876, with sumptuous new Pullman car expresses which outdid all rivals for comfort. The new line became well patronized, and its arrival added to the excitements of Carlisle Citadel Station, a frontier point where the expresses changed engines, the shiny black of the LNWR replaced by the royal blue of the CR, or Midland

LEFT D. Earle Marsh's express class I3 4-4-2T of the London Brighton & South Coast Railway, a type which astonished the engineers of the LNWR in 1909 by its frugal consumption of coal and water, when tested against their own 2-4-0 'Precedent' *Titan* between Rugby and Brighton.

red by the varying greens of its two Scottish allies. In addition to these, the local Maryport & Carlisle and the North Eastern (coming in from Newcastle) companies also used the station.

Especially from the 1870s to around 1914, the great interchange stations, such as Carlisle, York, Perth and Chester, were colourful, bustling places. The variety of different engine types and company liveries caught the eye. The walls were covered with advertisement placards for a great diversity of products. There was much impressive activity. Portions of the train were detached or added. Engines were changed or watered. All sorts of things in the way of goods and luggage were seen on the platforms. The railways had an obligation as 'common carrier' to transport all manner of items. It was not unusual to see an entire circus, or the stock and equipment of a farm, being trundled slowly through by one of the ubiquitous 0-6-0 types that

BELOW To the annoyance of company accountants, turntables had to be regularly rebuilt and extended towards the end of the nineteenth century, as engines became longer. This 2-4-0 of the E&MR (later Midland & Great Northern Joint) fits comfortably for the time being.

formed close on half the locomotive stock. The station was usually open to the public, and tickets were checked at a ticket platform outside the main station. A large and varied staff was employed, from the wheel-tapper with his hammer to the boy selling sweets from a tray; from the stationmaster himself to the lamplighter who topped up and lit the oil lamps inside the carriages before dusk. Beyond the knowledge of the passenger, each company had its own facilities close to these 'joint' stations: engine shed, carriage sidings and goods yard. More small engines fussed about on transfer trips between the yards. Officials of the Railway Clearing House monitored all intercompany movements and reported back to the (by now) huge head office by Euston Station.

ABOVE The preserved GNR single-driver, No. 1, in 1982. The engine, once used for hauling mainline expresses between London and York, remains in working order.

More Power Needed

Trains were longer and heavier than in the early period, especially after the mid-1870s, when all companies followed Midland practice – with different degrees of effectiveness – in improving passenger comfort. The consequences for railway accountants were important, as fewer passengers per ton of train pushed up operating costs. The consequences for locomotive design were also important. Unless trains were to be expensively double-headed, more powerful engines were essential. In the last decades of the nineteenth century, an extraordinary variety of locomotive types existed. But, livery and incidental details aside, they were mostly variations on a limited number of well-established themes.

There was still a clear distinction between goods and passenger engines. The goods engines at this time were slightly larger versions of the old 2-4-0 and 0-6-0 types, otherwise little changed. Heavy trains, such as the Midland and GN coal trains to

2-4-0 PRECEDENT LNWR 1874

Tractive effort: 10,400lb (4716kg)
Axle load: 25,760lb (11.7 tonnes)
Cylinders: two 17x24in (432x609mm)
Driving wheels: 79½in (202cm)
Heating surface: 1083sq ft (100.5m²)
Superheater: n/a
Steam pressure: 140psi (9.9kg/cm²)
Grate area: 17.1sq ft (1.6 m²)
Fuel: Coal – 8960lb (4 tonnes)
Water: 1800gall (2162 US) (8.2m³)
Total weight: 86,128lb (39 tonnes)
Overall length: 18ft 1in (5.51m)

LEFT Francis Webb's LNWR 2-4-0s were officially known as the 'Precedents', after the first engine in the class; however, to enginemen and enthusiasts, they were better known as 'Jumbos'. Here, No. 5048 *Henry Pease* takes on coal. Some of the 'Jumbos' remained in service for more than 50 years.

ABOVE Southern D-class 4-4-0 as BR 31746, photographed on a local train at St Catherine's, Guildford, in 1951. The D class, designed by Robert Surtees, under the aegis of Harry Wainwright, for the South Eastern & Chatham Railway in 1900, was a most reliable engine, and numerous examples survived virtually unaltered for over 50 years.

London, were usually hauled by two engines. Just around the turn of the nineteenth century, a notable feature, caused by production bottlenecks in British locomotive works, was the arrival of 2-6-0 mixed-traffic engines, imported from the USA by several companies, including the Midland, Great Northern and Great Central. Importation of foreign types was always rare, and such an influx was unusual. Their appearance was heavily anglicized, but the Midland examples did have generous American-style cabs. Although passenger engines frequently hauled goods trains, and vice versa, these were the first tender engines in Britain to occupy this in-between status.

Until the Midland's revolutionary developments of the 1870s, passenger engines were built to haul lightweight trains at a fair speed. Unlike the practice on European railways, most British lines operated frequent but short trains. This resulted in the continuation of the single-driver passenger engine, with its one pair of very large-diameter driving wheels. The most impressive of these were the Great Western's, built for the broad gauge by Gooch's engineering successors, Joseph Armstrong and William Dean; the most famous were the elegant Great Northern singles designed by Patrick Stirling. That designer's own favourite, his 'grand engine',

123
1 Z

LEFT The Caledonian Railway's one-off bogie 'single' No. 123, with 7ft (2.13m) driving wheels, built by Neilson & Co of Glasgow in 1886 and shown at the Edinburgh Exhibition of that year, was a participant in the 1888 'Race to the North'. Reboilered in 1905, it was retired in 1935 after running 780,000 miles (1,255,288km) and is the only preserved Caledonian express engine.

was the bogie 4-2-2 of 1870, with driving wheels 96in (244cm) in diameter and – unexpectedly – outside cylinders (the height of the driving axle made inside cylinders impossible). Somewhat to the surprise of American and European visitors, such engines worked mainline expresses into the twentieth century, and at high speed.

The 2-4-0 was also widely used in passenger service. Some hard-slogging but simple and robust engines of this type lasted a very long time: a Kirtley 2-4-0 of 1866, No. 158 of the Midland Railway, was still running on the LMS 77 years later as No 20002. Perhaps the most famous examples of the type were Francis Webb's LNWR 'Precedent' class, popularly known as 'Jumbos'. One of these, *Charles Dickens*, clocked up more than two million miles of running, all on the Manchester–Euston service, between 1882 and 1902. But heavy trains, with dining cars, sleepers or Pullmans, required more adhesive weight on the rails than the 4-2-2 or 2-4-0 could provide. As a result, from 1870 to 1899, the 4-4-0 engine dominated passenger traffic.

American Influence

Although the classic British 4-4-0 is thought of as having inside frames and cylinders and a low running-plate, with half of each wheel hidden by a splasher, this was not the first version of that wheel arrangement to run. The bogie, a four-wheeled frame provided with a degree of independent movement, was developed in the USA and taken up in Britain from the 1850s; apart from spreading the weight of the front end, it was supposed to guide the engine into sharp curves. Many designers were wary of it and never used it; its earliest designs were never quite satisfactory, and it continued to exercise designers right up to the 1930s.

A satisfactory bogie was, however, developed by Robert Stephenson & Co and first used in 1865 by William Adams on 4-4-0T engines for the North London Railway. British workshops built bogie 4-4-0s for export for several years before any were used by home companies. In 1860, the Stockton & Darlington bought from Robert Stephenson & Co a pair of outside-cylinder, inside-framed 4-4-0s for its trans-Pennine service to Penrith, the first tender type of this wheel arrangement for home service, although a 4-4-0T was produced for the East Kent Railway in 1857.

BELOW Designed by J.F. McIntosh and built at the company's St Rollox works in 1896, the Caledonian Railway 4-4-0 'Dunalastair' class caused a sensation in British railway circles because of the size and steaming capacity of its boiler. The class was developed over the next 20 years. No. 142, shown here, was from the enlarged fourth series of 1904.

ABOVE The Metropolitan Railway's 4-4-0T, built by Beyer Peacock in 1864–70, was the first locomotive designed for underground running. The copper-lined pipes running from the cylinders to the side tanks were for conveying condensed steam, and the bridge-pipe and vent allowed vapour to exhaust from the tanks. The system often worked better in theory than in practice.

4-4-0T METROPOLITAN 1864

Tractive effort: 11,000lb (5034kg)
Axle load: 35,336lb (16 tonnes)
Cylinders: two 17x24in (432x609mm)
Driving wheels: 69in (175.25cm)
Heating surface: 1013.8 sq ft ($94m^2$)
Superheater: n/a
Steam pressure: 130psi ($9.16kg/cm^2$)
Grate area: 19sq ft ($2.7 m^2$)
Fuel: Coal – 2240lb (1 tonne)
Water: 1000gall (1200 US) ($4.54m^3$)
Total weight: 94,416lb (42.8 tonnes)
Overall length: 20ft 9in (6.32m)

Outside-cylinder 4-4-0s went on to be used by numerous lines, culminating in the Midland Compound and Southern 'Schools' classes, although both of these also possessed a third, inside cylinder. On the Great Western, with its more generous loading gauge, a series of outside-framed 4-4-0s was produced, from the days of Daniel Gooch into the 1930s. The first Gooch 4-4-0s were on rigid frames, however.

The inside-cylinder, express 4-4-0 was first produced by Thomas Wheatley on the NBR in 1871, and within a few years the type was widely employed by other designers. Its basic form was reproduced in many variations by every company of any size. With its sweeping curves, imposing yet handsome, uncluttered appearance and carefully handled details, it represented the peak of aesthetic design for the Victorian locomotive. As early as the 1840s, Joseph Locke – a practical engineer if not a locomotive man – had praised the accessibility of outside cylinders and motion. To most Victorian locomotive designers, however, there appeared to be something almost unseemly in exposing the 'works' to public view.

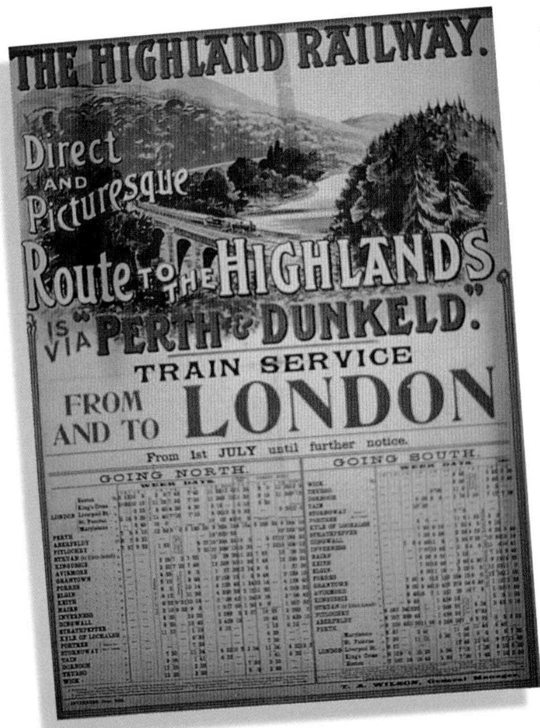

LEFT This poster for the Highland Railway's London service is now at the preserved Monkwearmouth station of the North Eastern Railway; however, in the NER's heyday, the route it features would have been that of the 'enemy', following the West Coast via Lancaster and Crewe.

Tank Engines Develop

During this period, a significant development was that of the tank engine. These had been known from the 1840s, and some early tender engines were converted to tank form, usually with a saddle tank fitted over the boiler. They remained relatively uncommon throughout the 1850s; however, by the 1890s, they almost outnumbered tender engines. Most services operated over relatively short distances with frequent stops, and for this work the tank engine was ideal. It could also be operated in reverse gear more satisfactorily than the tender locomotive and was independent of turntables. Well tank (within the frame), side and pannier tank types were also produced.

While the 0-6-0T was the most common type, the wheel arrangement of T-locos varied widely. Lines with longer commuter arteries, such as the London Tilbury & Southend and the Glasgow & South Western, built massive 4-6-4Ts (by the same designer, Robert Whitelegg); R.W. Urie of the South Western constructed a 4-8-0T; and the GWR had 2-8-0Ts for freight traffic. Some lines, such as the Rhymney Railway, had no need for anything other than tank engines. Sir John Aspinall's 2-4-2T for the L&YR numbered over 330, and the GW had over 800 of its 5700/8750 0-6-0T; only Ramsbottom's LNWR DX 0-6-0 outnumbered it as the most numerous single class, with 857 built.

Another celebrated tank type was the Metropolitan Railway's 4-4-0T, with steam-condensing apparatus, built from 1864 by Beyer, Peacock & Co of Manchester to

0-6-0T TERRIER LBSCR 1872

Tractive effort: 8400lb (3810kg)
Axle load: 18,368lb (8.3 tonnes)
Cylinders: two 13x20in (330x508mm)
Driving wheels: 48in (122cm)
Heating surface: 528sq ft (49m^2)
Superheater: n/a
Steam pressure: 140psi (9.9kg/cm^2)
Grate area: 15sq ft (1.4m^2)
Fuel: Coal – 1120lb (0.5 tonne)
Water: 500gall (600 US) (2.3m^3)
Total weight: 55,104lb (25 tonnes)
Overall length: 12ft (3.65m)

LEFT Broadside view of a Stroudley 0-6-0T 'Terrier' of the London Brighton & South Coast Railway, sold to the K & ESR in 1901.

work on London's underground railway, the first in the world. Contrary to supposition, it was possible for a tank engine to cover a considerable distance without taking on coal or water. In 1908, engineers of the LNWR were astonished when, on an exchange trial, a 4-4-2T, of the LBSCR's class I3, ran from Rugby to Croydon without the need to refill its tanks. Its water and fuel consumption were markedly less than that of the LNWR 'Precursor' 4-4-0 against which it was being compared. A Brighton man is reputed to have said: 'We could have run on what she threw out of her chimney.'

The GWR was still a broad-gauge line, and it continued to build broad-gauge branches until 1877. But, even in 1852, the extension of its line from Oxford via Banbury to Birmingham was laid to mixed gauge. Eventually, its directors bowed to the inevitable. Although it could operate quite happily as a self-contained system, the business of transfer from broad- to standard-gauge for all intercompany traffic, particularly goods traffic, was expensive and time-consuming. As long-distance travel became more comfortable and holiday resorts grew in importance, there was more interest among the companies in promoting cross-country passenger services. The through carriage was also becoming popular. Attached to two or three trains in sequence, it provided a link on intertown routes where there was insufficient demand to warrant a whole direct train service. The Great Western had so far excluded itself from all this. At last, on 20 May 1892, the final broad-gauge train left Paddington for the West Country. Already much of the broad-gauge track had been narrowed. Now, by 23 May, the task was completed. Long rows of old broad-gauge engines stood at Swindon waiting to be scrapped; more recent ones had been designed as 'convertibles' to fit the standard gauge. Deprived of its

ABOVE The Lancashire & Yorkshire had many industrial sidings and canal-side tracks, and, like other companies, built very short wheelbase 'pug' tank engines to negotiate the tight curves. This one, surviving into British Railways' ownership as No. 51202 of the London Midland Region, is a typical outside-cylindered, small-wheeled example of its kind. Because of their specialized but limited duties, many pugs had long working lives.

ABOVE The preserved GWR racer City of Truro on a special working at Banbury in 1992. Following refurbishment in the late 1980s, the veteran proved still to have a remarkable capacity for speed.

most distinctive aspect, however, the Great Western did not fall back into lassitude. Soon Swindon would show the world what it could do with locomotives built to the despised Stephenson 'cart-track' gauge.

RACING FOR PRESTIGE

Rivalry among railway companies was hardly news, but the 1890s turned it into news with the concept of railway 'races', and the newspapers of the day loved it. The West Coast route from Euston and the East Coast route from King's Cross – both to Aberdeen – converged at Kinnaber Junction, just north of Montrose, about 40 miles (64km) south of Aberdeen. North of here the line was owned by the Caledonian, and the North British had been granted running powers to Aberdeen. The West Coast companies – LNWR and Caledonian – and the East Coast – GNR, NER and NB – competed in August 1895 to achieve the fastest timing over the route, 541 miles (870.6km) for the former, 523.5 (842.5km) for the latter (the Forth Bridge had been opened in 1890). The first train offered to Kinnaber from the previous signal box on either line had the race sewn up. On the night of 20 August, both trains left London at 8 p.m.

LEFT An unusual fitting on this GWR 0-6-0 pannier tank engine, No. 2006 of Dean's 850 class, dating from 1881, was a bell, fitted American-style to the boiler top. This was for working on public roadways, on the tracks that lead to Birkenhead Docks.

The West Coast train reached Kinnaber just four minutes ahead of its rival. Including numerous stops for engine-changing, it had maintained an average speed of 59.9mph (96.4km/h); the East Coast had maintained an average 57.8 (93km/h). Although the trains were very lightweight, it was a remarkable achievement. In the five weeks or so of the races, the London–Aberdeen time had been reduced by over three hours. In normal service, this margin was not maintained, but the races had shown what was possible. Indeed, at this time Britain led the world for the number of high-speed runs.

Rivalry also broke out in the next decade on the lines from London to the West, where the LSWR and the GWR vied for the honour of transporting passengers and mails from Europe-

BELOW A broadside-on view of the Stirling GNR No. 1 at speed, at the head of a train of vintage LNER carriages, between Doncaster and London, on the centenary of the Doncaster locomotive works, the 'Plant', in 1938.

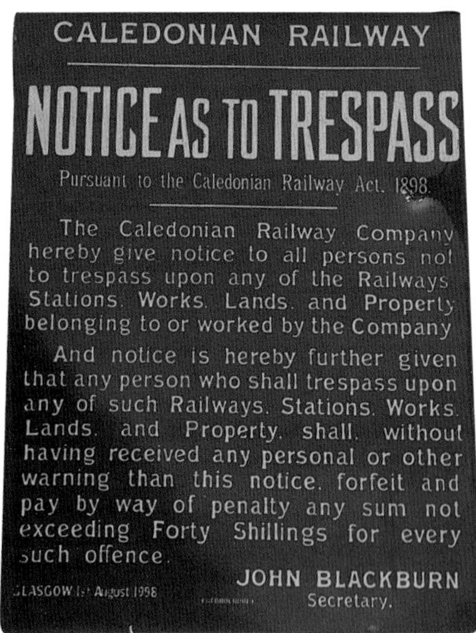

LEFT Trespass notices were there not only to warn people off, but to absolve the railway company from any legal claim by persons injured by straying on the line. An early law (1845) compelled all main-line railways to be fenced off.

bound transatlantic liners pausing at Plymouth. Both companies had termini there, and the two routes intersected each other at Exeter. Unlike the routes to Scotland, these were one-company lines all the way – 247.2 miles (397km) for the GWR and 230 miles (370km) for the LSWR – and the two CMEs, Dugald Drummond of the LSWR and George Churchward of the GWR, took a personal interest. Drummond himself went on at least one of the runs; Churchward left this to G.H. Flewellyn, a senior locomotive inspector. But he gave him the following typically Churchwardian instruction: 'Withhold any attempt at a maximum speed record till I give you the word. Then you can go and break your bloody neck!' It was on an 'Ocean Mail' special, on 9 May 1904, that the GWR 4-4-0 *City of Truro* attained a speed exceeding 100mph (160km/h) for the first time on British metals, racing down Wellington Bank towards Taunton.

On 1 July 1906, an American boat-train's horrific crash at Salisbury, caused by excessive speed, put an end to these excitements. Public opinion moved with its usual rapidity from enthusiasm for speed to fear of disaster. Maximum speed attempts were ruled out, and speed restrictions that had been winked at were again firmly enforced.

BELOW The combined wheel-splashers were a trademark of the North Eastern Railway's 4-4-0s. Wilson Worsdell's Q class of 1896 became LNER D17/2, and No. 1904 is seen here at West Hartlepool. Although the engines underwent considerable alteration in the 1930s, the class survived as late as 1959.

Improving Standards

By the 1890s, the railways had emerged from the trough of public disesteem. Gradually, things had improved. Although some companies, such as the Highland, still provided wooden seats

in third class, and some trains still seemed to crawl across the landscape and stand still for long, unexplained periods at country junctions, the general standard had improved considerably. By this time, corridor coaches were the norm on long-distance trains. Sleeping cars and dining cars had been introduced. Signalling and braking had been vastly improved. Comparative studies such as Foxwell and Farrer's *Express Trains, English and Foreign* of 1889 revealed how British railways were superior to those on the Continent, and not only in speed and frequency. In Britain, 93 per cent of the express trains carried third-class passengers; in France, Bavaria and Italy, the proportion was only 27 per cent. There was a new awareness that British trains could compare with the best that the rest of the world had to offer and that the railway companies could be much worse than they in fact were.

ABOVE The first Pullman cars in Britain were introduced from the USA by the Midland Railway in 1873, when sleeping and parlour cars were used on its new Anglo-Scottish main line via Leeds and Dumfries. This later example shows the distinctive styling and colour scheme, and the fine detail, of these sumptuous cars.

46521

3 • The Railway Towns

The need to build railway works, junctions and depots creates something new in British social life – the company town. In many ways they are preferable to the other new industrial communities which are springing up. The company owns everything, even the school and the church.

LEFT Oil was second only to coal as a fuel for the railways. Not only a vital lubricant, right up to the end of the steam age, it also lit many stations and signal boxes, as well as the head- and tail- lights of trains and the vast majority of signal lights. Over the years, an immense range of oil lamps appeared, variations on a single theme.

OPPOSITE In the 1940s, the LMS developed a range of locomotive types, several of which became British Railways standard designs. The Ivatt 2-6-0 light passenger engine, rated 2P, seen here at Kidderminster on the Severn Valley Railway, was one of these, intended for working branch line and local trains.

The arrival of the railway and the building of a station did not always mean a sudden leap in the fortunes of a town. For many places, the railway had a bad effect, drawing away an old market, or a local industry, to a more favourable location along the line. Even a resort town like Bath saw an actual drop in its population in the ten years following its acquisition of a station on the Great Western Railway. But certain places were transformed by the arrival of the railway, and some were created by it. These were the towns that housed the railway's own workshops and sometimes also its headquarters. A legend of dubious truth records that Isambard Brunel and his assistant Daniel Gooch, surveying the track works below the quiet old country town of Swindon in 1841, were having a picnic lunch when Brunel tossed a crust to one side and remarked, 'Here we shall have the locomotive works.' With its central position between London and Bristol, it was a natural choice; it was also to be a junction for the Gloucester line and the original plan was for engines of London–Bristol trains to be changed here, though in fact this did not happen much. Three hundred terraced houses were built of local stone, along with a church and a school, but the settlement quickly grew beyond that. By 1851 New Swindon had more people than Old Swindon. By the end of the century, fourteen thousand men were employed in the locomotive works and the associated factories where rails were rolled out, and wagons and carriages built and repaired. Eventually, industrial Swindon swallowed up its rural predecessor, and in 1900 they became a single municipality. As the Great Western system grew, it established other works, at Newton Abbot, Wolverhampton and Chester. But Swindon was always the prime centre: the office of the Locomotive, Carriage and Wagon Superintendent was here. It was a Great Western town, and from 1865–85, Gooch, later Sir Daniel and chairman of the company, was its Member of Parliament, in the Conservative interest. Swindon suffered from some of the defects and problems of a nineteenth-century industrial town. Sanitation was primitive, there was no piped water, and very soon disease became rife. The average life

ABOVE The smallest locomotive built at Crewe, *Wren* was used on the network of narrow-gauge tracks within the confines of the locomotive workshops, moving heavy parts and general supplies, and taking away waste materials for re-processing or dumping.

LEFT In what looks like a respite from shunting, the fireman of a GWR 0-6-0 pannier tank engine takes a rest on the brake platform of a wagon from the Italian FS system, that has come over on the cross-Channel train ferry.

LOCOMOTIVE DESIGNERS

TIMOTHY HACKWORTH (1786–1850)

In the eyes of some people, not least his son John who wrote his biography, Hackworth was the forgotten man of early locomotion. Born at Wylam, he followed in his father's footsteps to become foreman blacksmith at Wylam Colliery and participated in the building and maintenance of Hedley's engines. A practical engineer of great ability, he was a member of the little group of steam experimenters who included Hedley, Christopher Blackett and George Stephenson. Stephenson thought highly of his ability and secured him the position of engineer to the Stockton & Darlington Railway in 1825. Hackworth set up the company's Shildon workshops and also began building on his own account. His great contribution was to make effective use of the blast pipe, carrying exhaust steam from the cylinders, to increase the draught, and so the heat, of the fire. Colliery engines, travelling short distances, did not have to raise steam on the move, but the 25-mile (40-km) S&D line did require this. The 0-6-0 locomotive *Royal George*, which he rebuilt in 1827 from a defective 2-2-2, is generally regarded as the first effective freight engine in working more than short distances. His entry at the 1828 Rainhill Trials, *Sans Pareil*, was unlucky in the tests, breaking a cylinder and bursting a fusible plug in the firebox. In pulling power, though not in efficiency or speed, it probably outdid the *Rocket*. Hackworth was distressed by the failure and for a time there was bad blood between himself and the Stephensons, whose Newcastle works had cast the faulty cylinder. He gave up his post on the S&D in 1840, but built and sold engines until 1845. By that time his designs, with front-end fireboxes and high-angled cylinders, were looking distinctly old-fashioned, and being outperformed by more advanced locomotives.

Timothy Hackworth's business card, produced around 1830, shows an inside-cylindered 0-4-0 locomotive, with cylinders and firebox in rear.

expectancy in Old Swindon in 1829 was 36; twenty years later it had dropped to 30 – this was one of the facets of 'progress.' But the houses of Swindon, and its contemporary Crewe, built to the railway companies' specification, were superior in construction, materials and space to most of the jerrybuilt terraces being put up in other industrial towns at the same time.

BELOW It was a typical device to use the coats of arms of the terminal towns in the insignia of a railway company.

STRATEGIC LOCATIONS

Most industrial towns grew up because they were close to a source of raw material, such as coal, iron ore or china clay. The railway towns were different. The determining factor here was their position within the company system, normally fairly central and at a significant junction point. When the Grand Junction Railway, precursor of the London & North Western, decided in 1840 to move its locomotive works from the constricted site at Edge Hill, Liverpool, the choice of a new location was the farming settlement of Coppenhall, a 'greenfield site' near the old market town of Nantwich. It was a strategic choice. From here, branches left the main line from London to the North to serve Manchester, Chester and North Wales, and Liverpool. Crewe station, named after a local manor house, Crewe Hall, would soon become one of the country's busiest interchange points for passengers, while the marshalling yards beyond it served the same purpose for freight trains. Indeed Crewe became the epitome of the railway town. The works grew to become the biggest company-owned locomotive works in the world. A fully integrated production

system was set up here before the theory of 'mass production' was developed. It made iron at its own works from 1853 and set up a large steel-making plant in 1868. The adjacent brickworks turned out six million bricks a year. All this was wholly owned by the mighty LNWR, which was not only a railway company but an industrial empire on a scale which few if any companies could match anywhere. The company employed more than four thousand men in 1870. Twenty years later the number had almost doubled. As in Swindon, the prime figure was the Chief Mechanical Engineer. He had, and exercised, dictatorial powers, and not only on life inside the works. When this post was occupied by F.W. Webb, from 1873 to 1903, he installed his brother as the parish vicar, and the foremen saw to it that the services were well attended, even though most railwaymen, if of a religious persuasion, were Non-conformists. In 1877 Crewe became a borough, but in the first council elections, company officers standing for election were defeated. Webb was roused to rage and menace: 'If the people of Crewe do not study the company's interest I shall not be responsible for what the directors will do.' His intimidation tactics ensured a Conservative/Company majority until 1889, with himself as mayor from 1887–89. In the words of Professor Jack Simmons, 'Crewe was ruled from the general offices of the locomotive department.' Extension of voting rights and the introduction of the secret ballot however meant that the railwaymen could make their own choices. When Webb fired three workers, all local Liberals, for setting up a trade union branch in 1889, he had gone too far. To the discomfiture of the board, he was denounced in the *Times* by no less than William Ewart Gladstone, the former and future prime minister. The directors formally repudiated Webb's action, and from then on the CME gave up his efforts to manage local politics.

OPPOSITE There were several Waterloo stations in Britain. This Edwardian view shows the street entrance of Waterloo in the Liverpool suburbs, on the former Lancashire & Yorkshire Railway's commuter line to Southport.

BELOW Crane-fitted LNER Class J92 0-6-0T No. 8667 stands outside the crane engines' shed, and beside the remains of a four-coupled engine, at Stratford Works, East London, on 4 June 1947. Crane engines operated inside the works on a wide variety of lifting tasks.

AUTOCRATIC DEVELOPMENTS

Webb's effort to make Crewe a subservient company town was too crude to survive. But it should also be recorded that when he was mayor the company gave the town Queen's Park, and the autocrat of Crewe left almost all of his very large fortune to charities in the town. Paternalistic and dictatorial though they were, in both direct and indirect ways the railway companies were benefactors to the towns they created or expanded. It may have been through enlightened self-interest. Crewe and Swindon both had early Mechanics' Institutions, with libraries, reading rooms and opportunities both for discussion and education. A pool of intelligent and well-informed young men was necessary to feed the businesses' constant appetite for skilled workmen, clerks and apprentice engineers. The Crewe Mechanics' Institution had a scholarship scheme, sponsored by John Ramsbottom, Webb's predecessor, to send promising apprentices to Owen's College, the forerunner of Manchester University. But in Crewe especially, the purchase of radical newspapers and magazines, and the discussion of radical politics, was discouraged or forbidden. In

BELOW An LNWR 0-8-0, No. 9037, passes through Kensington (Addison Road) with a cross-London goods train in July 1939.

some cases the directors, conscious of their responsibilities and perhaps also with some pride in their towns, went beyond what many shareholders thought desirable. When in 1853 Edmund Denison, chairman of the Great Northern, wanted to build a church and school for the railway workers at Doncaster, he faced a storm of opposition. 'Is it intended to be a railway company or a Church Extension Society?' demanded one opponent, concerned for his earthly rather than his heavenly dividends. In the end the company paid for a school but the church was built by a private subscription from among the directors and certain shareholders more inclined toward charity.

The Lure of Small Towns

The scale of operations on the LNWR enabled it to maintain a second, smaller company town at Wolverton, where locomotives had been built for the London & Birmingham Railway and which later became the site of a carriage and wagon works. Sir Francis Head in his railway memoir *Stokers and Pokers* described it, fondly enough, as it was in 1849, '...it is a little red-

LEFT Inverness station in the 1900s. The night train from London has backed in at Platform 6, while the Wick and Thurso train is standing ready to leave from Platform 7.

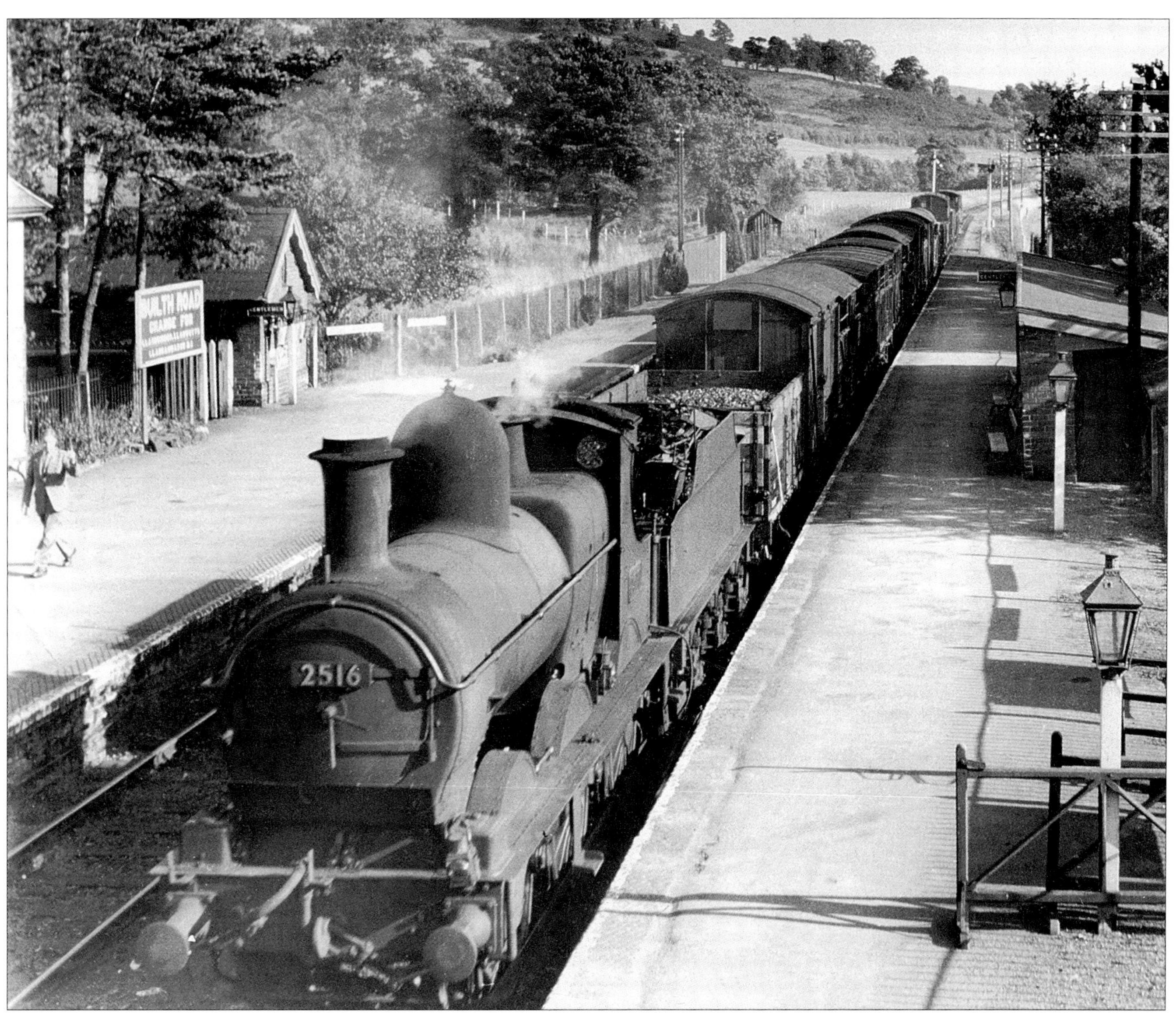

BELOW Builth Road was where the Cambrian Railway passed below the LNWR's Craven Arms–Swansea line. GWR 0-6-0 No. 2516 is on a north-bound goods train, heading for Moat Lane Junction.

THE GREAT EASTERN RAILWAY

Several railways were amalgamated in 1862 to form the Great Eastern. The oldest was the Eastern Counties Railway, formed in 1836 and intended to link Yarmouth and Norwich with London, though its own efforts had got it no further than Colchester by 1843, and three other companies, with which it operated in uneasy conjunction, completed the original plan. By 1845 Norwich and Yarmouth were linked to London, though rivalries and dissensions among the operating companies prevented the development of an effective service. It was 1854 before through trains ran from Norwich via Ipswich and Colchester to London. From its formation the GER had a virtual monopoly of railway transport in the East Anglian counties of Norfolk and Suffolk, and in most of eastern Cambridgeshire and Essex. In its final form, it had main lines via Cambridge to Kings Lynn; to Norwich and the North Norfolk resorts of Wells and Cromer; to Yarmouth and Lowestoft, and to Harwich. Although it served no great cities or mining and industrial districts, it had a good mix of traffics. The possession of a wide and rich agricultural region gave it a substantial, if seasonal, freight business. Yarmouth and Lowestoft generated substantial fish traffic to London and the Midlands. The company worked hard and successfully to promote Harwich as a port for northern Europe, building and operating its own steamers for passenger, mail and freight trade. In 1883 the development of Harwich–Hook of Holland traffic led to the opening of the enlarged harbour facilities at Parkeston Quay. For a time the GER exercised running powers over the

Great Northern and North Eastern railways to operate a 'York Continental' train from York to Harwich. In 1891 this became the first train to offer dining facilities to third-class passengers. Effort was also put into promoting the coastal towns as holiday resorts, and a summer 'Norfolk Coast Express' was run from Liverpool Street to Cromer, non-stop as far as North Walsham. Far from least, the GER had very heavy and substantial suburban services in north-eastern and outer London. The original ECR terminus at Bishopsgate had been replaced in 1875 by a new station at Liverpool Street, whose ten-platform capacity was further enlarged in 1892–94 by a further eight platforms; it was also provided with the Great Eastern Hotel from 1880. This commodious station always suffered from narrow access, restricted to four tracks, but the GER was an exemplary operator of punctual, if unpleasantly overcrowded at peak times, commuter services. It was the principal provider of the low-fare workmen's trains, and the extension of its suburban network defined the urban geography and the social mix of areas such as Walthamstow, Stratford and Ilford. Stratford, East London, was the company's main depot and the location of its locomotive works, established originally by the ECR in 1847, but enlarged greatly in the course of the nineteenth century. From 1878, Stratford built most GER engines. In its latter years the locomotive livery was royal blue with gold embellishments. The public eye was caught in 1900 by the opportunistically numbered locomotive 1900, a handsome and effective 4-4-0, first of the 'Claud Hamilton' class, named after Lord Claud Hamilton, the company chairman.

THE FINAL YEARS

After the wrangles of its old constituents were finally resolved, the Great Eastern became a quietly prosperous concern for most of the nineteenth century, suffering fluctuations of revenue chiefly in connection with good or bad growing seasons. The only serious intrusions on its territory were those of the lines which were formed into the Midland and Great Northern Joint line in North Norfolk in 1883. Between 1875 and 1900 it had a somewhat stormy relationship with the London Tilbury & Southend Railway, of which the old Eastern Counties Railway had been a part-owner. Given the opportunity to buy the LT&S in 1900, the Great Eastern made an inadequate offer that was duly spurned. In a later courtship in 1911, the GER was outmanoeuvred by the Midland, which snatched the Tilbury line for itself. Being sidelined in its own Anglian enclave, the Great Eastern attracted less attention than the other larger companies. In the amalgamations that came into force on 1 January 1923, it became part of the London & North Eastern Railway. Though Stratford built its last locomotive in 1924, Great Eastern engines, their blue liveries hidden under coats of successive LNER green and British Railways black, remained active into the 1950s.

A two-wagon freight, typical of East Anglian country branches in the last years of steam traction, ambles along behind a stove-pipe chimneyed ex-GER 0-6-0T.

brick town composed of 242 little red-brick houses – all running this way or that way at right angles – three or four tall red-brick engine-chimneys, a number of very large red-brick workshops, six red houses for officers – one red beer shop, two red public houses, and, we are glad to add, a substantial red school-room and a neat stone church, the whole lately built by order of the Railway Board, at a railway station, by a railway contractor, for railway men, railway women, and railway children; in short, the round cast-iron plate over the door of every house, bearing the letters L.N.W.R., is the generic symbol of the town.'

The high cost of land in London, as well as the inconvenience of having the works at a terminus rather than a central location, drove numerous companies to leave the metropolis. Only the Great Eastern continued to have its works at Stratford. The South Eastern moved out to Ashford, in Kent, in 1845, establishing first a repair works there but building new engines from 1853. Doncaster, to where the GNR moved its works (from Boston, Lincolnshire) also in 1853, was already an established town but in that one year it grew by almost one-quarter. Always known as 'the Plant', the GNR works alongside the station were not as vast as those at Crewe and Derby, but they made the railway company by a large margin the town's biggest employer. By 1900, when a new locomotive erecting shop was built, the Plant had 4500 workers and covered an extent of 200 acres (81ha). Sixty miles (96km) of sidings were needed to allow access to all points, hold the long lines of rolling stock awaiting repair and allow for the marshalling of coal trains. One aspect unique to Doncaster was its racecourse, and the works

RIGHT One of the Caledonian Railway's finest termini was the wrought-iron and glass structure at Wemyss Bay, built in 1903. Here trains connected with fast steamers for Rothesay and Innellan.

BELOW The departmental 0-6-0 saddle tank locomotive *Earlestown* was transferred to Wolverton when Earlestown wagon works, near Warrington, shut in 1963. It poses in front of the signal box controlling the line into the carriage and wagon works at Wolverton.

closed for a week each September at the time of the St Leger race-meeting, partly in order to accommodate the race traffic, partly because otherwise mass absenteeism would have ensued.

The Midland Railway's main centre was Derby. Unlike the other places, it was already an industrial town of some size when the Midland Counties, Birmingham & Derby Junction, and North Midland Railways all established lines here, linking Derby to Leicester, Nottingham, Birmingham and Leeds. They merged to form the Midland Railway in 1844 and their individual workshops were amalgamated into a single large works. While most railway companies had their main offices in London or another terminal location, the Midland made Derby its headquarters for everything, including the administrative and commercial aspects of the business. Despite this concentration of railway activity, the Midland never dominated Derby as, for example, the Great Western dominated Swindon. On the eastern side, about a mile from the centre, the station and the locomotive works were not integral with the town. To the annoyance of the company, the town council actively supported the building of a Great Northern

BELOW In the British Railways era, ex-GWR double-framed '9000' class 4-4-0 No. 9005 arrives at Oswestry station with a stopping train.

RIGHT Country junction: Lines from Harrogate, Hawes Junction, and Stockton converged on the York-Darlington main line at Northallerton. An ex-NER 0-6-0 numbered as British Railways 65038 waits in the bay while BR standard Class 3MT 2-6-0 No. 77001 pauses with a stopping train. Note the firebox and coal supply to prevent the water column from freezing up.

77001

ABOVE Two Great Western 0-6-0 tanks were sent to Helmsdale in Scotland to work the Dornoch branch of the former Highland Railway in the summer of 1960.

line linking Nottingham to North Staffordshire via Derby, and the Midland's general manager, James Allport, failed to be elected to the council in 1877 – this did not result in the tantrums and fixings that took place at Crewe.

Even into the twentieth century, the establishment of a railway works could have a dramatic impact on a small place. Horwich in Lancashire was a small cotton-spinning town when the Lancashire & Yorkshire Railway bought 350 acres (141ha) there in 1884 to establish a completely new locomotive works. Under the control of W. Barton Wright, chief locomotive superintendent, and his successor John Aspinall, later general manager of the company, the layout both of the works and of the adjacent streets was systematically planned. Typically, the streets of new houses – built and rented by private companies, not the railway – were named after engineers. The population tripled by 1891. Horwich was unusual in not being on a major main line, and so is perhaps least well known of the bigger 'railway towns', but it was central to the L&Y network. More visible to London-bound travellers was the London & South Western's new works at Eastleigh, Hampshire, established in 1891. At first this was a carriage and wagon works only, and unlike Horwich, the town grew up in a piecemeal and disorganised manner. It was not until 1910, when locomotive building was transferred to Eastleigh from Nine Elms in south London that the town really began to develop.

BELOW Former GER engines at Beccles in Suffolk, on 18 April 1949.

A MAJOR EMPLOYER

Although Derby was the only real 'capital' of a large railway among provincial towns, a number of other towns fulfilled this role for smaller railways. Inverness was the Highland Railway's centre for everything, though it was not a railway town in the sense of the railway being its reason for existence or main source of employment and revenue. Melton Constable in Norfolk, however, was entirely a railway town. The Midland & Great Northern Joint Railway, crossing the green fields of northern East Anglia, had its headquarters here. The small works opened in 1883. They built their first engine in 1896 and their last in 1910. After that it carried out repair work only, but Melton remained a railway town until the whole M&GN was closed in 1959. At

BELOW Waiting for the train at Wellingborough (London Road). The station name referred to the adjacent street; it was actually on the LNWR's Northampton–Peterborough cross-country line. It closed in the mid-1960s.

45360

the other side of the country, Oswestry carried out a similar role for the Cambrian Railways; the network was almost wholly in Wales, but the proximity of this rural English town to the North Wales coalfield and to the Great Western line to Wrexham and Chester may have triumphed over its peripheral location. The moving spirit was Thomas Savin, partner in a local drapery business, who became prominent in the expansion of the Welsh railway network and went bankrupt in the process.

Apart from the substantial employment provided by railway works and offices, the railway towns benefited from associated and spin-off industries. Crewe had a clothing factory producing uniforms for LNWR staff, and also a large printing works for timetables, posters and the innumerable other printed documents that a railway company needed. The same was true of other railway towns, large and small. Sometimes the lure provided to other industries was unwelcome to the railway operators, if the incomers drew on their pool of skilled labour and created a competitive wage market. The LNWR was rumoured to keep freight rates to and from Crewe especially high to discourage other industries from moving in. The Midland Railway is unlikely to have welcomed the arrival in 1907 of the Rolls Royce motor and engine business in Derby.

Even though they were not railway towns in the sense of being created or greatly enlarged by railway activity, certain places became very closely identified with railway operations in the mind of the travelling public. These were the principal interchange stations, the biggest examples – Crewe apart – being Carlisle, York, Perth and Chester, where several different

OPPOSITE Class 5 4-6-0 No. 45360 passes the neat station of Alness, on the Highland 'Further North' line, with an Inverness–Wick goods train on 3 June 1960. Its first stop will be Brora.

BELOW The highest station in the country was at Wanlockhead, terminus of a Caledonian branch from Elvanfoot on the Carlisle–Glasgow line. It was 1407 feet (429m) above sea-level. A Sentinel steam railcar prepares for the downhill run on 19 June 1936.

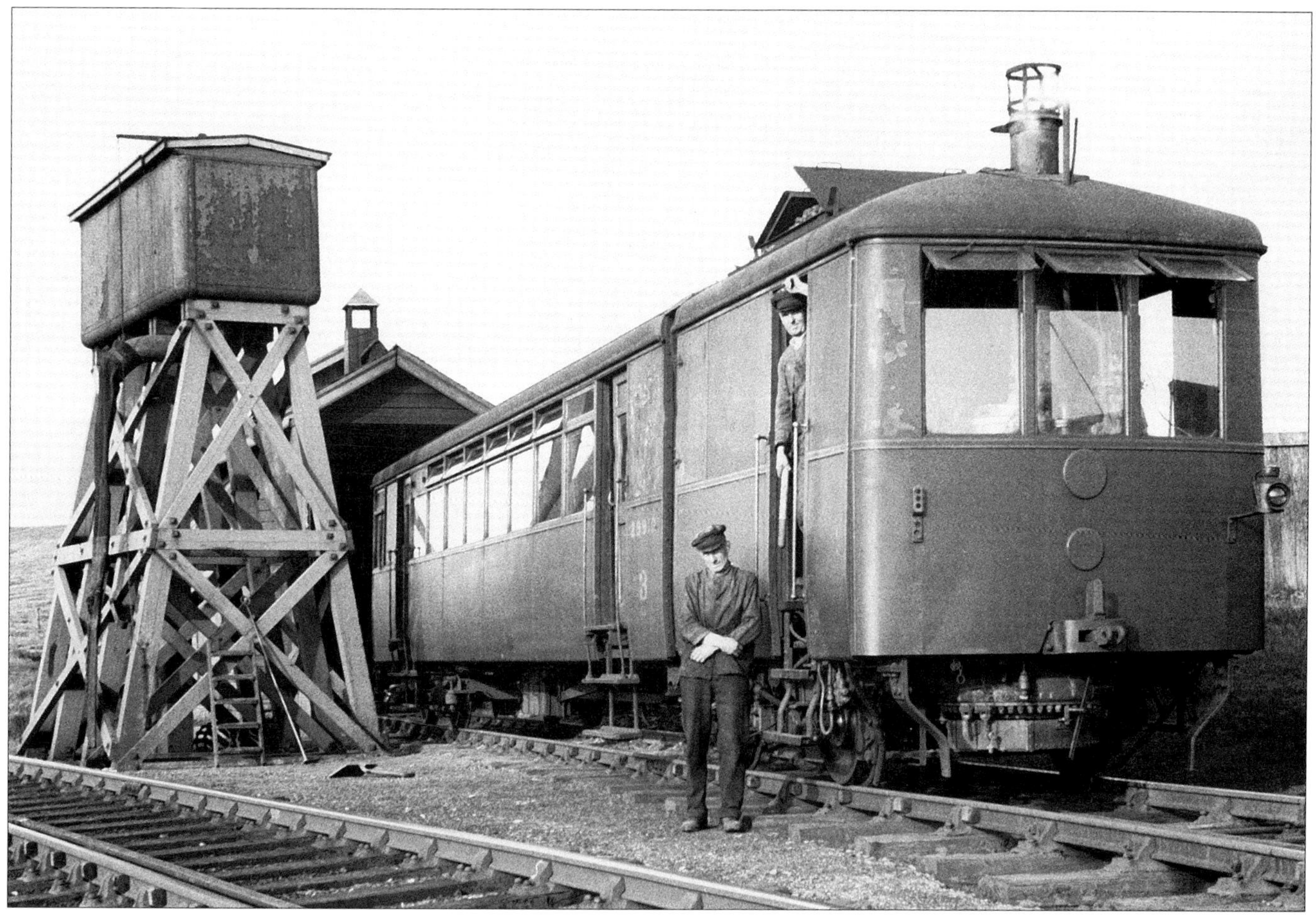

LEFT Horwich's station was a terminus at the end of a short branch from the L&Y's Chorley-Manchester line. The platform staff and friends take time to pose on a wet morning in the early 1900s.

companies met. Very large stations were needed to accommodate the traffic and most were extended and rebuilt several times. Between 1876 and 1922 seven companies ran trains into Carlisle Citadel station. In 1880 the station was rebuilt, four years after the Midland's main line reached the city. Its overall roof had an area of seven acres (2.8ha). But passenger operations were only part of what went on. Carlisle had eleven separate shunting yards, and seven goods stations, quite apart from various coal yards and seven locomotive depots. Though it had no railway workshops, apart from those of the Cowans Sheldon Company, which built railway

BELOW The track layout at the south end of York Station, in the early twentieth century, with six trains apparently waiting departure, though it is a specially posed publicity shot for the North Eastern Railway, which was justifiably proud of the spacious post-1874 station.

LEFT The multi-level complex of tracks at the approach to Wolverton from the south, to allow access to the LNWR carriage and wagon works, which can be seen beyond the storage sidings. The main line is on the right.

travelling cranes and turntables, over two thousand men were in railway employment there in 1901. York, though it had a carriage and wagon-building works from 1865, built few locomotives, but from 1854 to 1922 it was the headquarters of a major railway, the North Eastern (whose main works were up the line at Darlington). George Hudson was a York man and the favourable view of the city council towards railways was part of his legacy. Up to 1877 the station at York was hopelessly cramped and inadequate, but in that year the present building, with its great curved aisle, was opened, with thirteen (later 16) platforms. It was always entirely under North Eastern control, but six other companies had running powers into it, and paid the NER for these. York's role as a railway museum town began when the London & North Eastern started its museum in 1928; now the old motive power depot at Leeman Road houses the world's largest railway museum as part of the National Museums.

The Smallest Stations

At a number of places up and down the country, for operational reasons, small railway settlements were established. The great majority of these never became towns and some remained tiny hamlets. The most remote of all was Riccarton in the Scottish borders, the location of a junction of the Edinburgh–Carlisle railway and the branch line southwards through Kielder Forest to Hexham on the Newcastle–Carlisle line. Riccarton had no road access at all, and the North British Railway provided special trains to enable the stationmen and their families to do their shopping and go to school. At Tebay in Westmorland, the terrace of former railway houses can still be seen. Here the LNWR had a locomotive

BELOW Fifty years of railway life; 3000 locomotives. A plaque commemorating company paternalism and employees' industry on the dedication of Queen's Park, Crewe, in 1887. Centrepiece is a Webb 2-2-2-2 compound tank engine.

78054
BOAT OF GARTEN JUNCTION
CHANGE FOR SPEYSIDE LINE

LEFT Highland Junction: at Boat of Garten, the Highland Railway's original main line from Forres to Perth was joined by the Great North of Scotland's Speyside branch. British Railways Class 2 No. 78054 waits on the Speyside line with a train for Craigellachie. The Cairngorms loom in the distance.

LOCOMOTIVE DESIGNERS

DANIEL GOOCH (1816–89)

Born in the North-East, Gooch learned his engineering skills with Robert Stephenson & Co in Newcastle, and joined the new Great Western Railway at the age of 21 as its locomotive superintendent. Inheriting a stock of highly temperamental and experimental engines ordered by I.K. Brunel, he was plunged in at the deep end. The best of his engines was the 'Star' type 2-2-2 built by Stephenson, and this formed the basis of Gooch's own later designs. He was heavily involved in the building and organisation of the Swindon works, begun in 1841. From then on, the GWR built most of its own locomotives. Gooch's engines were noted for their speed, strength and stability. It cannot be said that his designs took full advantage of the 7-foot (2140-mm) gauge, but this was at least partly because the overall constraints of the fittings at the side of the lines, bridge heights and so on, determined by Brunel, made it impossible. He remained with the Great Western until 1864, when he resigned. His versatility as an engineer, typical of his generation, was shown in his supervision of the laying of the first transatlantic telegraph cable, using Brunel's ship Great Eastern. This earned him a baronetcy and he returned in the following year to the GWR, as chairman of the board, at a low stage in its fortunes. His management restored the company's financial strength, at the cost of indifferent services. He was elected as Conservative MP for Cricklade in 1865 and served for twenty years without ever making a speech in the House of Commons. The main achievement of Gooch's chairmanship was the building of the Severn Tunnel between 1873–86: at that time the longest in the world. He was the first man through when the two tunnelling sides met; and he died in harness, three years before the GWR's broad gauge main line was reduced to standard gauge.

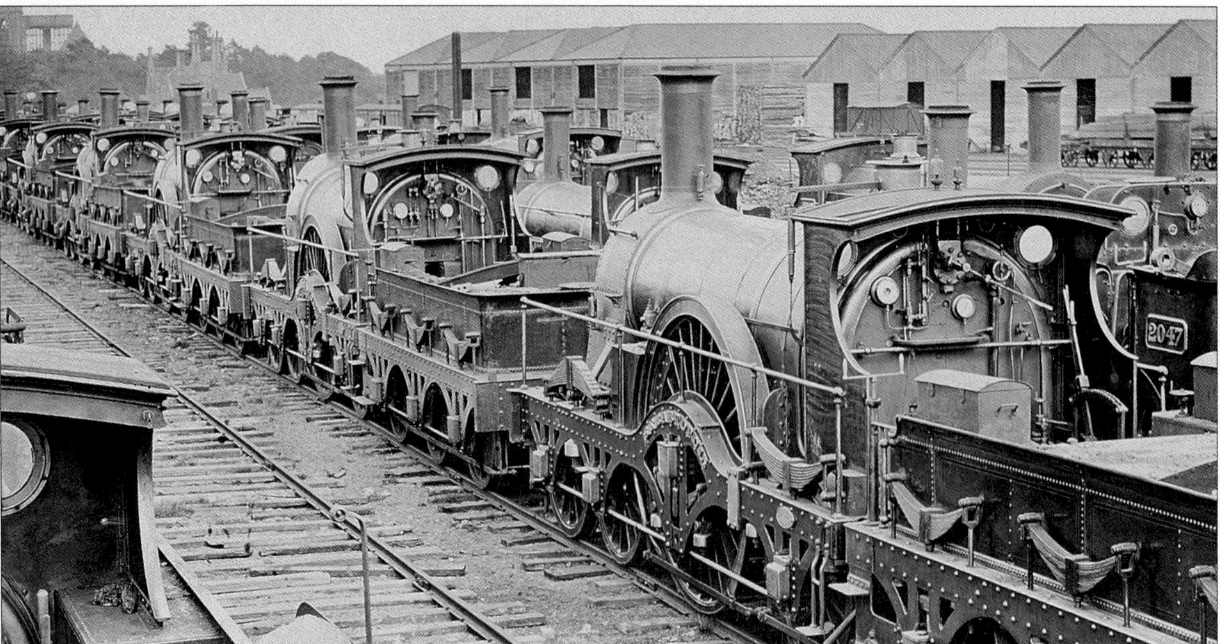

Redundant broad-gauge engines await scrapping at Swindon in 1892.

shed for the banking engines that pushed heavy trains up the gradient leading to Shap summit. Blair Atholl in Perthshire, previously a hamlet for the duke of Atholl's gamekeepers and shepherds, performed a similar role at the foot of the 'Big Hill' leading up to Druimuachdar Pass on the Highland main line. The village of Craven Arms in Shropshire was a railway settlement at the point where the Central Wales line diverged from the Shrewsbury–Hereford line; previously there had only been a roadside inn there. Riccarton no longer exists. But most of the other railway hamlets and villages survive. Often nowadays though they are far from the nearest railway. Halwill Junction in Devon where, as noted earlier, the London & South Western's Atlantic Coast Express from Waterloo carried out the last of its many dividings (with the Bude and Padstow portions separating), was also the end of a branch reaching south from Bideford and Barnstaple. All these lines have long since been lifted, but the village retains the 'Junction' in its name, as does Balquhidder Junction, in Perthshire. Here the tracks and pointwork of the Caledonian Railway's Callander–Oban main line and its eastward-running linking line to Perth are now no more than indentations in the heathery ground.

ABOVE At Weymouth Quay, the trains came right on to the pier to meet the Channel Island steamers after a slow run along a public roadway. The Great Western and London & South Western both used the station, though the GWR was the owning company. It was also convenient for the Pavilion, as this 1912 card view shows.

LEFT At the other end of England, the LNWR Windermere branch connected with the lake steamers. LMS 2-6-4 tank No. 42376 is ready to leave for Ulverston on a rather quiet day, around 1950.

7298
7298
L M S

4 • The Big Four

The twentieth century brings new challenges to the steam railway – world war, the advent of motor competition and the need for reorganization on a massive scale. It also sees the supreme achievement of steam-generated speed and power in Britain, with the magnificent A4 and 'Coronation' class locomotives.

LEFT R.J. Billinton designed the E4-class 0-6-2 radial tank engine for the London Brighton & South Coast Railway in 1898. 'Radial' refers to the bar allowing the pony wheels to adjust independently to sharp curves. Restored class member No. 473 *Birch Grove* is seen here on a winter day at Horsted Keynes on the Bluebell Railway.

OPPOSITE Preserved LMS 'Jinty' 3F 0-6-0T No. 7298 at Glyndyfrdwy, on the Llangollen Railway. The origins of this type go back to the Lancashire & Yorkshire Railway; although primarily a goods shunting engine, it was also used on passenger services on the Somerset & Dorset line and in some other areas.

Around the end of the nineteenth century, important innovations began to appear in locomotive design. British mechanical engineers were a tough breed: they had to be large-scale industrial managers as well as engine designers. Men such as Sir John Aspinall of the Lancashire & Yorkshire Railway planned and laid out large workshops (Horwich in his case) and controlled large numbers of men. His contemporary, Dugald Drummond of the LSWR, with works at Nine Elms and Eastleigh, and responsibility for locomotive running, also built his own private engine car (known to his staff as 'the Bug') to cruise over his far-flung domain. But these men, for all their power, did not dictate company policy. The demands being made by the traffic departments were ever greater, and the number-crunchers in the financial departments who desired operational cost-effectiveness were increasingly vocal and influential. Engine designers who had grown up with the 4-2-2 and

0-6-0 were being forced to consider much larger and more powerful tractive units for both goods and passenger working. Aspinall (later to became general manager of the line) was also a locomotive designer of distinction, whose 4-4-2 'Highflyers' romped through the Pennines with business expresses. In the bigger companies, all engineers had to face the 'big engine' challenge. In 1896, John F. McIntosh, chief mechanical engineer of the Caledonian Railway, created intense interest in railway circles when he introduced his new 'Dunalastair' 4-4-0. Still in the classic inside-cylinder style, it was distinguished by a boiler of 4ft 8in (142.2cm) diameter, the largest yet seen. An ex-driver, McIntosh produced an engine that was simple to operate and had ample steam-raising capacity. The 'Dunalastairs' did excellent service, and most engineers followed McIntosh's example.

The chief mechanical engineer with by far the largest locomotive stable was Francis W. Webb of the LNWR. The famous earlier designs of his long reign (1871–1903), the 'Cauliflower' 0-6-0 and the 'Jumbo' 2-4-0, were straightforward machines that responded well to hard driving. Soon, however, Webb became fatally interested in compound working. In this, the steam was used twice over, first at high pressure, then – exhausted from one set of cylinders into another – at lower pressure. In theory, it was a more efficient use of motive power and fuel. In practice, however, Webb's successive compound designs were tricky to drive and often temperamental

ABOVE This Caledonian Railway 0-6-0 was built by J.F. McIntosh in 1899, at St Rollox Works. Although essentially a freight class, the first 17, including the preserved No. 828, shown here at Aviemore, were painted in Caledonian blue and used on Clyde coast passenger services.

OPPOSITE One of F.W. Webb's 0-6-0s, called 'Cauliflowers' because of the LNWR coat of arms painted on the middle wheel-splasher, takes a train of coal wagons over the Settle and Carlisle line. These simple-expansion engines were much preferred by crews to Webb's compound locomotives.

LEFT Sir John Aspinall's Lancashire & Yorkshire Class L1 4-4-2 'Highflyer' of 1899 was Britain's second Atlantic type and was renowned for speed on the long-distance commuter lines radiating from Manchester.

in operation. On frequent occasions, they were seen attempting to start off with each pair of driving wheels revolving in opposite directions. It is remarkable that Sir Richard Moon tolerated what was undoubtedly an unnecessarily expensive and wasteful practice for so long – an indication of how much, even on the North Western, the CME was an unquestionable autocrat in his own domain. Webb's successors, George Whale and C.J. Bowen-Cooke, scrapped his engines as fast as they could and produced a range of simple-expansion locomotives that were vastly more reliable.

0-6-0 CAULIFLOWER LNWR 1880

Tractive effort: 15,000lb (6800kg)
Axle load: 24,897lb (11.3 tonnes)
Cylinders: two 18x24in (457x609mm)
Driving wheels: 61½in (156cm)
Heating surface: 1208sq ft (112m²)
Superheater: n/a
Steam pressure: 140psi (9.9kg/cm²)
Grate area: 17sq ft (1.6m²)
Fuel: Coal – 8960lb (4 tonnes)
Water: 3250gall (3903 US) (14.75m³)
Total weight: 74,704lb (33.9 tonnes)
Overall length: 15ft 6in (4.73m)

SCIENTIFIC INNOVATIONS

Part of the real shape of things to come was displayed on the Highland Railway, where in 1894 David Jones introduced the first 4-6-0 locomotives used in Britain, the very successful 'Big Goods'. But the main and continuing centre of innovation was Swindon, mechanical headquarters of the GWR. Here George Jackson Churchward, appointed locomotive superintendent in 1902, brought scientific principles to bear on design and construction. Unlike most of his peers, who – with unjustifiable arrogance and complacency – regarded British methods as naturally best, he was keen to learn and benefit from foreign practice, especially that of the Northern Railway of France, where the designer Alfred De Glehn had built some remarkable 4-4-2 Atlantic-type compound locomotives. The Great Western purchased three of these between 1903 and 1905, played with them intensively, and incorporated many features into Swindon practice, although not the compounding. Churchward found that the 'simple' use of steam answered his requirements effectively. The only British company to build successful compound engines in large numbers was the Midland, where Smith and Deeley as successive chief engineers built the 'Midland Compounds' that ran almost all the company's express trains.

ABOVE After the 1923 Grouping, some engines were transferred to new territory. Many Midland 4-4-0s went to the Glasgow & South Western Railway. This one is on a Kilmarnock–Dumfries stopping train.

The Midland was unusual in this respect. By the early 1900s, the 10-wheeler was regarded as essential by most lines for hauling mainline passenger trains. In many cases, the preferred version was the Atlantic, whose 4-4-2 wheel arrangement allowed for a wider firebox than the 4-6-0. The first British Atlantics were built by H.A. Ivatt on the Great Northern in 1898 and were known as 'Klondykes', as the Alaskan gold rush was on at the time. In 1902, Ivatt introduced a larger-boilered version, the first of which, No. 251, is preserved along with the first 'Klondyke', *Henry Oakley*. The Lancashire & Yorkshire, Great Central, London Brighton & South Coast and North British, among others, also favoured the Atlantic for mainline services. The 4-6-0's advantage over the Atlantic lay in its greater tractive power, with the coupled wheels bearing more of the engine's weight.

Not all designers succeeded with this type. Dugald Drummond, after a series of excellent and elegant 4-4-0 types, produced large, ponderous-looking 4-6-0s on the LSWR, including the aptly nicknamed 'Paddleboxes', the performance of which was generally less than sparkling.

ABOVE Britain's first Atlantic locomotive was the GNR's *Henry Oakley* of 1898, designed by H.A. Ivatt. These 4-4-2s were known as 'Klondykes' after the gold rush of the time.

4-4-2 HENRY OAKLEY GNR 1898

Tractive effort: 18,000lb (8160kg)
Axle load: 35,840lb (16.25 tonnes)
Cylinders: two 18¾x24in (476x609mm)
Driving wheels: 79½in (202cm)
Heating surface: 1442sq ft (134m²)
Superheater: n/a
Steam pressure: 175psi (12.3kg/cm²)
Grate area: 26.75sq ft (2.5m²)
Fuel: Coal – 14,320lb (6.5 tonnes)
Water: 3500gall (4203 US) (16m³)
Total weight: 129,920lb (58.9 tonnes)
Overall length: 26ft 4in (8.03m)

McIntosh, pioneer of the big boiler, produced a handsome inside-cylindered 4-6-0 for the Caledonian's heavy Anglo-Scottish expresses. The most famous was the 'Cardean' class, which performed well, but not outstandingly. It seemed that it was a hard type to get right, although Highland 'Castles' and GW 'Stars' demonstrated, in their different areas, that the 4-6-0 could be extremely successful. On the LSWR and the Caledonian, however, the older 4-4-0s were to outlive their bigger shed-mates by many years.

ALL CHANGE

On all lines, boilers became bigger, their pressure increased, chimneys and domes shrank, as the designers coped with fitting more power into the tight British loading gauge. The number of driving wheels increased. 0-8-0 locomotives were introduced on the North Eastern, 2-8-0s on the GWR and GNR, to replace the old double-heading on coal and minerals trains. Traffic was still expanding, and, despite the increase in power, the total number of engines in use continued to rise. The continuing increase in freight traffic led to the building of large

OPPOSITE A shunting engine and crew pose for the camera. LMS 2F Fowler dock tank 0-6-0T No. 11275, built in 1928, is in sparkling condition. Note the hooked shunting pole, used to attach and detach couplings while the wagons were on the move: a job requiring skill and muscle.

marshalling yards, with the innovation of hump shunting. At Feltham in West London (LSWR), Stratford in East London (GER) and Wath upon Dearne (GCR), among other places, vast arrays of sidings were laid out. Large tank-engine types were designed to move long wagon trains: on the London & South Western, R.W. Urie's 4-8-0T of class G16 was rated as amongst the company's most powerful engine types.

Changes on one front, in this case the greater weight and length of locomotives, demanded changes on others. Tender engines had to be turned at the end of their run, and, unless there was a convenient triangular layout, this meant using a turntable. Turntables built in 1880 to fit 4-4-0s might not be long enough for a 4-6-0 in 1905. New ones were often needed, and other engine shed facilities, such as coaling platforms, also had to be altered or extended. A distinctive feature of the steam railway was the water column at the platform ends of many stations, with its accompanying tank set on brick or metal supports. At some places where double-headed trains passed regularly, such as Crianlarich on the West Highland, these columns were set in pairs so that the train and pilot engines could take on water at the same time.

Heavier engines and trains, and higher speeds, made new demands on the permanent way. Major bridges had usually been built with such strength that they coped easily (some of

BELOW The Caledonian Railway built the 'Cardean' class inside-cylinder 4-6-0s in 1906 to haul mainline passenger expresses. *Cardean* itself was the regular engine on the Glasgow-Carlisle section of the 'Corridor', precursor of the 'Royal Scot'. The big eight-wheel tender allowed engines to run non-stop between Carlisle and Perth (151 miles/243km).

Brunel's brick bridges are still in use), but many smaller bridges had to be strengthened. The trackbed and rails also had to be of sufficient support and strength. Sleepers had usually been laid on a cinder base, thriftily using a railway by-product. Now, main lines were laid on quarried stone chips. There was concern not only about clearances, but also about the 'hammer-blow' inflicted on the rails by driving wheels, and new locomotive types had to be passed by the civil engineer before they were allowed to run. This caused a major row on the Highland Railway in 1916, when the civil engineer flatly refused to let the newly delivered big 'River'-class 4-6-0s set wheel on the line, and all six had to be sold off to the Caledonian.

ABOVE Ex-CR No. 905 leaves Glasgow with a southbound express. In CR days these locomotives had their own drivers, who were also responsible for care and routine maintenance.

Into the twentieth century, new steam-powered lines were still being built. Some of these were remote, such as the extensions to Mallaig and Kyle of Lochalsh in the western Highlands. But just before the end of the nineteenth century, the last main line into London (until the 21st-century Channel Tunnel link) was completed with the arrival of the Great Central Railway at Marylebone Station in March 1899. Known until August 1897 as the Manchester, Sheffield & Lincolnshire Railway, the Great Central was run with style and verve (its founding father, Sir Edward Watkin, had planned a Channel tunnel). But London and the East Midlands were already well connected via the Great Northern and Midland Railways. The speed and comfort of the GC expresses, drawn by J.G. Robinson's handsome Atlantics, the 'Jersey Lilies', attracted custom, but their traffic and revenues were always far less than those of their rivals.

The Modern Face of Steam

By around 1912, it could be said that the modern steam locomotive had arrived. All the essential features were present. It is worth pointing out that, although Britain produced the first locomotives, some of the most important technical features came from elsewhere. A vital and universally used addition to efficiency was the steam injector, developed by the French engineer Henri Giffard in 1859. This device forced water from the tender into the boiler against

BELOW From 1923 until the end of steam, the majority of Great Western fast passenger services were handled by the 'Castle'-class 4-6-0s, designed by C.B. Collett very much in the tradition of G.J. Churchward.

ABOVE The two-cylinder LNER B1 class, seen here in preserved BR No. 62005 at Goathland on the North Yorks Moors Railway.

the internal steam pressure. The valve gear which was used on most modern engines was based on that devised by the Belgian Egide Walschaerts, in 1844–48. Another Belgian, Alfred Belpaire, developed the flat-topped firebox which was used on many engines, from the 1880s up to the British Railways standard types. Although British engineers had tried superheating at various times in the nineteenth century, it was the German Schmidt superheater, developed in the early 1900s, which provided by far the best solution. The superheater took steam from the boiler and led it through a series of intensely hot flues, pushing up its temperature and expanding its volume, and so enabling less steam to do more work when it passed into the cylinders. It vastly improved locomotive performance. From then until the end of steam traction, improvements were a matter of detail and scale.

The new order was first revealed on the Great Western. Even before he assumed supreme command, the influence of Churchward was seen on the GW 'Atbara' 4-4-0s of 1898, but it

ABOVE Churchward's *The Great Bear*, shown here on the 'Cheltenham Tea Car Express', was Britain's first Pacific-type locomotive (1908) and the only one ever built by the GWR.

OPPOSITE A tank locomotive with express headlamps: preserved ex-LNER Class N2 0-6-2, in BR livery as No. 69523, is seen on the Great Central Railway. With condensing pipes for working in tunnel sections, the class was designed in 1920 to work suburban traffic north and south from King's Cross.

4-6-2 THE GREAT BEAR GWR 1908

Tractive effort: 29,430lb (13,346kg)
Axle load: 45,808lb (20.8 tonnes)
Cylinders: four 15x26in (381x660mm)
Driving wheels: 80½in (204.5cm)
Heating surface: 2831.5sq ft (263m^2)
Superheater: 545sq ft (50.5 m^2)
Steam pressure: 225psi (15.8kg/cm^2)
Grate area: 41.8sq ft (3.9 m^2)
Fuel: Coal – 13,440lb (6.1 tonnes)
Water: 3500gall (4203 US) (16m^3)
Total weight: 218,400lb (99 tonnes)
Overall length: 34ft 6in (10.52m)

was with the 'Cities' of 1903 that the hallmarks of a tapered boiler – an almost square-topped firebox and no dome – became familiar. In 1906 came the first of the celebrated four-cylinder 4-6-0 'Star' class, *North Star* (built first as an Atlantic), the direct ancestor of the later 'Castles' and 'Kings'. Like them, it was intended for express passenger work, but equally significant were the two-cylinder 'Saints', from which the LMS 'Black Five' was descended. The GWR engines were relatively expensive to build: when challenged by the company's directors on why it was that the LNWR could build three 4-6-0s for the price of two GW 'Stars', Churchward is reputed to have replied: 'Because one of mine could pull two of their bloody things backwards!' Interchange trials arranged by the LNWR in 1910 proved the superiority of the GW engines beyond doubt. George Whale's 'Experiment' class 4-6-0s were wholly outclassed by the GW *Lode Star* and *Polar Star.* The situation would be repeated in 1925 on the LNER and in 1928 on the LMS.

Nevertheless, on the LNWR, Bowen-Cooke and his predecessor George Whale had revolutionized the motive-power scene since 1903. One writer has called engines such as the

'Precursors' of 1904 and the 'George Vs' the Tin Lizzies of railway engines: cheap to build, straightforward to drive, uncomplicated to maintain, they hammered along with plenty of noise, rattle and smoke, but they had plenty of steam and speed too, and were solidly reliable. The enginemen loved them. Bowen-Cooke's four-cylinder express 4-6-0 of 1913, the 'Claughton', sought to combine some of the virtues of Swindon and Crewe; however, despite some very good test performances, its overall record was undistinguished, and the design was not developed by the LMS after 1923.

In 1908, Churchward also built the first British 4-6-2, or Pacific, locomotive, *The Great Bear*. It remained a one-off and was later converted to 4-6-0. The great era of the Pacific was yet to come, and its greatest engineers, Nigel Gresley and William Stanier, were still young men in 1908, working on the designs of others (in Stanier's case, those of Churchward).

BELOW Designed to work on the West Highland Railway, the preserved *The Great Marquess*, one of Sir Nigel Gresley's K4-class 2-6-0s of 1937, seen on the Freshfield bank, Bluebell Railway. The brief was to produce an engine with relatively light axle loading and considerable power. Speed was not a major concern.

LEFT The Great Central Railway's 2-8-0 goods locomotive of 1910, designed by J.G. Robinson, reached some unexpected places due to its selection as the 'war' engine for use in military campaigns in World War I. During the war, examples were built at various works, as well as at the GCR's own Gorton plant in Manchester.

Special War Services

When World War I broke out in August 1914, the railways of Britain were immediately placed under government control. For the first time, a single central authority, the Railway Executive Committee, was imposed over the 120 operating companies. Around a third of the railways' male staff volunteered for war service, and the phenomenon of the lady porter and signalwoman appeared. Railway workshops switched to building tanks and making munitions. Vast numbers of special trains were run, the most celebrated being the 'Misery', which ran every night between Euston and Thurso carrying naval personnel to and from the Grand Fleet's base at Scapa Flow. (The nickname was heartfelt.) It took more than 22 hours for its journey of 728 miles (1172km).

Between 1914 and 1919, intensive traffic and reduced maintenance took a heavy toll on the railways. At the end of the war, most were in a decrepit state, short of equipment and money. All were owed large sums by the government, following their provision of special war services. Despite many protestations of gratitude for the companies' work, the government proved to be a slow, reluctant and incomplete payer, and some companies, including the North British, almost collapsed while waiting their due. Disgruntled railway staff held their first national strike in September–October 1919. To the fury of the companies, the government granted an eight-hour working day and substantial pay rises.

BELOW In 1900, James Holden of the Great Eastern Railway introduced the 'Claud Hamilton' class 4-4-0 for express services, including its longest non-stop run, 131 miles (242km) between Liverpool Street and North Walsham, 'The Norfolk Coast Express'. The original engine is seen here on exhibition in LNER colours.

ABOVE The GER made numerous experiments with oil rather than coal fuel, and a number of the 'Claud Hamilton' 4-4-0s were fitted out as oil burners, with tank tenders. With North Sea oil still undiscovered, coal was always the cheaper option for British steam railways.

In 1919, for the first time, the British government included a Minister of Transport, Sir Eric Geddes, once deputy general manager of the North Eastern Railway. His presence indicated the intention to have a national transport policy, but this did not come about. To the central controllers, however, it had seemed clear that to have more than 120 railway companies in a relatively small country was wildly uneconomic, as well as highly inefficient. Each one, however small, had its hierarchy of officers, its workshops and depots. Often competing with one another for the same traffic, many had little chance of remaining profitable in the postwar world. Already the electric tramcar had caused the abandonment of many suburban services; now the petrol-engined bus and truck were coming on to the scene in large numbers. Throughout the war, the railways, under government regulation, were refused

LEFT Another preserved example of the once-ubiquitous 0-6-0 type is the North British *Maude*, built in 1891 and classed J31 by the LNER. Rebuilt in 1915, it went to France for army work in 1917–18, then worked in Scotland until 1966. It is now on the Bo'ness and Kinneil Railway.

ABOVE The Southern Railway's 'King Arthur' class of 4-6-0s, 'Knights of the Turntable', was designed by Richard Maunsell in 1925 to provide the company's basic express passenger traction. Preserved No. 777 *Sir Lamiel* was always one of the star performers and is seen here at Rothley as BR 30777.

permission to increase their freight charges. In 1920, when they at last went up, they nearly doubled overnight. As common carriers, the railways were forced to publish a scale of charges. The road hauliers could charge what they liked and found it easy to undercut the railways. It was clear that some rationalization of the railways was necessary.

Amalgamation and the Railways Act

The railways passed out of government control on 15 August 1921. Four days later, the Railways Act came into force, enjoining the amalgamation of all railway companies into regional groups by June 1923. An Amalgamation Tribunal was set up to coordinate matters and resolve disputes. A number of amalgamations (called the Grouping) followed swiftly, while discussion still went on about the eventual shape of things. By January 1923, however, the work was completed. Four great railway companies replaced the previous multiplicity. Of the larger constituents, the London, Midland & Scottish Railway embraced the LNWR, L&Y, Midland, Caledonian, GSWR and Highland. The London & North Eastern Railway comprised the GN, GC, GER, NER and NB. The Southern Railway comprised the LSWR, LBSCR and SECR. The Great Western Railway alone retained its former title, with its empire now enlarged by all the Welsh companies, such as the Cambrian and the Taff Vale.

Only three joint systems – the Cheshire Lines, the Somerset & Dorset and the Midland & Great Northern – and a handful of very small independent standard-gauge lines were outside the ambit of the Railways Act; they continued to be run as before. The Big Four would last until the railways were nationalized in 1948.

The amalgamations and takeovers were not accomplished without argument, difficulty and even heartache. The old companies had often engendered fierce loyalty among their staff, together with contempt for rivals. The problems were particularly acute in the newly formed LMS, the biggest single railway business in the world, where ancient hatreds between LNWR and Midland still flourished. One-time chiefs became divisional heads, answerable to men who had been their commercial or mechanical rivals. Was the proud engineering tradition of Darlington to bow to that of Doncaster? Or Crewe to Derby? The answer was yes – but it took time for the new scheme of things to settle down. Traffic managers had to decide between competing routes in some cases. The Southern, now with two routes to Portsmouth, downgraded the old Mid-Sussex line through Horsham in favour of the former LSWR direct line via Guildford and received such a blast of bad publicity that it became the first

OPPOSITE In BR livery, Sir William Stanier's ex-LMS Pacific *City of Lichfield* puts out full power on the climb to Beattock Summit with the down 'Royal Scot.'

BELOW One of two preserved LNER three-cylinder class Q 0-8-0s, seen here at Thomason Foss on North Yorkshire Moors Railway.

railway company to set up a modern-style public relations department to put its own side of the story.

The Great Western apart, it took some years for an esprit de corps to emerge among the new companies. The almost family atmosphere of such lines as the GSWR and the Hull & Barnsley could not be preserved. Staff relations were poor, with managements refusing to talk to the trades unions. Although the new chiefs tried to familiarize themselves with their regional outposts, they were inevitably seen as remote figures. On the LMS, Sir Josiah Stamp, President of the Executive from 1927, who had a carriage fitted out to take him round the system, was regarded with nervous hostility by the staff. His visits were seen as 'sacking tours'. Stamp's great ambition, in the tradition of Sir Richard Moon, was to reduce the costs of the company by standardization and by economies – and if the latter meant grubby trains and unpolished engines, then so be it.

BELOW Preserved LNER class A2 Pacific No. 60532 *Blue Peter* takes the 10.15 Leicester–Loughborough on the restored Great Central main line – the 20-mile (33.8km) trip rather easier than its original service.

Hard Hit by the Depression

For eight years from 1929, the railways suffered, like the rest of the country, from the slump in trade and industry known as the Great Depression. Pay for all grades was reduced by 2.5 per cent in 1929. The basic traffic in coal, iron ore and steel fell disastrously. Many staff were laid off. With reduced revenues,

4-6-0 ROYAL SCOT LMS 1927

Tractive effort: 34,000 lb (15,420kg)
Axle load: 47,040lb (21.3 tonnes)
Cylinders: three 18x26in (457x660mm)
Driving wheels: 81in (205.75cm)
Heating surface: 2081sq ft (193.3m²)
Superheater: 445sq ft (41.3m²)
Steam pressure: 250psi (17.6kg/cm²)
Grate area: 31.2sq ft (2.9m²)
Fuel: Coal – 11,200lb (5 tonnes)
Water: 3500gall (4203 US) (16m³)
Total weight: 190,400lb (86.3 tonnes)
Overall length: 27ft 6in (8.38m)

there was less opportunity for new investment. Although it was also a decade of technical progress, with high-performance locomotive types appearing, there was less replacement of veteran types than would otherwise have been the case. This was even more true of the carriage and wagon stock. The typical goods wagon or van remained a basic four-wheeler without provision for automatic or continuous brakes. The industrial recovery of the later 1930s was led by new 'light' industries, running on electrical power and situated with an eye to road, rather than rail, links. The rail connection was no longer vital.

The railway companies, like other big businesses, found that it was desirable to cultivate a public image that was sometimes at variance with their actual average performance. The natural way to do this was by focusing public attention on a select number of prestige routes and trains. All of them did this to some extent. The Southern introduced the 'Atlantic Coast Express', from Waterloo to the north Cornwall resorts, on 19 July 1926. In 1929, it inaugurated the all-Pullman 'Golden Arrow' service on the London–Dover–Paris route. The LMS ran many named trains including the longest-distance scheduled service, the overnight 'Royal Highlander' from Inverness to Euston. Its crack train was the 10 a.m. 'Royal Scot' from Euston to Glasgow and Edinburgh, long known to operating staff as 'The Corridor', as it had

ABOVE The original LMS 'Royal Scot' type 4-6-0 of 1927 was an immensely impressive machine, though its subsequent rebuilding in the 1940s made it a far more effective and efficient one.

BELOW Rebuilt 'Royal Scot' No. 46102, *Black Watch*, sets off from the now-closed Edinburgh Princes Street station with a local train for Glasgow Central.

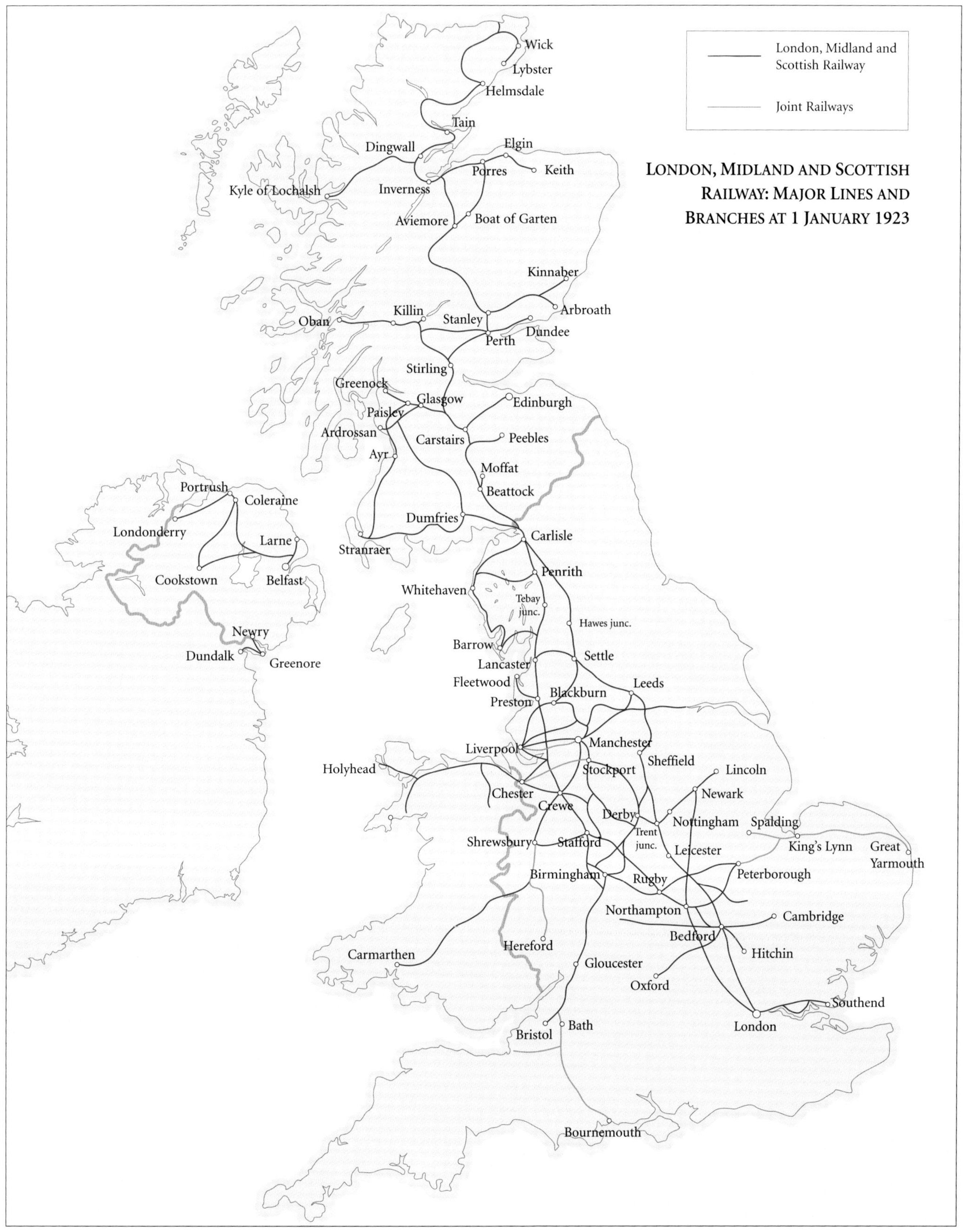
London, Midland and Scottish Railway
Joint Railways
London, Midland and Scottish Railway: Major Lines and Branches at 1 January 1923
Wick
Lybster
Helmsdale
Tain
Dingwall
Elgin
Forres
Keith
Kyle of Lochalsh
Inverness
Aviemore
Boat of Garten
Kinnaber
Arbroath
Oban
Killin
Stanley
Dundee
Perth
Stirling
Greenock
Glasgow
Edinburgh
Paisley
Ardrossan
Carstairs
Peebles
Ayr
Moffat
Beattock
Portrush
Coleraine
Londonderry
Larne
Cookstown
Belfast
Dumfries
Stranraer
Carlisle
Penrith
Whitehaven
Tebay junc.
Hawes junc.
Newry
Dundalk
Greenore
Barrow
Lancaster
Settle
Fleetwood
Leeds
Blackburn
Preston
Liverpool
Manchester
Sheffield
Holyhead
Stockport
Lincoln
Chester
Newark
Crewe
Derby
Nottingham
Spalding
Trent junc.
Shrewsbury
Stafford
Leicester
King's Lynn
Great Yarmouth
Birmingham
Rugby
Peterborough
Northampton
Cambridge
Bedford
Hereford
Hitchin
Carmarthen
Gloucester
Oxford
Southend
Bath
Bristol
London
Bournemouth

been one of the first corridor trains. For no very obvious reason, the GWR picked the town of Cheltenham for its fastest train, 'The Cheltenham Spa Express', which began in 1923 and was popularly known as the 'Cheltenham Flyer'. For a period, this was the fastest train in the world, with a scheduled run between Swindon and Paddington of 77.3 miles (124.4km) in 70 minutes. Its best recorded time was made on 2 June 1932, with an average of 81.7mph (131.5km/h). The most famous of the named trains was the LNER's 10 a.m. King's Cross–Edinburgh, the 'Flying Scotsman'. Like the 'Royal Scot', it had a long pedigree. From 1 May 1928, this train made the longest non-stop run in the world, with no scheduled halt between start and finish of its journey. Despite economic uncertainty and ever greater road competition, Britain's railway companies could thus claim to lead the world in a number of ways.

ABOVE The GWR's 7200 class 2-8-2T of 1934, its most powerful tank engine consisted of rebuilds of older 2-8-0T classes 4200 and 5200.

RATIONALIZATION

Rationalization and reallocation of rolling stock and locomotives often improved services. Lines which had still been using wooden six-wheel vehicles from the previous century were equipped with steel bogie coaches; even if these were second-hand from elsewhere, they were a great improvement. Locomotives sometimes ran far from their one-time haunts. Midland

BELOW G.J. Churchward's two-cylinder 'Saint' class of 1907.

Compounds on the old Caledonian and GSW lines gave sterling performances, often with loads far greater than originally envisaged for them. The LNER built a new batch of 4-4-0 'Directors' of the Great Central's design for use in Scotland. There was still no national policy for locomotive design. Each of the Big Four kept its own locomotive works, although the smaller ones were normally reduced to repair and maintenance depots.

An interesting difference in philosophy emerged between the designers of the LMS and the LNER. Under the dominating influence of Lord Stamp, the LMS aim was to construct locomotives which could be employed anywhere on a system that stretched from Wick to Bournemouth. Gresley, chief mechanical engineer of the LNER from 1923, believed in matching locomotive types to particular routes. Whilst the LMS policy had greater logic

BELOW The Southern Railway's four-cylinder 'Lord Nelson' class 4-6-0 appeared in 1926 and was in mainline service for 30 years. All were refitted with wide chimney and multiple-blast. In this 1948 scene, No. 861 *Lord Anson* heads out of Victoria with an express.

GREAT CENTRAL
506
BUTLER-HENDERSON

LEFT The Great Central 'Director' class 4-4-0s were introduced by J.G. Robinson in 1913 and handled that company's relatively lightweight but fast expresses on the main line from Marylebone to Sheffield. They mark the final development of the characteristically British inside-cylinder 4-4-0. One member of the class, No. 506 *Butler-Henderson*, survives in preservation.

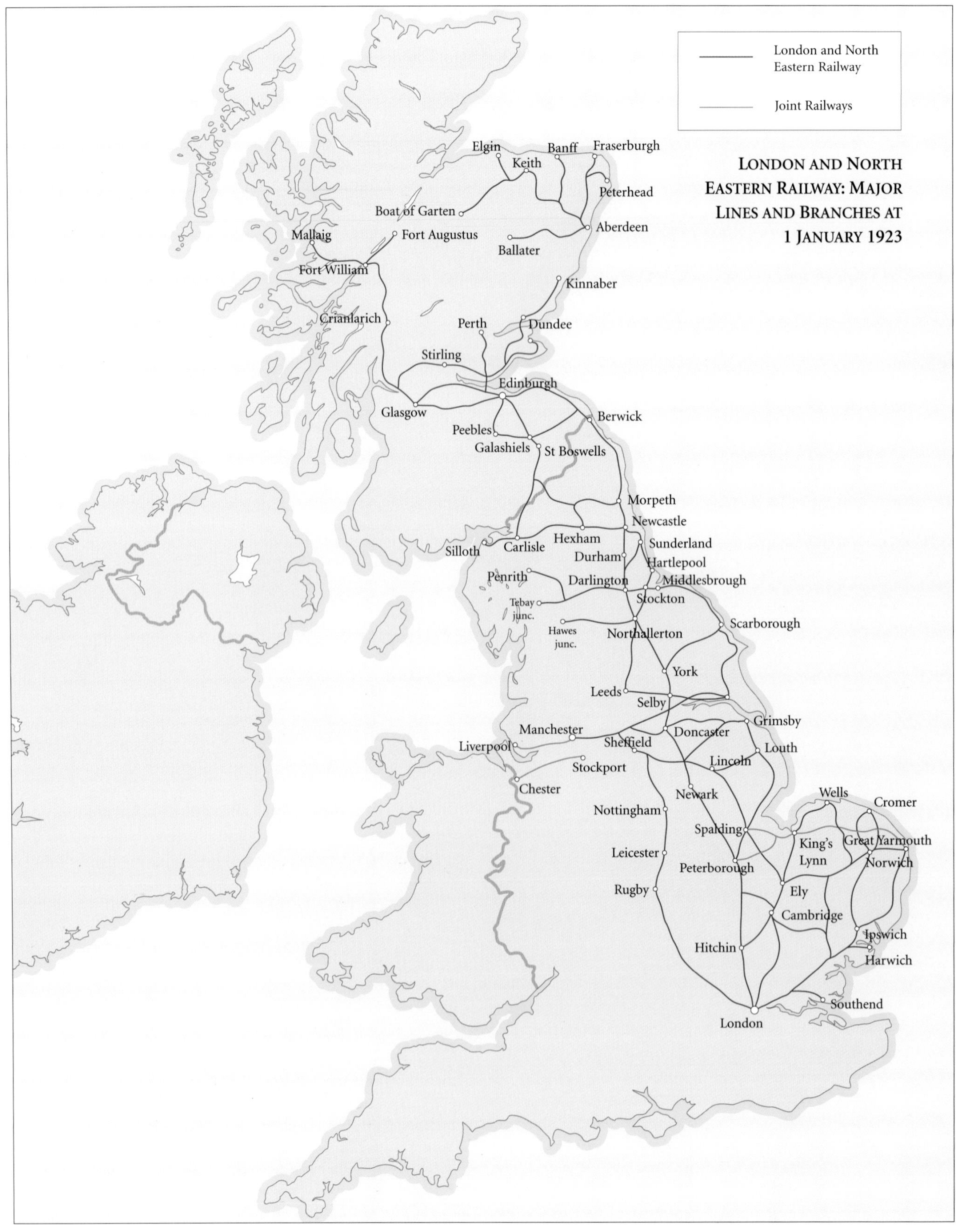
London and North Eastern Railway
Joint Railways
LONDON AND NORTH EASTERN RAILWAY: MAJOR LINES AND BRANCHES AT 1 JANUARY 1923
Elgin
Banff
Fraserburgh
Keith
Peterhead
Boat of Garten
Aberdeen
Mallaig
Fort Augustus
Ballater
Fort William
Kinnaber
Crianlarich
Perth
Dundee
Stirling
Edinburgh
Glasgow
Berwick
Peebles
Galashiels
St Boswells
Morpeth
Newcastle
Hexham
Sunderland
Silloth
Carlisle
Durham
Hartlepool
Penrith
Darlington
Middlesbrough
Stockton
Tebay junc.
Hawes junc.
Northallerton
Scarborough
York
Leeds
Selby
Grimsby
Manchester
Doncaster
Sheffield
Louth
Liverpool
Lincoln
Stockport
Chester
Newark
Wells
Cromer
Nottingham
Spalding
King's Lynn
Great Yarmouth
Norwich
Leicester
Peterborough
Ely
Rugby
Cambridge
Ipswich
Hitchin
Harwich
Southend
London

behind it, the LNER's gave it a more varied and distinctive locomotive stock and was much more beloved of railway enthusiasts. (Prior to the introduction of Gresley's Beyer-Garratt locomotive in 1925, the most striking example of an engine built for a specific route was the Midland's solitary 0-10-0, known as 'Big Emma' or 'Big Bertha', which spent its entire career from 1920 to 1956 banking trains up the Lickey Incline.)

Each company set about building new locomotives, and the new urge for favourable publicity was soon followed by some of the old rivalries. Each new express type had to be bigger or more powerful. This trend began on the Great Western in 1923 with the appearance of the first 'Castle', *Caerphilly Castle,* hailed as the most powerful express engine in Britain. Designed by C.B. Collett, Churchward's successor from 1923, it was in every way in the

ABOVE The Midland Railway's 0-10-0 was a one-off, built in 1919 to bank heavy trains up the 1:38 Lickey Incline of its Bristol–Birmingham main line. Common in many other countries, ten-coupled engines were an extreme rarity on British lines until the 'Austerity' 2-10-0 of World War II.

LEFT Preserved GWR Class 43xx 2-6-0 No. 7325 at Kidderminster, Severn Valley Railway. Great Western 'Moguls' go back to pre-1914, but this one was built in 1932. Although it was intended as a mixed-traffic engine, fast goods services were its main task.

ABOVE The L&Y 'Crab' 2-6-0, of 1922, was a useful general-purpose engine, showing that its designers had learned from the failure and successful rebuilding of the 4-6-0 type that preceded it. No. 42765 is seen here on Summerseat viaduct, East Lancashire Railway.

2-6-0 5P4F CRAB LMS 1926

Tractive effort: 27,000lb (12,245kg)
Axle load: 21,280lb (9.6 tonnes)
Cylinders: two 21x26in (533x660mm)
Driving wheels: 66in (167.5cm)
Heating surface: 1412sq ft (131.2m^2)
Superheater: 308sq ft (28.6m2)
Steam pressure: 180psi (12.7kg/cm^2)
Grate area: 27.5sq ft (2.5m^2)
Fuel: Coal – 11,200lb (5 tonnes)
Water: 3500gall (4203 US) (16m^3)
Total weight: 150,080lb (68 tonnes)
Overall length: 25ft 6in (7.77m)

Churchward tradition. In 1926, when R.E.L. Maunsell introduced the 'Lord Nelson' four-cylinder 4-6-0, the Southern's publicity machine trumpeted it as 'the most powerful passenger engine in the country'. In 1927, Collett brought out the 'King' class, the theoretical tractive effort of which was slightly greater and thus won back the accolade.

The LMS – after having gone through a succession of CMEs, and having done nothing more enterprising than build more of the Midland Compounds and some smaller mixed-traffic engines such as the sturdy Horwich-designed 'Crab' 2-6-0 – found itself short of powerful express locomotives in 1927. A compound Pacific was in an advanced state of design at Derby, but the LNWR faction, with memories of Webb, opposed this plan. A GW 'Castle' was borrowed, unknown to Fowler, and showed that a simple-expansion 4-6-0 could keep time with the West Coast expresses. Top management was convinced; the Pacific was abandoned and an express 4-6-0 was urgently demanded. Despite his command of major works at Crewe, Horwich, Glasgow and Derby, the CME, Sir Henry Fowler, turned to the privately owned North British Locomotive Company in Glasgow for the rapid production of 50 of the imposing three-cylinder 'Royal Scot' 4-6-0, which was to a very large

LEFT The LNER's last fling: A2 Pacific No. 525 *A.H. Peppercorn*, named after its designer, stands newly finished at Doncaster in December 1947, on the eve of railway nationalization.

extent based on the 'Lord Nelson' design. This engine's claim to promotional fame was a boiler pressure of 250lb (113kg). All these various express types performed their basic task adequately, which was to pull a train of up to 500 tons (508 tonnes) at express speeds, then requiring an average of between 60 and 65mph (97 and 105km/h), over long distances.

Chalk and Cheese

Even in the 1930s, 4-4-0s were still being built. The two types could hardly have been in greater contrast. The 'Dukedogs' of the GWR were built to cope with the light axle-loading requirements of the Cambrian lines; they used the outside frames of the obsolete 'Bulldog' class with a 'Duke' class domed boiler. With inside cylinders and outside cranks, they inevitably had an old-fashioned air. The 'Schools' class of the Southern, introduced by R.E.L. Maunsell in 1930,

BELOW Originally No. 3283, this 'Duke' class 4-4-0 was built in 1897, re-boilered in 1905, and withdrawn in 1949. It was photographed at Aberystwyth in 1930.

ABOVE Sir Nigel Gresley designed two 2-8-2 'Mikado' types for the LNER, the P1 goods engine of 1927 and the famous P2 express class, of which *Cock o' the North*, in 1934, was the first. This contemporary picture shows its original part-streamlined form. Later members of the class would be fully streamlined on the A4 model.

2-8-2 P2 LNER 1934

Tractive effort: 44,000lb (19,955kg)
Axle load: 45,360lb (20.57 tonnes)
Cylinders: three 21x26in (533x660mm)
Driving wheels: 74in (188cm)
Heating surface: 3490sq ft (324.2m^2)
Superheater: 635sq ft (59m^2)
Steam pressure: 220psi (15.5kg/cm^2)
Grate area: 50sq ft (4.6m2)
Fuel: Coal – 20,160lb (9.1 tonnes)
Water: 5000gall (6029 US) (22.75m^3)
Total weight: 246,400lb (111.7 tonnes)
Overall length: 37ft 11in (11.58m)

Maunsell in 1930, was also designed for a specific route, the tightly bending Hastings line, on which 4-6-0s were not allowed to run. With three cylinders, smoke deflectors and wide chimneys, they looked like express engines and performed similarly. Forty were built, and they ultimately ran on many routes apart from the Hastings one, often matching the performance of the 'Lord Nelsons'.

One company was already operating Pacifics. The GNR had built its first Gresley 4-6-2 in 1922, just before the Grouping and also just before Sir Vincent Raven's 'City' class 4-6-2 for the North Eastern. The appointment of Gresley as first CME of the LNER confirmed that his design – which in any case was superior – would be the standard. In locomotive exchanges of 1925, however, the GW 'Castles' showed superior performance to the Gresley A1s, and Gresley and his team made a number of detailed modifications. By the time of the non-stop 'Flying Scotsman' of 1928, the A1s, some of them fitted with corridor tenders to enable a non-stop change of engine crew, were excellent performers. In 1928, Gresley also brought out his 'Super-Pacific', class A3, and these were doing first-rate service on the East Coast main line well before Stanier moved from Swindon to join the LMS in 1932 and set about providing the West Coast with a comparable stud of Pacifics.

The choice of Stanier was due not only to his abilities, but also to his Swindon training. The LMS's top brass had been greatly impressed by the power and economy of the GWR's *Launceston Castle* when it was borrowed for test purposes in 1928. Now Swindonian techniques and forms began to appear from the LMS works at Horwich, Crewe and Derby.

OPPOSITE TOP The zenith of LMS Pacific design was attained in the 'City' 4-6-2s. Here No. 6254 *City of Stoke on Trent* passes Wavertree Junction, Liverpool, with a London express in the last years before nationalization. These engines had relatively small tenders, but operated over lines well supplied with water troughs.

Even before that, 1932 saw a widespread speeding-up of schedules and the introduction of new named trains such as the 'Liverpool Flyer' and 'Manchester Flyer' between these cities and Euston, hauled by 'Royal Scots'.

BELOW A preserved taper-boilered 0-6-0 GWR No. 3205 at Llangollen, exactly the kind of line for which it was designed.

French Inspiration

Just as De Glehn had given Churchward much food for thought in the 1900s, so another distinguished French engineer, André Chapelon, gave inspiration to Nigel Gresley in the early 1930s. Chapelon's speciality was the internal streamlining of locomotives to make steam flow with the minimum of restraint and the maximum of efficiency from boiler to cylinders. His work was influential in Gresley's design for the P2, Britain's only 2-8-2 'Mikado'-type express locomotives. The first of the six, *Cock o' the North*, appeared in 1934. With smaller driving wheels than the Pacifics (74in/187.9cm, compared to 80in/203.2cm), they were intended to operate on heavy

LEFT The LMS 4-cylinder 'Princess' class Pacific prototypes were built in 1933. A production batch, of which No. 46203 *Princess Margaret Rose* was one, followed in 1935, after some of the faults of the first models had been corrected. No. 46203 is seen here at Kingmoor, Carlisle, on an up express.

OPPOSITE The appearance of the LNER 3-cylinder A4 Pacifics was a sensation in 1935. Later, the streamlined valances over the wheels and motion would be removed, but this illustration of No. 4482 *Golden Eagle* shows the original appearance (*Mallard* is also restored to this form).

Edinburgh–Aberdeen expresses; and with a tractive effort of more than 43,000lb (19,501kg), they were easily the most powerful passenger type produced in Britain. Although not built for high speed, they ran readily up to 85mph (137km/h).

The Pacifics were much faster. In March 1935, an LNER A3 Pacific, *Papyrus*, on a Newcastle–London test run, reached 108mph (174km/h), beating *City of Truro*'s 1904 record, but Gresley had more surprises in store. In September of the same year, which marked 25 years

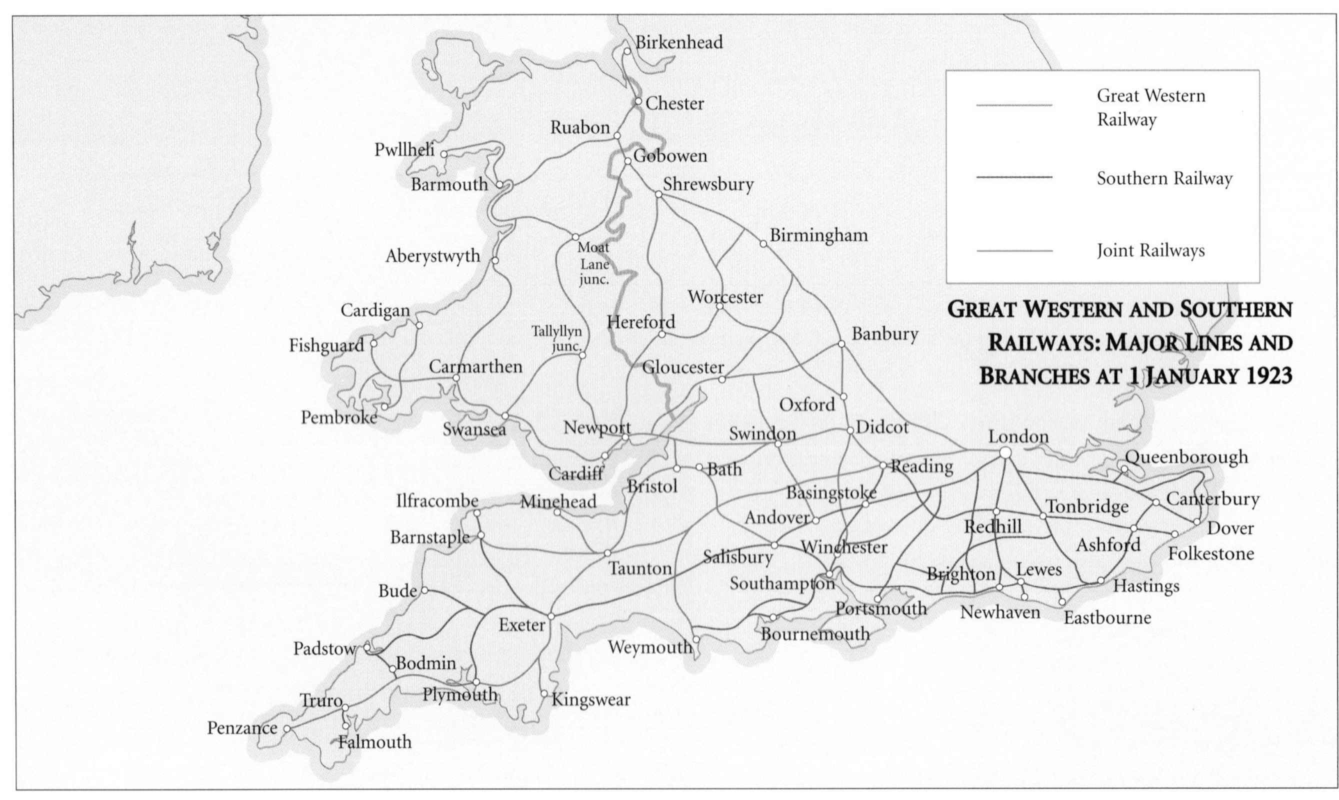

of George V's reign, the LNER inaugurated a new express between London and Edinburgh, the 'Silver Jubilee', making the run in six hours. The world had not seen a train like this before. The locomotive was a new 4-6-2 design, the A4. Though based on the well-proven A3, it looked strikingly different. It had a wedge-shaped front (which owed something to Gresley's friend Ettore Bugatti, the Italian racing car builder), a whaleback top, smoothed sides and a deep valance that covered much of the wheels and motion. The seven carriages were also streamlined. But the vital streamlining was in the steam passages concealed within the A4's silver-grey body. On the press run of the new train, the first of the class, *Silver Link*, ran from south of Hitchin to Holme, outside Huntingdon, at speeds consistently in excess of 100mph (161km/h), with a maximum of 112.5mph (181km/h).

On 3 June 1938, Gresley (by then Sir Nigel) used the excuse of some braking trials on the old Great Northern main line to find out just how fast one of his A4s could go. With a 240-ton (244-tonne) train and a steel-nerved King's Cross driver, John Duddingston, at the regulator, the answer, supplied by *Mallard*, was 126mph (203km/h). It was not achieved without damage to the engine: the middle cylinder big-end was broken. But *Mallard*'s record has never been surpassed by a steam locomotive.

The LMS, too, had its triumphs. Stanier had produced his first Pacific type, No. 6200 *The Princess Royal*, in 1933. The two prototypes were carefully monitored, and a number of design changes, especially to the boiler, were made before others were built. The aim was to

BELOW Class N on the LNER designated 0-6-2T, a large range, containing sub-types designed from the 1890s to the late 1930s. No. 7999, an N7/4, seen here at Corfe Castle on the Swanage Railway, was built in 1924.

have an engine that could run on one tenderful of coal from London to Glasgow, and to make the outward and return trips, a total of 802.8 miles (1292km), within 24 hours. The 'Mid-day Scot' loaded up to 530 tons (538.5 tonnes), more than double the weight of the 'Silver Jubilee', and had the summits of Shap and Beattock to climb. This was the true task and measure of the Stanier Pacifics, but the LMS also responded to the 'Silver Jubilee' with the 'Coronation Scot' of 1937, hauled by the 'Coronation' 4-6-2s, a streamlined development of the 'Princess Royal' class. On this train's trial run, 20 June 1937, No. 6320 *Coronation* snatched the speed record with 114mph (183km/h), held until *Mallard*'s epic achievement a year later. The location of maximum speed – just two miles (3.2km) south of the facing cross-overs at Crewe, where the train was due to stop – required very rapid braking. There was considerable relief among the engineers on board when it was safely accomplished.

ABOVE Gresley's second Pacific, the LNER A3 class of 1928, were known as the Super-Pacifics. Raised casings behind the chimney cover the superheater headers.

COMPETING GENIUSES

Enthusiasts still debate the respective merits of the Gresley and Stanier Pacifics (the latter's streamliners were later rebuilt as more conventionally shaped engines). Both chiefs produced one-off 'experimental' engines, with the LMS steam turbine Pacific proving more effective and durable in service than the LNER's 'hush-hush' 4-6-4 No. 10000, of 1929, with a super-high-pressure boiler. Gresley produced a solitary Garratt-type 2-8-0+0-8-2 in 1925 and in the pre-Stanier years the LMS brought out a 2-6-0+0-6-2 class (1927) – neither was a great success. In 1936, Gresley also produced the highly successful express freight V2 class 2-6-2, sometimes known as the 'Green Arrows': 184 were built.

LEFT Britain built Beyer-Garratt locomotives by the hundred for export, but only a small number ever ran on standard gauge here. The LNER had one; the LMS employed 33 on the Toton–Brent coal trains. Built between 1927 and 1933, they were not highly successful, partly because LMS engineers insisted on using standard parts not meant for articulated locomotives.

LEFT GWR 4-6-0 No. 6990 *Witherslack Hall* approaches Quorn on the restored Great Central line. It is pulling a breakdown train, including a steam crane. The 'Hall' class, from 1928, was the GWR's standard mixed-traffic engine and the immediate ancestor of Stanier's LMS 'Black Five' of 1935.

Gresley will remain most celebrated for his Pacifics and the Mikados. But Stanier's lasting achievement was with two more workaday types, a goods 2-8-0 and the celebrated 'Black Five', a mixed-traffic 4-6-0 which was built in large numbers (842 by 1949) and which, true to LMS philosophy, worked with equal effectiveness on freight or passenger trains over every part of the system. The 'Black Five' owed much to GW practice, particularly the GW 'Hall' class of 1928, which fulfilled a similar role on the Great Western. When war broke out in 1939 and the railways were once again put under extreme pressure, the Stanier 2-8-0 and 4-6-0 types proved invaluable.

BELOW Preserved A4 *Mallard* on the Scarborough Spa Express excursion train at York. On the side of the locomotive can be seen the plaque recording its achievement of the highest speed by a steam engine (won by a whisker from a German 4-6-4).

8P
6240

5 • The Railway in the City

As more and more lines and stations are built in the cities, the townscape is increasingly transformed. The railways often bring change for the better – but sometimes for the worse. Great stations and palatial hotels help to transform city centres, but viaducts, embankments and locomotive depots create social divisions and areas of pollution.

LEFT A 1950s sartorial study. Stationmaster Turrell at Euston wears a topper and tails, locomotive inspector Smith has a Homburg and brown coat, driver Gray wears a peaked cap and overalls, and fireman Moffat wears no hat (but presumably overalls). The engine is LMS Pacific No. 46240 *City of Coventry*.

OPPOSITE Euston departure for Ulster – Stanier 'Pacific' No. 46237 City of Bristol with the 6.30pm express train to Stranraer, connecting with the Larne steamer, on 3 March 1949. This engine was formerly streamlined, as can be seen from the flattened smokebox top.

In North America and some parts of Europe, access of the railway into towns and cities was often simple enough: the railway track was laid along the broad main highway and the train, with bell ringing vigorously, came trundling in at a slow pace. In Great Britain that would not do. From an early stage, a law said that railways had to be fenced off. Roads were usually narrower in any case. In order to get into a large town, property had to be purchased for the line, sidings, yards and stations. The whole activity of railway building required careful surveying of the ground and the underlying geology, and detailed inquiry into land ownership. This latter aspect could be particularly difficult in densely populated urban areas. In the earliest days of steam railways it was less of a problem than it became later. The population of England tripled during the nineteenth century, with most of the increase concentrated in cities, and these consequently spread out mightily. At the same time, of course, this

ABOVE A 1938 scene at Birmingham (New Street). Ex-LNWR 2-4-2 tank engine No. 6636 is at Platform 1 with a local train. In the foreground is an LMS laundry hamper, probably with dining car table-cloths and napkins.

development of outer cities and suburban areas, particularly around London, offered potential for high-intensity suburban train services.

The attitudes of cities to having railway stations varied greatly. Cambridge kept its railway at a distance, to the profit of hackney carriage and later taxi drivers. Oxford's station was slightly closer to the centre but by no means in it. York allowed its ancient walls to be breached to get the railway close in. Edinburgh sanctioned a deep cutting right under the castle walls and a huge station in the middle of the city. Glasgow Central was also, as the name suggests, right in the city centre. In general, all large municipalities came to accept the necessity of letting the railway pass right through, and in return the railways sometimes provided the city with handsome architecture in the big stations, as well as the amenities of opulent hotels.

Station Sharing

In a few cases – Derby is the best example – the city also persuaded several railway companies to combine in using a single station. This was also the most convenient thing for passengers, as it made changing trains and catching connections much easier. But for various reasons this was not always possible. The companies themselves were not keen on shared stations: they liked to control their own lines and systems. Sometimes the topography was wrong. Bradford had two central termini, Exchange and Market Street, at different levels. New lines might come

ABOVE The narrow platforms at London's Charing Cross Station stretched on to Hungerford Bridge over the Thames. In this 1907 coloured photograph, South Eastern & Chatham 4-4-0 No. 591 is ready to go with a lengthy train.

in long after a station had been built, and their promoters might object to buying extra miles of expensive real estate just to link up with another railway. Often the best that might be hoped for was that stations might at least be close to each other, like the LNWR and GWR stations in Oxford, or the Somerset & Dorset and GWR stations in Bath. But this did not always happen. In Aberdeen, the 'southern' Caledonian and North British Railways used a joint station. The Great North of Scotland Railway's terminus was a mile and a half (2.4km) away. When the south train was late, the GNSR waited only for the mailbags to be hustled along. To the unfortunate passengers, it seemed as if the trains to the north were flagged away as soon as they came into sight. In 1867, the GNSR finally joined in using a new joint station. Sharing a station did not necessarily mean friendly relations between the companies. The LNWR, the Chester & Holyhead, the Shrewsbury & Chester and the Birkenhead, Lancashire and Cheshire Junction companies owned Chester, opened in 1849. The LNWR, then led by Captain Huish, declared war on the

LEFT At the sprawling station of Manchester Victoria, in LMS days, 'Crab' mixed-traffic 2-6-0 No. 2841 backs on to its train. The tender, narrower than the locomotive, is lost to sight on the curve.

MATTHEW KIRTLEY (1813–73)

Appointed as the Midland Railway's first locomotive and carriage superintendent in 1844, Kirtley held the post for almost thirty years. He had held the same office on the Birmingham & Derby Junction since 1841, and among his first jobs was to organise a single Midland Railway locomotive works from the separate establishments already existing at Derby. A north-easterner like so many of the first generation of locomotive engineers, he was an apprentice to Timothy Hackworth on the Stockton & Darlington Railway, before becoming an engine driver. He drove the first train into Euston Station on the London & Birmingham Railway in 1838. Kirtley's locomotives, mostly 0-6-0 freight and 2-4-0 passenger types with outside frames, were notable for their solidity and many remained in service for seventy years or more. From 1856 to 1859, with one of his assistants, Charles Markham, he was responsible for the design of what became the standard British firebox for burning coal, with an arch of firebrick and a deflector plate. In some other respects he was a conservative designer, retaining buffers with wooden heads long after most others had adopted iron. He was one of the first to construct large numbers of a single class. His '480' class of goods engines numbered 232 and they remained familiar sights on London coal trains for decades. The longest-lived was No. 778, built in 1869, which was finally withdrawn as British Railways' No. 58110 in 1951, after 82 years of useful service. The Kirtley tradition in some ways lasted for as long as the Midland Railway itself, with a range of quite small but well-built locomotives hauling lightweight trains, and working double-headed with heavier loads. But he did not use the famous 'Midland red', which came later. His engines were painted a deep blue-green.

A Midland veteran, 2-4-0 No. 827 of Kirtley's '800' class, built by Neilson's of Glasgow in 1870, and rebuilt by S.W. Johnson in 1876, as LMS No. 60, in 1932. It was withdrawn in 1936.

LEFT An interior shot of a locomotive roundhouse with engines grouped around the central turntable – Barrow Hill shed at Chesterfield is the only surviving working roundhouse in the country.

Shrewsbury & Chester, which, in association with another line, was trying to capture some of the LNWR Chester–Birmingham traffic. The S&C ticket clerk was bodily thrown out of his office, and all its signs and posters torn down – this in a building of which it was joint owner. From late 1849 to May 1852 the campaign of blatant intimidation and obstruction went on, until the S&C and its ally, the Shrewsbury & Birmingham Railway, negotiated a merger with the Great Western, which itself wanted access to Chester for its Birmingham–Birkenhead line. At that point Huish had to accept the failure of his campaign: even he could not intimidate the Great Western.

Apart from London itself, with its proliferation of terminal stations all round the central area, and no proper long-distance through services, there were other extreme examples of cities with multiple termini. Swansea, with six termini opened between 1850 and 1863, by six different companies, had more than any city other than London. The concentration of railways here was influenced mostly by freight traffic, to do with mining, ironworks and the huge increase of coal export traffic through Swansea Harbour. However, a combination of difficult topography – which would have made it difficult to find a site for a single big station – and fierce hostility among the companies, ensured there would be no single 'Swansea Central' for the convenience of passengers. In most cases, a single city station

BELOW The locomotive roundhouse of the London & Birmingham Railway at Camden Town, London is familiar to Euston-bound passengers. Built in 1847, it is one of the oldest railway buildings to survive, though no longer used for railway purposes.

During the last years of the steam era, three grimy LMS 'Class 5' 4-6-0s have come up from the locomotive shed to wait for duty at Manchester Victoria, while a fourth stands at the platform with a parcels train.

44734

would have been possible, but the government's 'let them get on with it' policy towards railways meant that only a very strong-minded town council could force the big companies to do things they did not want to do. In some places, like Newcastle and Hull, the early amalgamation of local companies into a monopoly – the North Eastern in these cases – also helped in establishing a single central station. Even before the North Eastern Railway was established, George Hudson was chairman of the two lines approaching the Tyne gap from south and north, the Newcastle & Darlington Junction, and the Newcastle & Berwick. It was his enterprise that brought the construction of the two-deck high level rail and road bridge in 1844–50.

A Double-edged Sword

The twin towns of Newcastle and Gateshead give a good example of how the railway could provide improvement or blight. The high level bridge greatly improved access between the two communities. Newcastle gained a fine new Central Station, further enhanced by the building of the Station Hotel in 1854, and contributing to the distinction of the new city centre. At first the station was a terminus, but its western side was opened up with the building of the King Edward VII Bridge in 1906, enabling north–south trains to run straight through. The line to the north was taken in a wide curve round the edge of the city centre. Railway tracks and viaducts split Gateshead, where lines from south and east converged. It was not provided with

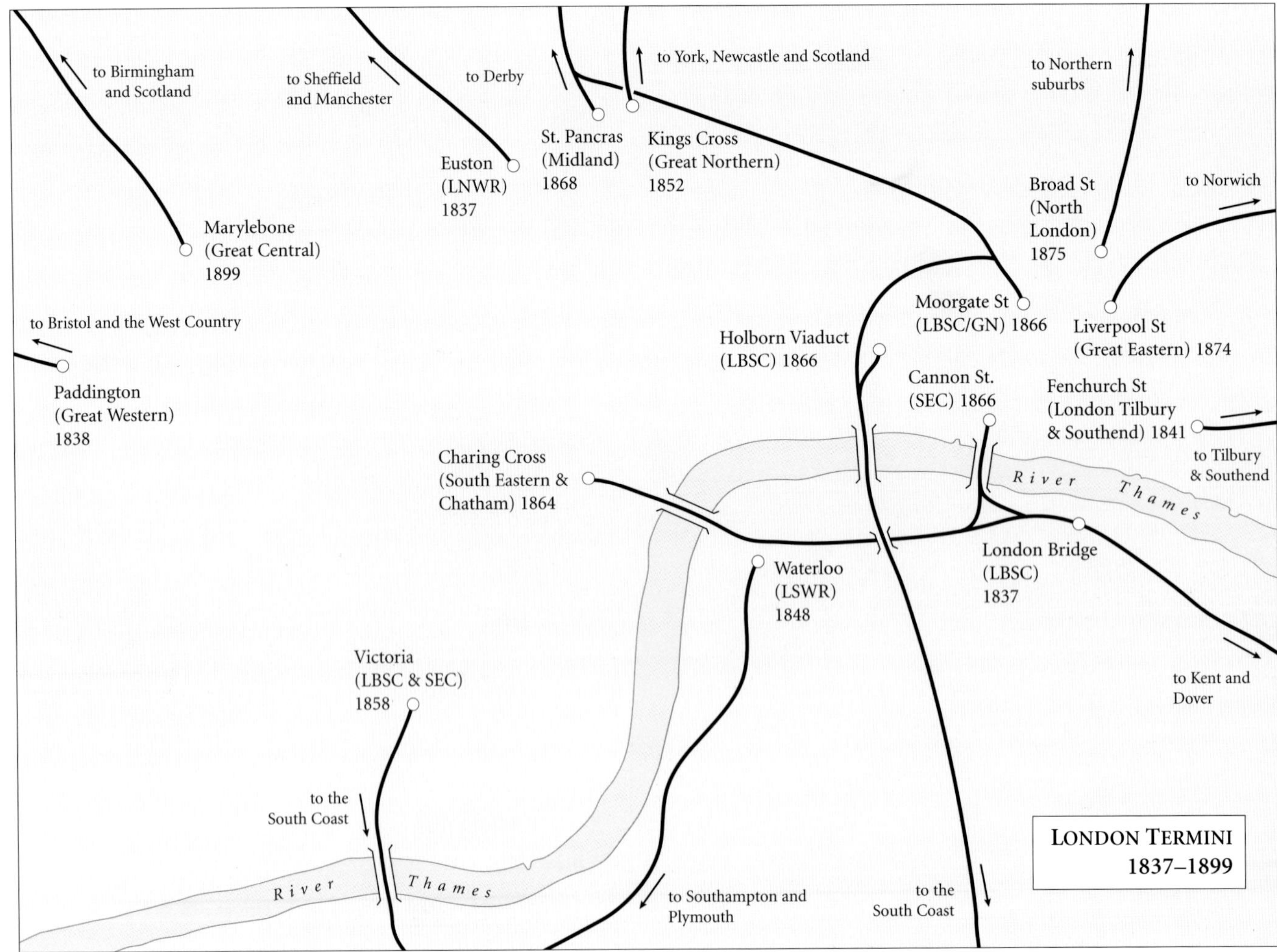

London Termini 1837–1899

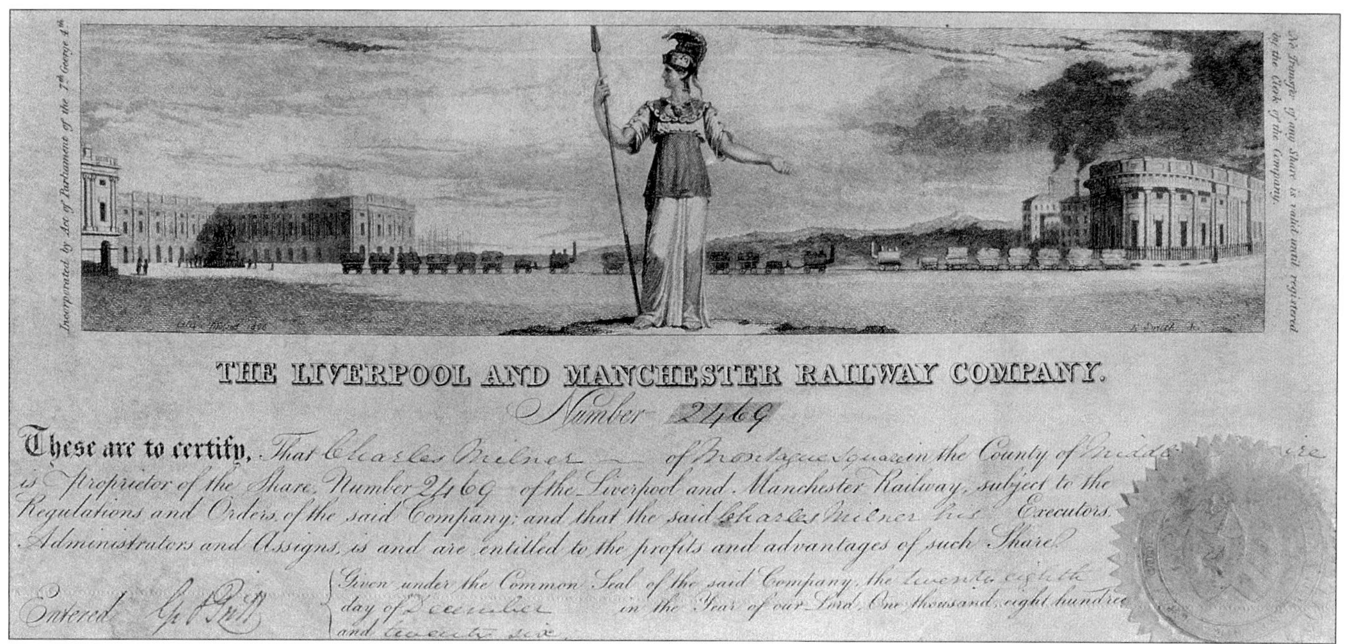

Incorporated by Act of Parliament of the 7th George 4th

No Transfer of any Share is valid until registered by the Clerk of the Company.

THE LIVERPOOL AND MANCHESTER RAILWAY COMPANY.

Number 2469

These are to certify, That Charles Milner of Montague Square in the County of Middlesex is Proprietor of the Share, Number 2469 of the Liverpool and Manchester Railway, subject to the Regulations and Orders of the said Company; and that the said Charles Milner his Executors, Administrators and Assigns, is and are entitled to the profits and advantages of such Share.

Given under the Common Seal of the said Company, the twenty eighth day of December in the Year of our Lord, One thousand eight hundred and twenty six.

Entered

ABOVE Scenes from the terminal cities, with trains linking them and Britannia presiding, are engraved on this share certificate printed for the flotation of the Liverpool & Manchester Railway in 1830.

a large station and travellers had to go to Newcastle Central for all long-distance services. Gateshead was the site of a large locomotive depot and also of an engine repair and building works, which provided employment but also ensured that the town was shrouded in smoke and soot. The town council often made requests for improvements to the service, to which the NER paid scant attention. When the second Tyne bridge was built, Gateshead lost its mainline station altogether. Whilst many other industries contributed to the soot-laden atmosphere, the railway had a literally divisive effect on towns like Gateshead and Stockport, where the shadow of viaducts, the cutting of lines through close-packed housing and the frequency of junctions

LEFT Ex-LSWR Class T1 0-4-4T at Southampton Central, with a stopping train to Portsmouth & Southsea, in August 1937.

LEFT For a long time after the end of steam, this warning sign (now at the Beamish Open Air Museum) still indicated an unguarded level crossing. The outline of a moving steam engine was unmistakable in a way that a diesel or electric locomotive could not be.

all combined to create areas of urban blight. Railway access to city centres almost always brought problems. If the terrain was level, large numbers of level crossings were needed – Hull is a good example – or the railway could be set up on a long viaduct, which obviated the difficulties of level crossings at the cost of walling off one part of the city from another. From the city's point of view, the best way of getting the railway to the centre was by tunnel. This was not a solution welcomed by railway companies as tunnelling was invariably more expensive than laying a surface line, and also required much more construction time. In some cases the lie of the land made tunnelling necessary anyway, and Birmingham was fortunate in this respect. Its first stations, at Vauxhall (1837) and Curzon Street (1838), set up by the Grand Junction and London & Birmingham Railways respectively, were at the edge of the central area (only set up as a borough in 1838, the city had not yet acquired its monumental Victorian buildings). As more lines converged on the rapidly-growing city, the London & North Western, having absorbed the GJR and the L&BR, tunnelled into the centre to build New Street station right in the middle, and this was also used by the Midland Railway. Also by tunnel access, the Great Western built Snow Hill station in the central area. Both of these were through stations, not termini, and the old termini were closed as passenger stations, to become freight-only depots.

LEFT An unusual scene at Waterloo on 28 May 1953, with an ex-LNER Class V2 2-6-2, No. 60908, heading the 9 a.m. train to Exeter and the West. Failures among the Bulleid 'Pacifics' resulted in 'foreign' engines being drafted in to maintain the express services.

LOCOMOTIVE DESIGNERS

JOHN RAMSBOTTOM (1814–97)

A versatile engineer, Ramsbottom was also a highly efficient manager. The growth of the London & North Western Railway's Crewe works owes more to him than to anyone else. He was born in Todmorden, Lancashire, where his father owned a steam-powered cotton mill, and was apprenticed to the Sharp, Roberts locomotive works in Manchester. In 1846 Francis Trevithick (son of Richard Trevithick), a capable designer but poor manager, was sacked as locomotive superintendent of the North-Eastern Division; Ramsbottom was appointed in his stead, and immediately set about a programme of reform, re-organisation and development. Written instructions on plans from his first years, such as, 'Dimensions must be worked to', shed some light on earlier working practices. In 1862 he became chief mechanical engineer of the entire LNWR, at that time the world's biggest railway company. Despite the demands of running a large factory and workforce, Ramsbottom was able to employ his inventive talents. He was the originator of the water-scoop, as described in the main text, and its use spread to other companies and countries. Prior to that, in 1856, Ramsbottom had introduced an improved form of safety valve. The previous type, using a spring balance, was not tamper-proof, and drivers keen to get a few extra pounds of pressure sometimes weighed them down. This was impossible with the Ramsbottom valve, which was widely used. His first notable invention had been an improved piston ring, in 1852. Apart from a substantial salary, royalties from his inventions made him a very wealthy man. He was open to other people's ideas too, and was one of the first locomotive superintendents anywhere to employ the steam injector. Patented in France by Henri Giffard in 1859, it was being fitted to Ramsbottom's new 'Lady of the Lake' 2-2-2 express-engine class that same year. Also in that year he brought out the DX goods 0-6-0 class, which eventually numbered 943; one of them, in 1866, was the thousandth locomotive of the Crewe Works. Under Ramsbottom, the Crewe works set up its own steel-making plant, but his entrepreneurial zeal brought trouble from the private locomotive builders when he tried to build engines for companies other than the North Western. Ramsbottom retired from the LNWR in 1871, following an argument over his pay with the company's formidable chairman, Sir Richard Moon. As a consulting engineer, he remained involved with Britain's railways for another twenty years, and used his Crewe experience to advise the Lancashire & Yorkshire Railway on the layout of its new Horwich works. Ramsbottom, despite his efficiency, left a reputation as a genial and philanthropic individual.

Ramsbottom features on this LNWR 'Precursor' of 1879 include safety valves, injector and water scoop.

An Unfortunate Location

Sheffield was among the less lucky cities in the placing of its stations. Originally bypassed by the Derby–Leeds line of the North Midland Railway, it was at first served only by a branch terminating in what the *Railway News* called a 'miserable station' at Wicker. The completion of Woodhead Tunnel through the Pennines brought an east–west link with Grimsby and Manchester, and Victoria station was completed on this line in 1851. It was some way from the centre. A local attempt in 1864 to raise money for a north–south line, passing under the centre and providing a new central station, was a failure. In 1870 the Midland Railway's line from Chesterfield finally gave Sheffield direct connection to the south, and was followed by the Midland route to Manchester via the Totley tunnel. But the Midland station was also away from the centre, and Sheffield never did get its 'Central'. The railways had the whip hand because they alone had, or could raise, the necessary capital for major works. But they only embarked on such projects where they could see their own advantage. A vastly expensive tunnel under Sheffield's city centre would have done little to increase the revenues of the Midland or Manchester Sheffield & Lincolnshire (later Great Central) railways. Travellers had no choice but to make their way to stations built to suit the railways' convenience. Manchester, despite its early start with the Liverpool & Manchester Railway in 1830, also never achieved a proper central station, although there was a station called Central. The city ended up with four main stations, south and west of the central area. The LNWR had London Road (the present Piccadilly), providing

ABOVE During the General Strike of May 1926 rail services were at a virtual standstill. Troops were drafted in to run some essential trains. A seaman artificer stands on the footplate of LSWR '700' class 0-6-0 No. 692 with an amateur fireman.

RIGHT An LMS class 4F 0-6-0 shunts vans at Wellingborough's main station on the former Midland main line, as a 'Class 5' pulls out with a northbound stopping train. The railway line defines the eastern edge of the town.

services to Crewe and London. This station was shared with the Manchester Sheffield & Lincolnshire, an uncomfortable arrangement that led to obstructions and fisticuffs in 1857 when the MS&L allowed access to the Great Northern, which provided an alternative route to London. Victoria Station, opened in 1844, came into ownership of the Lancashire & Yorkshire Railway when various lines amalgamated in 1847. The LNWR also used Victoria for trains to Liverpool and Leeds, but limited accommodation and the LYR's refusal to allow joint ownership led to the LNWR building the larger Exchange Station alongside Victoria in 1884. Four years before that, the Cheshire Lines Committee, jointly owned by the Midland, the Great Northern and the MSL had opened Manchester Central. Victoria and Exchange were both through stations, but this was useful only for local services. Manchester never acquired the cross-city link-line that would have provided long-distance through services, and travellers changing trains had to allow for a cab or bus ride through crowded streets from station to station.

ABOVE Ex-GWR 0-6-2T No. 5656 at Swansea (High Street) on 12 July 1957.

FLYING SCOTSMAN
BRITISH RAILWAYS
60133

LEFT A busy scene at London King's Cross as A.H. Peppercorn's Class A1 4-6-2 No. 60133 Pommern of British Railways' Eastern Region prepares to depart with the 10 a.m. 'Flying Scotsman' for Edinburgh. The year is 1949. The 'Pacific's' double chimney can clearly be seen.

LEFT After the remodelling of Bristol Temple Meads Station, Brunel's original train shed, with its terminal tracks, was largely used for carriage storage, and its platforms, though numbered, were rarely used for scheduled services.

In the cities of Britain, only the great cathedrals (where they existed) offered public space on a scale comparable to the larger railway stations of the nineteenth century. The stations were something altogether new. Public access to the concourse was free. At first they were simply large spaces where passengers could queue at the platform gates until the staff opened them, shortly before the train left. In addition to the basic ticket office, refreshment and waiting rooms were provided from the beginning, graded from first to third class, and with accommodation to match, from plush and leather through horsehair and moquette to bare

BELOW The curve of Newcastle Central and the elegance of its iron architecture are captured in this high-level view, taken in the 1900s, looking along the main southbound departure platform, with a train of clerestoried carriages.

ABOVE A handsome engraving of Newcastle's High Level Bridge, with two trains crossing, decorates the business card of Robert Stephenson & Co. Although locomotive construction was the principal business, the company proclaims its ability to build any kind of machinery.

wood. Left luggage and lost property offices were provided from very early on. Lavatory facilities were available. These were essential, as the trains themselves had no toilet compartments until the later 1880s. Telegraph offices were open to send messages on ahead. The first station bookstall was established at Fenchurch Street Station, London, in 1841. In 1848, W.H. Smith & Son contracted to supply books and newspapers at LNWR stations, for a minimum rent plus a proportion of receipts above an agreed level. At large stations, other vendors gradually appeared, selling fruit, flowers, sweets and tobacco. Boys with trays plied the platforms, selling chocolate and oranges. In the later nineteenth and the twentieth centuries, many railway companies also earned money from advertising. This was often subtly placed. Even on stair treads, passengers were confronted with such repeated messages as VIROL – FOR GROWING BOYS, or, as the sharp-eyed John Betjeman noted, IRON JELLOIDS, 'insisting, as one ascends, on the weakness of one's heart and its need for the stamina which those pills supply.'

Station Names

The naming of city stations took various forms. The original, most prosaic, and much the most common, was simply to call the station after the street on which it fronted, the example set by the first stations, Curzon Street in Birmingham and Crown Street in Liverpool. Similarly, some stations were named after a city district, like Norwich Thorpe, or Paddington in London. Another was to stake a claim for centrality (however specious) as in Cardiff, Glasgow, Leeds,

ABOVE Cardiff General Station in 1957 – ex-GWR 4-6-0 Manton Grange has just arrived with the Saturday 9 a.m. train from Bournemouth, on 13 July.

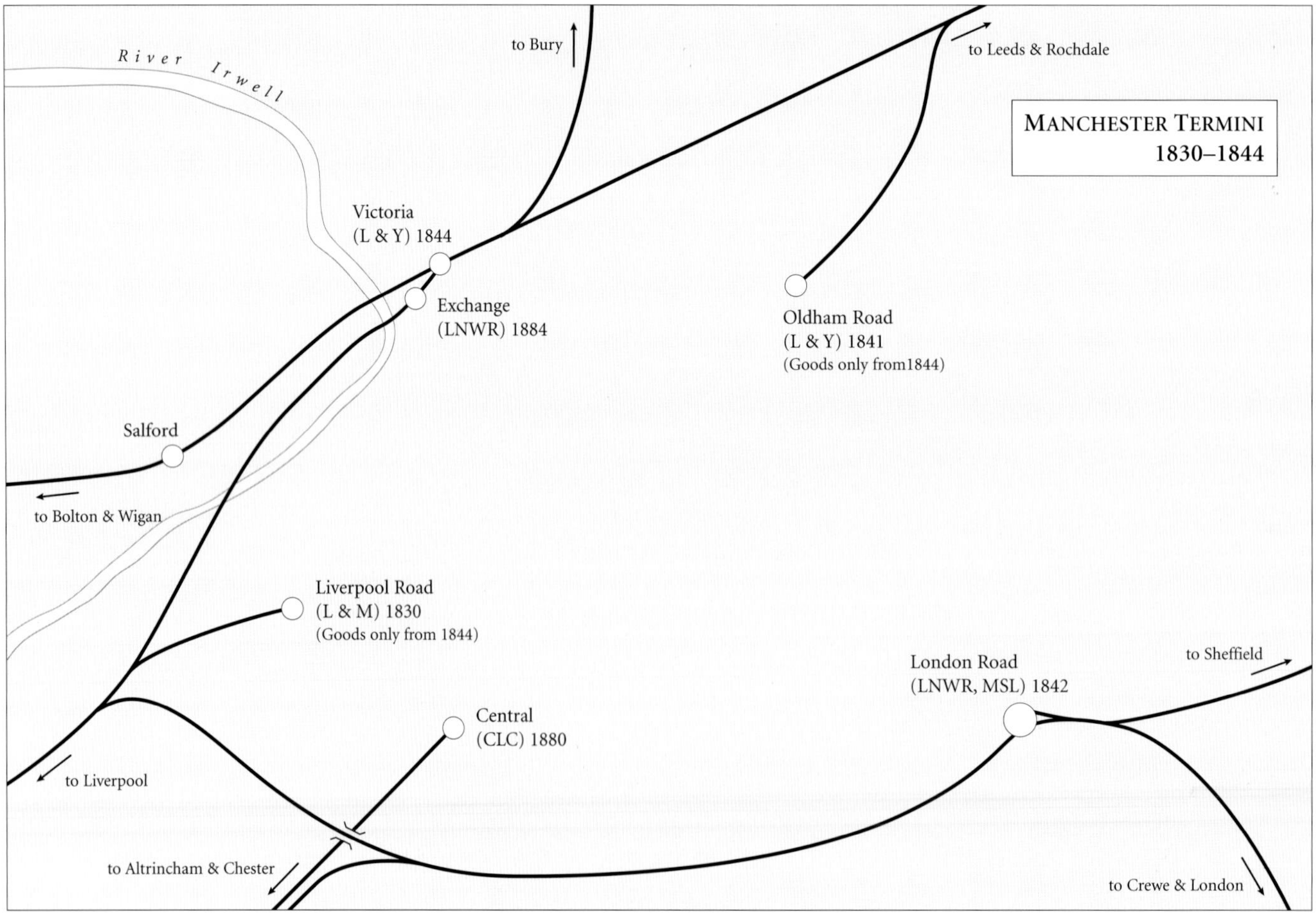

Newcastle and Manchester. 'Exchange' was used to emphasise the convenience of changing trains in Manchester but in Liverpool simply marked the location. The Midland took advantage of its short name to identify its own stations in Nottingham, Sheffield, Rugby and other places, and company names were also found in Wigan North Western, Nuneaton Trent Valley (and also Lichfield). Certain joint stations were known as 'General', including Perth and Shrewsbury. Grand associations were also invoked. Queen Victoria, herself always somewhat nervous of railways, was acknowledged in several large stations. London, Manchester, Norwich, Nottingham, Sheffield and Swansea all had Victoria Stations. Perhaps the most unusual is Edinburgh's Waverley Station, which gained its name from Sir Walter Scott's first and most famous novel. Waterloo in London, which may have seemed rather triumphalist to incoming travellers from France, just happened to front on to Waterloo Road.

London was of course the prime example of a city of termini with no central linking line. A single 'London Central' would have been a monster of impracticable size even in the early days,

with signalling still at a rudimentary stage. A Royal Commission on London Railways ruled out such a prospect in 1846, and also rejected proposals for bringing lines close into the central area of the city. The Commission wanted to see an outer circular line built, like the *Ceinture* in Paris, but this was never fully accomplished. Meanwhile the number of terminal stations grew to fifteen. Between 1863 and 1884, the majority of these termini were linked by the 'Inner Circle', now the Circle Line of the London Underground, though it did not pass under the Thames to

ABOVE A 'G' class 4-4-0 of the North Staffordshire Railway, now No. 598 of the LMS, at Stoke on Trent in the early 1920s. The North Staffordshire, or 'Knotty', survived as an independent line until the Grouping of 1923.

LEFT Edinburgh Princes Street was that city's terminus of the Caledonian and later LMS railways. Only its hotel now remains. Ex-Midland compound 4-4-0 No. 40904 was photographed there on 29 June, 1953.

THE LANCASHIRE & YORKSHIRE RAILWAY

Sir John Aspinall

Like the Great Eastern, this was a big provincial company, though as it sprawled from west to east across the lines of the LNWR and GNR, it could hardly be said to be unobtrusive. Its headquarters were in Manchester, and its commercial size and volume of business may be gauged from the fact that it was fourth among British railway companies in number of locomotives, though only eleventh in its total route mileage. Those locomotives were very largely 0-6-0s and tank engines, handling the intensive freight and local passenger traffic of the industrial and mining districts of the two counties that it served. Its original stem was the Manchester and Leeds Railway, which obtained its Act of Parliament in 1837 and was completed across the Pennines by 1840, including the 1125-yard (1029-m) summit tunnel. The original terminus was Oldham Road, Manchester, replaced by Victoria in 1844, a through station that enabled cross-country services to run through Manchester. The Manchester & Leeds changed its name to the Lancashire & Yorkshire in 1847. Through the nineteenth century it continued to grow by a mixture of building new lines and acquisition of existing ones, though it kept to its northern region and did not develop grand ambitions as the Manchester Sheffield & Lincoln Railway did. Its management was not ambitious and its service indifferent, but it regularly turned in a handsome dividend for the shareholders. There was another side to this, however. Hamilton Ellis in *British Railway History* commented that: 'It would have been hard to find, in all England, anything worse among main-line railways than the service provided at this time by the Lancashire and Yorkshire Railway…monumentally bad, quite in keeping with the obsolescent, clanking, broken-down old locomotives, and the ugly, decrepit carriages with which it was worked.' From the 1880s, the company began to mend its ways, and made considerable capital investment in new works, improved junctions and multiple track sections at bottlenecks, as well as new locomotives. Although modernisation policies had begun before his arrival in 1886, a key figure was J.A.F. (later Sir John) Aspinall, who joined originally as chief mechanical engineer. In this capacity he was responsible for the 4-4-2 'Highflyers' and the large class of 2-4-2 tank locomotives that enabled the L&Y to run a vastly improved service both on longer range trains like the Liverpool–Manchester expresses and on local commuter and workmen's trains.

Like other companies, the Lancashire & Yorkshire used steam railcars for short branch workings. An L&Y unit, as LMS No. 10612, stands at Horwich station in the late 1920s.

COMPANY PROFILE

Aspinall completed the development of the new Horwich locomotive works, replacing the former cramped works at Miles Platting in Manchester set up by the MLR in 1846, and which had been destroyed by fire in 1873. In 1889 he was appointed general manager of the company, one of the few locomotive engineers (Daniel Gooch being another) to make this transition. Although dividends dipped, the company's volume of business increased greatly, and without the work of George Armytage, chairman from 1887 to 1918, and Aspinall, who retired in 1919, the company would in all likelihood have gone under, to be swallowed up by the LNWR.

The L&Y controlled docks at both sides of the country, Goole on the Humber, reached by a joint line with the Great Northern, and Preston and Fleetwood on the Lancashire coast, as well as Liverpool. It owned more cargo vessels than any other British railway company, and also operated a passenger service to Northern Ireland. In anticipation of the 1923 Grouping, the L&Y amalgamated with the London & North Western in 1922.

LEFT The Great Central and Great Northern Railways both used the GC's Nottingham Victoria station, built between 1894 and 1898. The offices, with clock tower, were designed in Dutch renaissance style, with the addition of a wide awning extending over the entrance roadway.

the two big stations on the south bank, London Bridge and Waterloo. Architecturally the finest of London's steam age termini was Euston. Writing in 1952, when steam trains still ran and old Euston Station's Great Hall still stood, John Betjeman said of it, 'Never had there been and never has there been since in England so magnificent a piece of railway architecture. This huge hall is now ruined with filthy little kiosks and enquiry bureaux built in a jazz-modern style by the L.M.S. But not even these destroy its proportions.... To compare with Euston, there is nothing.'

BELOW At Haworth (now on the Keighley & Worth Valley Railway) ex-LMS 2-6-2 No. 41273 leaves with the 17.37 to Oxenhope, on 15 May 1954. Designed by H.A. Ivatt, the class dates from 1946, and 130 were built.

ABOVE Glasgow had the busiest suburban network outside London, with intensive services run both by the LMS and LNER. In this scene from the pre-electric years, ex-LNER Class V1 2-6-2T simmers at Bridgeton Central, with the 12.16 p.m. train to Dalmuir Park via Westerton, on 20 June 1960.

But the train sheds beyond Euston's grand frontage were undistinguished compared with the great iron halls of Paddington and St Pancras. In most cases the London termini also held the head offices of the railway companies, so that the LNWR was synonymous with Euston, the GNR with King's Cross, the Great Eastern with Liverpool Street. Most also built a large hotel beside the station, with direct access from the main concourse. In some cases, including the Midland Railway's St Pancras and the South Eastern's Charing Cross, the hotel formed the main frontage, concealing the train shed behind it. The architect of the Gothic extravaganza at St Pancras, Sir Gilbert Scott, had wanted to use the style in government offices, and said of his railway hotel: 'My own belief is that it is possibly *too good* for its purpose.' London saw every variety of the railway in the townscape. Tunnels pierced upland areas like Primrose Hill, with trains bursting forth from imposing entrance/exit arches. The Great Western approached Paddington through wide, shallow cuttings. The Greenwich Railway, later part of the South Eastern & Chatham, reached London Bridge by means of a viaduct of 878 brick arches, and these structures were also often found on other South London lines, giving interior glimpses at first floor level of the terraces of New Cross and Brixton. The Metropolitan Railway, opened in 1863, ran in vertical-sided cuttings and shallow tunnels built on the cut-and-cover principle. Its lines ran under streets because of an Act of Parliament, in the early days of railways, which compelled railways to purchase any buildings situated above a tunnel. The world's first underground railway, with the first underground stations, it provided a smoky, sulphurous experience. For the passengers, the ordeal was usually quite short, but the enginemen and guards spent hours in the murk, and the tank locomotives did not have cabs. Some insouciant doctors in the 1860s held that the Metropolitan's pungent atmosphere was beneficial to patients with lung diseases: these unfortunates were sometimes brought down into the stations to breathe in fumes which undoubtedly helped to shorten their lives.

The Growth of Suburbia

London was the first place to be served by what came to be known as suburban railways. In the early days, inter-city transport had been the primary intention. But the London & Greenwich Railway, opened in 1836–38, was not a trunk line; it was deliberately intended to link the south bank communities to London. The Greenwich railway did not lead to a sudden surge in development, but as the railway network grew, it became apparent from around 1860 that the steam railway offered a new opportunity to city workers – to live in the country and work in town, using the speed and directness of the train. This was a consumer-led activity, and some companies reacted faster and more energetically than others. Before that, however, the railways had started to run 'workmen's trains'. These were early-morning, late-evening services, using

RIGHT LMS 2-6-4T No. 42551 enters Heaton Norris with a Manchester-Stockport local, on 6 August 1954. On the right the warehouses still bear the name of the London & North Western Railway, more than 30 years after its incorporation into the London Midland & Scottish.

BELOW With green fields in the foreground and an industrial Pennine townscape – perhaps Bolton? – as the backdrop, an LNWR 0-8-0 makes its purposeful way with a train of colliery-owned coal trucks.

LONDON AND NORTH WESTERN RAILWAY COMPANY'S GOODS WAREHOUSE
42551
HEATON NORRIS

ABOVE The functional lines of Victoria Station, London: the South Eastern & Chatham side. The tank engine has drawn in the rolling stock of a train at Platform 2 and waits for it to depart. An express has arrived at Platform 6.

the most basic rolling stock, usually old four-wheelers, to bring what was known as the 'mechanic population' into London to work. Despite the teeming East End, the rise in property values and the demolition of urban slum areas had forced large numbers of the working population to move to further-out places such as Peckham Rye and Brockley in the south, and Walthamstow and Edmonton in the north. For a daily return fare of two pence, the workmen's trains made it possible for men and women to get to their work in the city centre. In 1875, the Great Eastern was issuing 53,000 workmen's weekly tickets. Neither the timing nor the comfort of these trains, however, was right for the middle-class office worker.

The Commuter is Born

At first the trunk lines paid little attention to the outer suburbs. When in 1838 the London & South Western Railway opened, it built a station called Kingston to serve the old town of Kingston on Thames, though it was some way from the town. Speculative building began to fill in the empty land between the railway and the town. Twenty years later this was considered to be a place in its own right, and briefly acquired the name of Kingston on Railway before receiving the more traditional-sounding Surbiton from an old farm in the area. It was the first suburb to be created – albeit without intention – by the railway. Kingston itself was given a more convenient station on a branch. Soon most of the lines running south and west of London were developing branches in order to capture this new twice-daily short-haul traffic. A new word was borrowed from American usage – the commutation ticket, or reduced-price season ticket: its holder became a commuter. Then as now, commuter traffic had its negative aspects: too many passengers wanting to travel at the same time, needing trains that were not

RIGHT The cavernous-seeming interior of Edge Hill Tunnel, Liverpool, in an Ackerman print of 1830. This print had to be withdrawn, as locomotives were supposed to be rope-hauled through the tunnel. It seems an odd place for spectators, but perhaps the artist felt that human interest was necessary.

ABOVE At Nottingham Victoria on 24 April 1948, ex-Midland Railway 4-4-0 No. 419 heads the 10.38 a.m. stopping train to Northampton.

required again until the next rush-hour period. This caused congestion and was very difficult to organise in a cost-effective way. The railways had to invest in special locomotives and rolling stock to cater for the traffic. A great boost in the numbers of tank engines resulted. Their shorter length, the ease with which they could be driven backwards, with no need to run out to be turned on a turntable at the terminal depot, and their lower construction cost combined to make them more suitable than tender locomotives for handling commuter trains.

The London Tilbury & Southend Railway (taken over by the Midland in 1911), operating along the northern bank of the Thames estuary, acquired a distinctive tank engine type in 1880, a 4-4-2T with outside cylinders, designed by William Adams and featuring his typical stove-pipe chimney. Twelve were delivered in that year, and the historian Kenneth Leech described them as, 'probably the largest tank engines in the country in 1880…the first tank engines specifically designed for hauling passenger trains at what were then fast speeds.' A further 24 were built up to 1892. They were named after stations on the line, which occasionally confused unwary passengers who thought the names, painted on the side tanks, indicated the destinations.

These were excellent locomotives, with working lives extending to 50 years and more, though altered in various respects in the course of their careers. Service demands were heavy, with the 'business trains' loading up to 230 tons (234 tonnes) and running to a 50-minute schedule over the 42 miles (67km) between Southend and Fenchurch Street. A truly Cockney touch, reminiscent of the 'pearly kings', was the elaborate dressing up of engines to commemorate special events, especially coronations.

ABOVE Southern Railway 'King Arthur' class N15 4-6-0 No. 776, *Sir Galagars*, shunts the empty stock of a boat train towards Southampton Town Quay, in August 1938.

Suburban services developed around the major cities, with Glasgow having the largest network after London. Two cross-city routes were developed, with low-level stations beneath the main-line termini of Queen Street (North British) and Central (Caledonian). The Glasgow & South Western terminus of St Enoch also had a large suburban service. Inner suburban services became victims of the electric tramcar almost as soon as they were established. But lines that served commuters and shoppers in the cities' further hinterlands, like those which linked Ilkley and Keighley to Leeds and Bradford in

the West Riding of Yorkshire, or Southport to Liverpool, continued to be well used. In the second and third decades of the twentieth century some very large tank locomotives operated the heaviest trains on the Southend line from London Fenchurch Street and the Fairlie line from Glasgow St Enoch: 4-6-4 'Baltic' types, both designed by Robert Whitelegg. On the Southend line, despite their speed – one was timed at 90mph (144km/h) – and power, they were too long and heavy to be really useful. The busiest suburban and inter-urban lines began to be electrified from 1890, but far into the twentieth century commuter trains were hauled by a variety of steam tank engines, both ancient and modern.

ABOVE Clarence Road Station, Cardiff, on 18 July 1957. Ex-GWR 0-6-0 pannier tank No. 6411 finds little custom for the 3.12 p.m. train to Penarth.

RIGHT The gas-holders outside St Pancras are familiar, but the locomotive is a 'foreigner': the Southern Railway 'West Country' 4-6-2, No. 34005 *Barnstaple*, with the 1.50 p.m. Manchester Central–London, during the inter-regional locomotive exchanges of June 1948.

LEFT Passengers wait for the 6.45 p.m. push-pull service between Nottingham and Mansfield to come to a stop at the island platform of Hucknall, Notts., on 14 August 1947. The engine is ex-Midland 0-4-4T No. 1350.

44793

6 • Parcels and Wagon Loads

Coals from Newcastle, pottery from Stoke, tweeds from Galashiels, milk from Melksham. Reaching into almost every corner of the kingdom, the steam railway is the nation's common carrier, with no load too small or (if it can be somehow fitted into the loading gauge) too large.

LEFT One of the few tramway-style steam railways in Britain was the Wisbech and Upwell Tramway, part of the Great Eastern. The rich fenland provided the line with a considerable goods traffic. Engine No. 7130 trundles a goods train by the roadside near Wisbech in June 1937.

OPPOSITE In the last years of steam, a grimy Class 5 4-6-0 hauls a long goods train on the Midland main line. Introduced by the LMS in 1935, this two-cylinder mixed-traffic class, eventually more than 850-strong, did sterling service in every part of the country. For many, its sturdy looks typify the later British steam locomotive.

Coal was the mainstay of the steam railway in two ways, first as the fuel of the locomotives. The companies bought their coal as locally as possible to minimise the expense of running their own coal-supply trains. To bring coal to depots at Penzance, Norwich or Inverness was an addition to operating cost, though coal itself was relatively cheap. Seasoned travellers claimed to be able to tell the line by the whiff of its smoke. The Great Western burnt hard Welsh steam coal and this was a significant factor in the performance of its engines. Yorkshire coal was softer and flakier, more productive of smoke and soot, as travellers on the LNER might notice. The softest coal came from the Kent coalfield, and not the least of O.V.S. Bulleid's achievements was to fit his 'Pacifics' with fireboxes that efficiently consumed the products of Betteshanger and Shepherdswell. The nearest thing to a national standard was the coal known as 'Blidworth B' from the Nottinghamshire colliery of that name,

ABOVE The busy LNER goods yard and engine shed at Sleaford, Lincs., on 23 August 1936. Numerous wagons from other companies attest how far produce traffic went across the system.

which was used by British Railways in steaming tests and in evaluation tests of other kinds of locomotive coal.

Coals on Track

Coal also formed the principal bulk traffic. Where coalfields were, the density of the rail network increased. Most notably in South Wales, between Swansea and Newport; in the West Riding of Yorkshire, around Doncaster and Barnsley; in Nottinghamshire and Derbyshire between Chesterfield and Trent; in Lancashire around Wigan and St Helens, the railway geography was complicated in the extreme. Each colliery required its own feeder line and sidings, and the narrow valleys were seamed with tracks at different levels. The frequent junctions and the undulations caused by underground subsidence made for slow running. Most collieries assembled their trains using their own tank locomotives, and these were then taken by a railway company's engine, normally an 0-6-0, to the nearest marshalling yard. Until nationalisation of the coal mines in 1948, most collieries owned their own wagons, which had to be returned empty. Coal traffic went in four main flows – to the docks for export; to heavy industry, to gas and electricity production; and for domestic use. Coal was a major export from the 1850s to the 1930s. The railway companies carried it to the sea and often owned the dockyards where it was transferred by conveyor machinery into the holds of cargo ships. A prime example was the Barry Railway in South Wales, whose existence was stimulated by the high dock charges and congestion at Cardiff, the biggest coal port. Despite fierce opposition from established railways in the region, it opened in 1889 and served its own new 73-acre (29.6-ha) dock; it was further enlarged in 1898. By 1914 Barry was exporting more coal than Cardiff and Penarth combined. In 1922 the Barry Railway became part of the GWR. Another great dock complex was created by the Great Central Railway at Immingham, on the south bank of the Humber. Opened in 1912, it had 150 miles (240km) of sidings and covered 1000 acres (405ha). Ironically, nowadays Immingham imports coal. Forty miles (64km) inland, at Wath in the South Yorkshire coalfield, a huge marshalling yard had been laid out in 1907. Capable of sorting five thousand wagons within a 24-hour period, it was almost exclusively concerned with coal traffic. Four large 0-8-4 tank locomotives were built in 1908 to shunt long train-loads there.

BELOW Road haulage services were biting heavily into the railway's freight traffic by the 1930s, and Sir Nigel Gresley's LNER class V2 3-cylinder 2-6-2 *Green Arrow* (named in connection with an express freight service), was designed as an answer, in 1936, to speeding up inter-city goods trains.

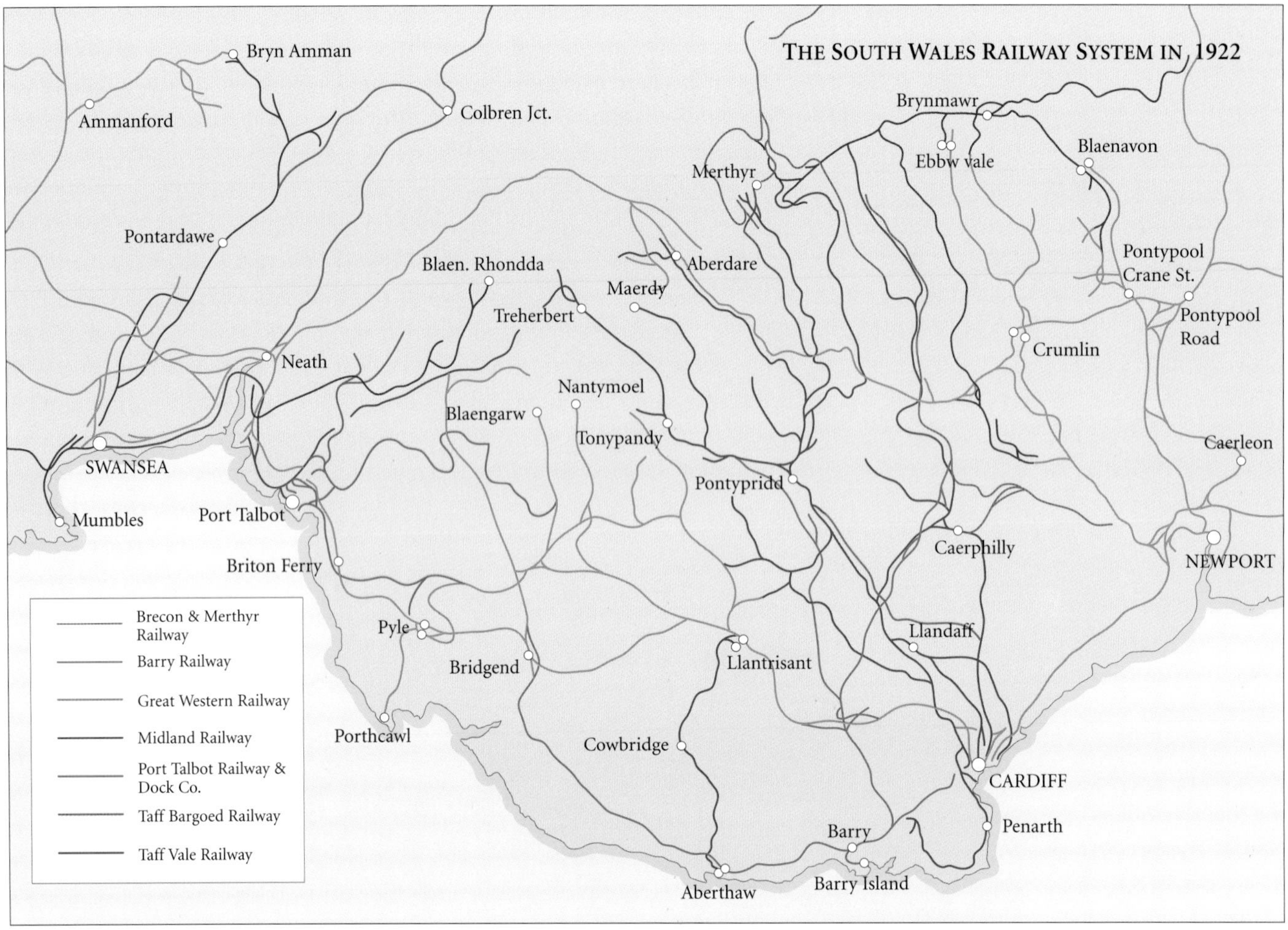

THE SOUTH WALES RAILWAY SYSTEM IN 1922

Bryn Amman
Ammanford
Colbren Jct.
Brynmawr
Ebbw vale
Blaenavon
Merthyr
Pontardawe
Blaen. Rhondda
Aberdare
Maerdy
Treherbert
Pontypool Crane St.
Pontypool Road
Crumlin
Neath
Nantymoel
Blaengarw
Tonypandy
Caerleon
SWANSEA
Pontypridd
Mumbles
Port Talbot
Caerphilly
NEWPORT
Briton Ferry
Pyle
Llandaff
Bridgend
Llantrisant
Porthcawl
Cowbridge
CARDIFF
Penarth
Barry
Barry Island
Aberthaw

Brecon & Merthyr Railway
Barry Railway
Great Western Railway
Midland Railway
Port Talbot Railway & Dock Co.
Taff Bargoed Railway
Taff Vale Railway

Bulk coal trains were the main reason for prompting the design of larger freight locomotives. In 1903, the Great Western produced Britain's first 2-8-0 goods engines, for hauling South Wales coal to London. They were capable of pulling 1000-ton trains, of one hundred wagons. Engines of 0-8-0 wheel formation had been around for some years before that, including a four-cylinder compound designed by F.W. Webb on the LNWR in 1892. The Great Northern had introduced the '401' eight-coupled engine in 1901. Its chairman reported to the half-yearly shareholders' meeting in 1902 that: 'If you will go back two years and compare the year ending 30 June 1902, with the year ending 30 June 1900, you will find that the train mileage has diminished by 1,255,000 miles.... We have now in daily use quite a number of the larger engines that we have been building. We shall have a further quantity in all probability this half-year, and the effect of this is we are able not only to take a heavier load, but, by concentrating the loads, to reduce the number of trains on the line, which is itself a great advantage.' At this time the GNR was also

BELOW One of the Southern's heavy eight-coupled tanks of Class G1b, used for marshalling freight trains, in the yards at Feltham on 21 October 1936.

building some 20- and 30-ton wagons. But the 0-6-0 remained the most common British goods engine and most coal trains consisted of far less than one hundred wagons. Then, and for long afterwards, all goods trains were loose-coupled, with no continuous braking system. While the train was moving, brakes could only be applied to the engine and tender wheels, and those of the brake-van. When a long downhill stretch was ahead, the train had to be stopped while the guard pinned down the brake-lever on each individual wagon. It then proceeded very slowly down the grade, to stop at the foot for the partial braking to be released. The progress of a goods train was thus very slow. On busier lines, loop sections were essential to allow passenger trains to overtake. Goods engines thus spent a great deal of time standing still. The brake van, with its ducket side windows, coal stove, wooden seat and rudimentary desk for the guard to write his journal, was a vital item. Ballast was added to its frame to give it additional weight, and a wheel operated the brakes. Originally a four-wheeler, some later versions had six or eight wheels, the latter on long brake-vans with two four-wheel bogies. The Southern Railway even experimented with concrete-framed brake-vans, to give additional weight and braking force.

Many Materials

Throughout the years of the steam railway, heavy industry remained the backbone of the British economy. Coal sustained it, but a huge variety of other raw materials, components and finished products were carried. Mineral trains carried iron ore, bauxite, sand, road-stone and

BELOW Dusk falls over the serrated roofline of the old Euston in March 1938, and the blank-sided stock of the down 'West Coast Postal' stands at Platform 2, soon to be hurried northwards behind a 'Royal Scot' 4-6-0.

CAMBRIAN RAILWAYS

Though it always existed in the shadow of the Great Western, the Cambrian carried on an independent life as the largest of the Welsh railway companies until it finally became a constituent company within the GWR at the 1923 Grouping. Its origins were in the Newtown (then a flourishing textile centre) and Llanidloes Railway, linking these two communities in 1859 before any other railway had come near. Two dynamic figures in nineteenth-century Welsh industrial life, David Davies and Thomas Savin, were responsible for the building of this line. It combined with a number of other small railways in 1864 to form the Cambrian Railways: the Oswestry and Newtown; Newtown and Machynlleth; and Oswestry, Ellesmere and Whitchurch Railways. Though Newtown was the hub of the system, the works were eventually set up at Oswestry (see main text). In 1865 the Aberystwyth & Welsh Coast Railway joined, and from 1888 the Cambrian also worked the Mid Wales Railway, which ran from a remote junction, Moat Lane, on the Oswestry–Welshpool–Machynlleth line, to Talyllyn where it met the Brecon & Merthyr line at another rural junction. En route it crossed the LNWR Craven Arms–Llanelli line, with a linking spur, and met a Midland branch from Hereford at Three Cocks. The final constituents of the Cambrian system were the short Van Railway (built 1861), the Mawddwy Railway (1866) and the Tanat Light Railway, almost twenty miles (32km) long, built in 1904 at the height of the interest in light railways before the advent of the motor car. Two narrow-gauge lines also were incorporated, the still-existing Vale of Rheidol line (opened 1902), and the defunct Welshpool & Llanfair, opened two years later. The extension of the system farthest east was at Whitchurch, in Shropshire, where it connected with the LNWR Shrewsbury–Crewe line. The initiative in building these lines, at least those of standard gauge, was not from the communities they served, which were all small towns with populations of 5000 or less. Instead, it came from the contractors who financed them in the hope that providing through services and 'opening up' the country would provide its due reward. The greatest benefit was felt by the coastal resorts of Cardigan Bay, now put in railway contact with the West Midlands and other centres of population, but the holiday traffic was never very large.

The nature of the terrain, the lightness of traffic, and the lack of funds, all combined to make the Cambrian a basically single-track system, with crossing loops provided at the majority of stations, though some were single-platform halts. The company went bankrupt twice, in 1868 and 1884. During its independent years its shareholders never enjoyed the sort of dividends paid out by big English companies or by the South Wales coalfield lines. In 1913, the Cambrian carried

[illegible] saddle tank Plasfynnon, built in 1863, and given its cab in 1897, heads a mixed train in 1904.

some three million passengers and 947,000 tons (960,000 tonnes) of freight, on a system with 241 miles (386km) of route. It also transported 373,000 head of livestock.

A TRAGIC ENDING

A serious accident at Abermule, when two trains collided head-on on the single track, clouded the final years of the Cambrian. Seventeen people were killed on 26 January 1921 when the Aberystwyth–Whitchurch express, with through carriages for London and Manchester, hit a Whitchurch–Aberystwyth stopping train, which had been allowed to leave Abermule with the wrong tablet for the single-line section between that station and Newtown. All the rules relating to single-line working had been broken. The casual nature of station procedures was severely criticised in the ensuing inquiry. Two years later the Cambrian was incorporated into the Great Western, under favourable conditions that, perhaps, made its long-suffering shareholders pleased to have clung on through all the vicissitudes.

LEFT Now a wayside platform between Oxford and Worcester, the Cotswold station of Shipton-under-Wychwood once had a busy goods yard, as this pre-1920 view shows. There is no motor vehicle: horse and steam between them move the freight.

limestone, between docks, quarries and industrial plants. Iron and steel works lit up the night sky above many towns from their blast furnaces. Coatbridge, Motherwell, Barrow, Corby, Wrexham, Bishop Auckland, Rotherham, Scunthorpe, Port Talbot and Llanelli were among the metal-working towns where railways played an important part, with lines snaking round mills and furnaces, miles of sidings and large locomotive depots housing few passenger engines but hundreds of freight types.

With the establishment of the Railway Clearing House, it became possible to trace the movement of goods from one company to another. Traffic grew rapidly, and from 1852, the revenue from goods haulage overtook that of passenger traffic and remained the prime source of railway income until virtually the end of the steam age in 1962. The peak year – outside wartime – was probably 1913, when some 367 million tons of freight were carried by rail. For many country stations, it was goods revenue that kept them going. Only the smallest did not possess a siding or two, a loading bank, a goods shed and a crane. Daily, or maybe only twice weekly, a local pick-up goods train would come through, hauled by one of the ubiquitous 0-6-0s or perhaps by a pensioned-off passenger engine, such as the handsome LSWR T9 4-4-0s in the south-west, or

BELOW Beauty show for wagons – the Butterley Co. of Nottingham displayed this 12-tonner, built for private owners, in 1923. While the railway companies mostly built their own rolling stock, private owners bought from independent builders.

ABOVE Re-enacting a once-typical dockland scene, preserved ex-LNER class Y7 0-4-0 'pug' No. 68088, in British Railways livery, crosses the swing bridge at Boston Docks in November 2000. These tiny engines were vital for tightly curving dock and canalside lines.

their distant relations, the later series of the Caledonian 'Dunalastair' 4-4-0s, in Scotland. Both types lasted into the 1950s. The standard freight vehicles were four-wheelers, a covered van and an open wagon, though the contents of the latter were often covered in tarpaulin, to prevent theft as well as to protect them from the weather. Though the companies much preferred full wagonloads, they accepted 'smalls' – individual items kept together in a van to be sorted at the pick-up train's terminus. The preparation of trunk goods trains was thus a complicated business that required a numerous staff. 'Smalls' had to be consolidated into wagonloads all for the same town or distribution point. Individual wagons then had to be marshalled into the right assembly and sequence for the next move. This might be to a transfer yard, where one

LEFT Tall masts rise above an 0-4-2 dock tank engine at Aberdeen, on 23 June 1955. The engine is LNER class Z4 No. 68191, former class X of the Great North of Scotland Railway. Dock engines had to be able to negotiate tight curves, and the short wheelbase was essential. The GNSR had two of these, Nos. 43 and 44, built by Manning Wardle in 1915.

company handed over to another, or to another marshalling yard or to the final destination. On the LNWR Crewe became the key transhipment point from 1901, when a huge shed was built to deal every day with hundreds of mixed-load vans. Every city and town had one or more goods depot. Their vast brick warehouses, often still bearing the initials of one of the 'Big Four', or even a predecessor, can still be seen near many city termini. In the cobbled yards of these depots, horse carts and later motor trucks congregated to collect items for local delivery. Horses lasted for a remarkably long time, used both for deliveries and for moving single

BELOW A Great Central class 8A (Q4 of the LNER) 0-8-0 on a London-bound coal train south of Rugby, a year or two after the 1923 Grouping.

wagons in the shed-yards and sheds. In 1951, the nationalised British Railways still owned more than seven thousand working horses, and the last ones were pensioned off in 1959. Capstans and hand-levers were also used to move wagons, as steam locomotives were prohibited from entering the fire-prone goods sheds.

'PROBLEM' CLASS 2-2-2

Tractive effort: 6840lb (3102kg)
Cylinders: 16x24in (440 x 660mm)
Driving wheels: 91.5in (2322mm)
Heating surface: 1098sq ft(102m²)
Steam pressure: 120psi (8.4kg/cm²)
Grate area: 14.9sq ft (1.4m²)
Total weight: 60,480lb (3102 kg)

ABOVE The 'Problem' class was also known as the 'Lady of the Lake' class, from the name of the first of its sixty engines. Designed by John Ramsbottom, all were built at Crewe, and were highly advanced locomotives for their time in 1859.

A Long Journey

The system normally worked efficiently, sustained by a vast amount of paperwork in the pre-computer era. Non-priority freight could take some days to reach its destination, but this was understood and reflected in the charge. A wagonload of slates from Llanberis (LMS) in Snowdonia, destined for a builder's yard in Lincoln, directly across the country, would be brought down the branch line to Caernarvon by a pick-up goods train. Then it would be attached to a Caernarvon–Chester goods train that would also pick up vans and wagons from Anglesey at Menai Bridge or Bangor. At Chester it would be added to a non-stop Crewe train and at Crewe it would be shunted again onto a Derby-bound through freight train running via Burton on Trent. From Derby it would be taken on a transfer working to Trent Yard, and finally attached to a Trent–Lincoln goods train running via the old Midland line that still crosses the East Coast main line on the level at Newark. It would end its journey at the LMS goods depot in Lincoln – six different trains, though a single operating company.

LEFT Milk was a time-sensitive goods item, given priority treatment and transported by express trains. Milk churns could be seen at hundreds of country stations.

It is possible to see how even the complete wagonload might be uneconomic for the railway, and why, by the mid-1950s, the purchasers might decide to send a lorry. In 1952, the railways had 956 marshalling yards, mostly of small capacity. By 1968, the last year of steam traction, the number had dropped to 184.

Responsibility for carrying the great bulk of the country's freight entailed having a range of

41708
16A

Lightweight goods: a 'half-cab' ex-Midland Railway Class 1F 0-6-0T, one of 262 built between 1874 and 1892, and numbered as British Railways 41708, hauls a charter freight near 50 Steps bridge, on the Swanage Railway, in 2001.

ABOVE A former LNWR 'George V' express 4-4-0, LMS 25334, on a Cambridge–Bletchley goods train in October 1937.

specialist vehicles to carry particular items. Every railway had large numbers of part-open sided vans for transporting sheep and cattle, but the LMS also kept an elephant van at Rhyl, for the use of circuses and zoos. Special vans for carrying theatre props were stabled at Oldham (Mumps) when not in use. The Southern Railway – one of whose predecessor companies, the South Eastern, had suffered a famous bullion raid in 1857 – had bullion vans, as did the other big companies. Extra-long, or low-slung, wagons were available for carrying particularly bulky loads. Great ingenuity sometimes had to be exercised when 'out of gauge' items had to be carried. Sometimes it was impossible, but usually a way was found. Tank cars, which made an early appearance, were used for bulk liquid transport; with the growth in use of fuel oil, these became very numerous. Oil trains usually had a match-wagon between the locomotive and the tanks, to minimise any risk from sparks reaching volatile fumes. Salt was another commodity carried in special vans, from the production zones in Cheshire and Droitwich. These could be distinguished by having peaked, rather than rounded, roofs, similar to the vans that carried goods via the cross-Channel train ferries onto the European railways. The latter also had dual air and vacuum brakes. Perhaps the most exciting special vans for the traffic-watcher were the gunpowder vans, carrying explosive material to and from factories such as the Nobel plant at Irvine, Ayrshire; they were fitted with extra springs and pads, and shunted with unusual care.

BELOW Dual braking systems are fitted to this LBSC shunting tank of class E1, to handle continental rolling stock.

Perishable Items

The other great liquid traffic was in milk, first

carried on the Liverpool & Manchester Railway in 1832. Later in the century, among the most familiar items on a country platform would be a few milk churns. The Southern alone owned more than a million of these in the 1920s. It was essential that milk should be delivered fresh, and, as with other perishable items, the railways responded with a proper urgency. Milk traffic on a large scale began around 1865, and the first country depot was opened at Semley station (LSWR) in Dorset in 1871. Here and at similar installations the collected milk could be chilled, poured into churns and loaded in ventilated vans for rapid haulage to London – hence the name of the Express Dairies company. Initially passenger trains transported milk but separate milk trains began to run in the 1890s. Stainless steel tank cars were introduced in 1927, and in the following year the railways carried 280 million gallons (1,270 million litres), not only to London but also to other major cities. Fresh fish was dealt with in a similar way. Fish vans from as far north as Wick would be got to London overnight. The principal whitefish harbours, Aberdeen, Fleetwood, Grimsby and Lowestoft, sent complete fish trains to London and Manchester, and these received priority over passenger expresses. The driver of a train following behind had to take extra care to avoid the slipping of the driving wheels on rails well greased by fish oil and scales. Perishables sometimes had to be kept warm. Banana vans were the only goods vehicles with provision for train heating, to preserve their cargo in frosty weather. When a banana ship was due at Garston Dock, Liverpool, ten trains of these vans would be held in readiness. Special running conditions were observed to ensure that being jerked about in transit did not bruise the fruit. In terms of tonnage, the biggest perishable item was potatoes, and King's Cross and St Pancras goods stations both had large potato markets attached. Seasonal vegetables, fruit and flowers were rushed to London from the growing districts and from Weymouth, the port for the Channel Islands. Even more exotically, the Great Northern ran special trains in 1913 to convey up to 100,000 Sudanese quails at a time from Manchester Docks to London. The North Eastern pioneered the use of special vans for carrying racing pigeons. The 'pigeon special' would arrive at some remote station where, at the appointed moment, the staff would release the birds from their racks of cages to race back to their home lofts.

ABOVE Size as a virtue: an LNER poster of around 1925, promoting the big new company – and its new locomotives – to the wider public.

GEORGE JACKSON CHURCHWARD (1857–1933)

The development of the twentieth-century steam locomotive in Britain owes more to Churchward than to any other individual. The son of a well-off Devon farmer, he chose engineering as a career and was apprenticed to the South Devon Railway, a constituent of the Great Western, moving to Swindon in 1873. He was to remain there for the rest of his life, graduating through the ranks to become carriage works, then locomotive works, manager, before emerging as the principal assistant to William Dean, the chief mechanical engineer, in 1897, and finally taking over the top job in 1902. Churchward was a great engineer but not a great original engineer. In the words of Professor W.A. Tuplin: 'All that he did was to realise that, by 1900, every variation in the conventional steam locomotive had been tried out by somebody, somewhere or other, and that, if he made the best use of the knowledge acquired from all this vast experience, he might expect to take the design of the steam locomotive about as far as it could ever go.' The key phrase is, of course, 'made the best use' – Churchward's genius was vital in assessing the best practice and incorporating it into an effective design, a far from easy task. Dean had given him ample scope for experiment and in 1902 he knew what he needed to do. At the same time he set out to standardise fittings and equipment within and across the new locomotive classes for which he was responsible. He also established Britain's first and, for a long time, only locomotive testing plant, at Swindon. American and French practices were closely examined through technical drawings and the purchase of three French 'Atlantics'. The Swindon works were remodelled and extended, and new tools were introduced that machined moving parts with a greater degree of accuracy than before. The key elements of the Churchward *ensemble* comprised a tapered, American-style 'wagon-top' boiler, a high Belpaire firebox, outside cylinders with long travel and valve gear inside the frames (originally Stephenson's but changed to Walschaerts' with the 'Star' 4-cylinder class of 1907). The running plate was so high as to need almost vestigial splashers, and there was no dome, but a brass safety-valve casing was set on the rear of the boiler. In essence, this was the shape of things to come, but when the 'Saint' 4-6-0s were introduced in 1902, there were cries of horror from the advocates of traditional design. But, especially when fitted with super heaters – Churchward was quick to catch on to this after Wilhelm Schmidt's successful development in Germany, though he favoured a lower degree of super heat than Schmidt – the new breed of Great Western locomotives were unquestionably the best in the country. Churchward remained in office until 1922, and his successor C.B. Collett carried on the same principles. The celebrated 'Castle' 4-6-0 class of 1923, a combination of rebuilt 'Stars' and new engines, confirmed that Great Western superiority was maintained in the 1920s, until both the LMS and the LNER borrowed examples. And, over twenty years after Churchward showed the way, they themselves began to use similar principles in such engines as the A3 'Pacifics' and 'Royal Scot' 4-6-0s. After his retirement, Churchward continued to live at Swindon and often visited the works. His death was caused by one of his own locomotives, the approach of which he failed to hear as he walked along the track.

LEFT Originally intended for Sweden, the D-93 0-8-0s were bought up by the Barry Railway and gave good service.

Perishable in a different sense were daily newspapers. The railways had made national distribution and mass circulation possible, and newspaper trains were among the fastest services. In fact, in most ways, newspaper and postal trains resembled passenger rather than freight trains in the speed of their operations and both items were very often carried in vans attached to passenger trains. For a long time the fastest train in Britain was the little-known 2.32 a.m. Marylebone–Sheffield, via Brackley, Rugby, Leicester and Nottingham, which raced along the former Great Central metals at an average speed of over 60 mph (97km/h) including stops. Usually hauled by an ex-GC 4-cylinder 4-6-0 (the LNER B3) in the 1930s, it consisted of one composite passenger coach and up to ten newspaper vans.

BELOW The preserved LMS two-cylinder 2-8-0 No. 48305 at Switherland, Great Central Railway. Introduced in 1935 as a mainline freight entine, in World War II, many were built for military use until the advent of the 'Austerity' 2-8-0.

POST-HASTE

Another very tightly timed service was the Travelling Post Office, as virtually all mail went by rail. Mailbags were as common a sight on large railway stations as milk churns (though more closely watched). Guards' vans had lockable cages for mailbags. Other trains might carry one or more post office vans in addition to the passenger stock. From as early as 1838–39, at certain places on the side of the lines, mailbag pick-up posts were set, so that the train could snatch up a stout leather bag of mail in a net let out from one of the TPO vans, without having to stop. It was also possible for bags to be dropped from the trains, the whole exercise often carried out at around 70 mph (113km/h). By 1935, there were 132 points where such apparatus was installed. The

ABOVE Veteran of the 1895 'Race to the North' between the East and West Coast routes from London to Scotland, and painted in LNWR 'blackberry black', is No. 790 *Hardwicke*, at the Dinting Railway Centre on 3 Ocober 1982.

first exclusively postal train ran between Paddington and Bristol in 1855; later there were two Post Office-only trains, the TPOs from London to Aberdeen via Crewe and from London to Penzance, which ran through the night, with staff sorting mail as the trains went along. Many other trains carried one or more mail vans, in which letters were sorted on the move. In the mid-1930s, over 150 sorting vans were in regular use.

In the days of the LMS, the northbound 'Postal' consisted of from 13 to 15 vans, a load of over 500 tons (508 tonnes). Six of these were equipped as sorting vans and the others held pre-sorted mail. It left Euston at 8.30 p.m., and ran non-stop to Rugby, picking up bags automatically at Harrow, Hemel Hempstead, Bletchley and other intermediate stations. At Rugby it took up northbound mail from two trains newly arrived from Peterborough in the

LEFT The station crane was an essential fixture. This one at Biggar, Lanarkshire, was set on an old LNWR tender frame.

east and Swindon (via Banbury) in the west. Its next stop was the low-level platforms at Tamworth. A Birmingham-bound train from Lincoln and Derby had just left northbound mailbags at the high-level platform, from which they had been whisked down by a metal chute. The 'Postal' went on to reach Crewe at 11.42 p.m. At this nodal station, numerous trains had already arrived bringing mailbags from the west and south-west. Hectic activity ensued in the six-minute stop, during which previously sorted mail for the north-west of England was taken out, and a huge amount more loaded on board. The engine was changed. From Euston the train was normally hauled by a 'Royal Scot' 4-6-0; for the steep gradients ahead, the motive power was almost invariably a 'Princess Royal' or 'Duchess' 4-6-2. If not one of these, then double-heading would be required. The southbound 'Postal' here crossed the northbound train and the Glasgow and London sorting crews changed over, to complete their night shift on the way

BELOW LMS 0-8-2T No. 7885 at Bescot Yard, Birmingham, in 1935. Coal wagons dominate the scene.

home. At 11.48 p.m. it left, with its next stop Preston, where mail from Liverpool and Manchester was waiting. More automatic exchanges were made as it went through Lancaster. A stop in the small hours at Carlisle picked up mail brought across by an LNER train from Newcastle. With its loading completed now, sorting went on. It was the next section that W.H. Auden famously described in his poem-text for the 1936 documentary film *Night Mail*:

This is the Night Mail, crossing the Border
Bringing the cheque and the postal order

At Carstairs Junction, the train was divided. The 'Pacific' took one section on to Glasgow. A Class 5 4-6-0 would take the other section forward to Perth and Aberdeen. Mail for the Highlands was unloaded at Perth. The furthest-flung TPO was a former Highland Railway vehicle, which worked until 1961 from Perth to Helmsdale on the Highland line.

20TH CENTURY FREIGHT

Heavier freight trains and increasing road competition through the 1920s and 30s brought elements of modernisation to the enduring nineteenth-century scene of small engines and goods trains without automatic braking. The fastest freight trains acquired automatic brakes,

BELOW A LNWR Class DX 0-6-0 goods engine, designed by John Ramsbottom and built at Crewe Works, with a train of remarkably assorted stock, much of which looks quite antique even for the time, which appears to be the 1890s. Most long-lived engines were rebuilt with new boilers, but this one is of original construction.

and a number of other express goods trains were designated as part-fitted, with a proportion of continuously braked wagons next to the engine. The positioning of the oil lamps on the smokebox and buffer beam identified these trains to signalmen and other staff. Several bigger freight locomotive types took to the rails. The Great Central brought out a 2-8-0 in 1911, mostly for its coal traffic, and the Somerset & Dorset Joint Railway also acquired a 2-8-0, built by the Midland's Derby Works, to cope with coal and minerals traffic on the steep slopes of the Brendon Hills south of Bath. Bigger things appeared on the LNER, though the 'Mikado' 2-8-2 P1 class of 1925, intended for heavy freight, consisted of only two engines. In 1936 the much more numerous V2 2-6-2 class, of which 184 were ultimately built, appeared. The first of the class, and only one to be named, No. 4771 *Green Arrow*, inaugurated a new express freight service of the same name. The V2s

ABOVE Publicity pictures like this, of *Cardean* racing along with the 'Corridor', the Glasgow Central–Euston express, seduced a generation of schoolboys with the glamour of steam power.

LEFT A Great Western indicator board for the overnight 'Postal' train, from the 1930s. The photographer noted that it was in fact attached to a carriage of the 18.45 mail train at Penzance.

RIGHT The Somerset & Dorset Railway's locomotives were designed by the Midland, one of the joint owners. Most powerful were the 2-8-0s. This scene from Bath Green Park shed shows on the left the original No. 81, one of six built by the Midland Works in Derby in 1914. Beside it is a larger-boilered version (originally No. 87), one of five built by Robert Stephenson & Co. at Darlington in 1925.

13807

COMPANY PROFILE

THE LONDON & SOUTH WESTERN RAILWAY

The South Western, as it was generally known, began in 1834 with the incorporation of the London & Southampton Railway. Even before its first main line was complete it changed its name to L&SWR, by an Act of Parliament of 4 June, 1839. Clearly Southampton, and an early branch to Gosport, opened in 1842, were not the limits of its ambitions. Its first London terminus was at Nine Elms, south of the Thames and some way from the centre of things. On 11 July 1848 a new terminus was opened, fronting on to the Waterloo Road, much more convenient for the city workers who were already becoming an important part of the railway's business. By this time, the company also had a somewhat roundabout route to Salisbury via Bishopstoke (later Eastleigh) and Romsey, opened in 1845. The same year saw a branch from Woking to Guildford, and, more oddly, the acquisition of the Bodmin & Wadebridge line, in remote Cornwall. But the company intended to live up to its name. In 1847 it also took control of the broad-gauge Exeter and Crediton line, and had extended it to Bideford by 1855.

A highly important development took place in 1860 when the South Western acquired a direct route to the west. By something of an anti-Great Western coup, it took the proposed Salisbury and Yeovil Railway under its wing, and in 1857 completed a direct line to Salisbury from Basingstoke via Andover. By July 1860 the line from Yeovil to Exeter (Queen Street) was complete, and the L&SWR emerged as a serious rival to the Paddington empire. But the grand plan was by no means finished. From Yeoford on the Barnstaple and Bideford line, a branch was built to Okehampton. The South Western duly absorbed this line and its 1874 extension to Lydford, from where it obtained running powers on the Great Western's Launceston to Plymouth line. From 12 May 1876 the South Western was running through trains from Waterloo to Plymouth, and the stage was set for the races to come between it and the Great Western for the prestigious transatlantic passenger trade. A branch from Okehampton divided to serve the North Cornwall resorts, the 'Atlantic Coast' of future publicity campaigns.

A RAILWAY ROW

Frontier warfare broke out in December 1858, when the South Western began to operate the Direct Portsmouth line which had been built as a speculation, between the railheads at Godalming and Havant. From Havant into Portsmouth, running powers over the LB&SC Railway were needed. Annoyed at the threat to its own Portsmouth trains, it refused, and fights between rival gangs of navvies, as well as a lawyers' beanfeast, ensued, before a new working agreement was finalised.

The old terminus at Nine Elms was also the company's works site, and locomotives were built there from 1843. The first locomotive engineer was Joseph Woods, followed by Daniel Gooch's brother John V. Gooch. The South Western had several notable locomotive engineers, including Joseph Beattie, William Adams, Dugald Drummond and R. W. Urie. In January 1923 it became the largest constituent part of the Southern Railway, with a total route mileage, including joint lines, of just under 1020 miles. At the end of 1922 it also possessed seventeen steam vessels for the Isle of Wight, Channel Islands, Cherbourg and St Malo traffic. At that time it also owned 911 locomotives, ranging from the new class N15 express 4-6-0 to a trio of venerable Beattie tank engines.

Joseph Beattie's 2-4-0 express engine Ariel, built at Nine Elms in 1864.

could handle the nightly London-Edinburgh 'Scotch Goods' which frequently loaded up to 600 tons (610 tonnes) and travelled at 50 mph (80km/h) plus. But with 74-inch (1879-mm) driving wheels, they were really mixed-traffic locomotives and were often put on express passenger duties. On the LMS, a new class of articulated Beyer Garratt 2-6-6-2 engines was introduced in 1927 to work coal trains between Toton in Nottinghamshire and Brent yards in north London. This was a bold step, and formed Britain's only Garratt class (33 in all) though the LNER had built a one-off 2-8-8-2 in 1925. While Garratts did excellent work abroad, the British ones did not particularly shine. The cause of this has been put down to the Derby engineering

ABOVE Southern Railway 'Z' class 0-8-0 heavy shunting tank No. 955, at work in the yard at Ashford, Kent, in October 1938. This 3-cylinder class of eight locomotives was introduced by R.W. Maunsell in 1930.

LEFT The Hull & Barnsley's heaviest power was this eight-coupled type. No. 117 was built by the Yorkshire Engine Co. in 1907.

ABOVE An ex-War Department 2-8-0, British Railways No. 77260, passes North Cave, on the former Hull & Barnsley line, with a long goods train for Hull.

department's insistence on standard LMS parts being used where possible, which did not suit the Garratt design. The LMS had greater success with its standard 2-8-0 of 1935, of which ultimately 630 were built, making it the second most numerous tender locomotive class after the same company's 'Black Five' mixed traffic engine. They were most often employed on block loads of coal and minerals though they also hauled inter-city mixed freights.

A Job for Life

Freight activity, mostly conducted away from the eyes of passengers, and very often at night, accounted for a high proportion of railway staff. The railways were among the country's largest employers. In 1938, they employed more than 580,000 people; in 1948, it was 629,000. The great majority were male. Nearly two million of the population thus depended on the railways for their daily bread. It was a man's world: apart from wartime emergency, women's posts were usually restricted to office work, cleaning, catering and opening the gates at level crossings – and women's voices were favoured for making broadcast announcements at major stations. Demarcation existed between the different departments of the civil engineer, the mechanical and electrical engineer, the locomotive running superintendent and the traffic and accounting managers, though each offered a career path. In the locomotive running department, a new recruit began as an engine cleaner, also doing other work around the shed, from shovelling cinders to lighting up the fires. In sequence he would then become a fireman, a 'passed fireman' with a driver's ticket and then a driver. After the times when a driver had his own engine – which lasted into the late nineteenth century on some lines – locomotive crews were organised in 'links', that is, groups of crews allocated a specific set of duties. 'Top link' was the long-

LEFT An ex-LSWR A12 class 0-4-2, No. 628, with a goods train at Marchwood, on the Totton-Fawley branch, in August 1938.

distance passenger trains. The new driver had another set of ladders to climb, which explains why in so many photographs of express engines, the driver is an elderly man. A few drivers progressed to become inspectors.

On the station side, a boy might start by filling oil lamps, which were still widely used throughout the system in the 1950s, and progress to the post of top-hatted stationmaster in a city terminus. The engineering works offered apprenticeships, usually linked with classes at the local technical college.

The promotional pyramid narrowed sharply. Most lamp boys, if they stayed on, would end their career as signalmen or porters rather than as stationmasters. The life of the railway had become so diverse in the twentieth century that the actual enginemen were a small minority of the employees. In 1938, around 20,000 locomotives were in use, one engine for every twenty-nine staff.

BELOW Great Western 0-6-0 pannier tank No. 9795 at work in the yard at Salisbury, in August 1937. Though Salisbury was very much in LSWR territory, the GWR line from Westbury carried substantial freight traffic from South Wales, which the LSWR took on to Southampton.

PARKESTON
№ 61264

7 • The Passenger Train

In 1938, the year that *Mallard* hits a record breaking speed of 112.5mph (181km/h) between Grantham and Peterborough, steam railways have 6,698 stations open to passengers. In these twelve months, 1,205,586,000 passenger journeys are recorded, an average of around 25 train journeys for every man, woman and child in the country.

LEFT The South Eastern & Chatham Railway had its own terminus at Bexhill-on-Sea, the branch joining the Hastings line at Crowhurst. The London train is at the departure platform in this scene from around 1900. Ample baggage space was needed for prosperous holiday-makers.

OPPOSITE Preserved LNER B1 4-6-0 No. 61264 heads a Leicester train at Woodthorpe on the restored Great Central main line. The green livery harks back to a period in British Railways when the operating regions were allowed to apply their own colour schemes to passenger engines: in this case, London & North Eastern green.

A glance at the railway map of Britain in the 1930s, and even in the early 1960s, shows a network far greater in extent than at present. Although uneconomic branch lines were closed every now and then, their total mileage was very small. Many of them were city railways, like the Edinburgh–Leith or Nottingham suburban lines, killed off by competition from electric trams and then diesel buses. The Big Four saw their rural lines as feeders to the main lines; they also inherited much of the attitudes of their predecessors, with a strong urge to protect their own territory. They also inherited a sense of service. As the monopoly long-distance transport system until the advent of the motor coach, they accepted a duty to provide the country's transport links. Branch line services in many cases were infrequent, but they existed. Country towns such as Cirencester, Oakham, Crieff and Lampeter took their place on the railway network for granted. Cirencester was one of many towns of moderate size, like

ABOVE W.P. Reid's imposing North British 4-4-2s dominated Scottish express services on the East coast from 1906 into the 1930s. Here, LNER No. 9906 enters Carlisle with an express train off the Waverley Route from Edinburgh in 1934.

Banbury, Workington, Newark and Ardrossan, which had two stations serving different lines. Some of these were in direct competition: the inhabitants of Ardrossan could once take either the Caledonian or Glasgow & South Western to reach Glasgow; those of Windsor can still choose between what were originally the Great Western route to Paddington and the South Western route to Waterloo. At some frontier points, there was little evidence of inter-company collaboration. Travelling south on the Highland line from Forres, part of the LMS system from 1923, passengers would see at the small junction station of Boat of Garten a huge notice suggesting that the right thing to do was to change trains and proceed south via the LNER. This would have involved a very slow cross-country detour of about 90 miles (145km) and a further change, in order to reach Aberdeen, before going southwards.

The principle of through trains, run across the territory of more than one company, was established in the 1830s when the Liverpool & Manchester and Grand Junction railways agreed on the L&M operating Manchester–Birmingham trains on the GJR line. It might seem that

commercial common sense would make it obvious that there should be cross-country services as soon as the network of lines made it possible. In fact the development of these was slow and limited. At first there was no system for selling a through ticket, and no method for assessing the fare and how it should be divided among companies. The Railway Clearing House came to play a vital part here. But in 1852, a traveller proposing to go from Exeter to Newcastle would have had to take the Great Western to Gloucester; and the Midland from Gloucester to Birmingham. Here he would have a choice of routes, but he might select the London & North Western to Manchester and then the Lancashire and Yorkshire to Leeds. Finally the North Eastern would take him from Leeds to Newcastle. The whole journey would take two days, with an overnight stay in Manchester. A 'through' ticket was impossible to buy, as the GWR did not join the Railway Clearing House until after 1860. The traveller did, however, have an invaluable aid in *Bradshaw's Monthly Railway Guide*, a compendium of all companies' timetables, first issued in 1842 and surviving until 1961.

4-6-2 DUCHESS LMS 1938

Tractive effort: 40,000lb (18,140kg)
Axle load: 49,952lb (22.6 tonnes)
Cylinders: four 16½x28in (419x711mm)
Driving wheels: 81in (205.75cm)
Heating surface: 2807sq ft (260m²)
Superheater: 856sq ft (79.5m²)
Steam pressure: 250psi (17.6kg/cm²)
Grate area: 50sq ft (4.6m²)
Fuel: Coal – 22,400lb (10.1 tonnes)
Water: 4000gall (4804 US) (18m³)
Total weight: 235,200lb (106.6 tonnes)
Overall length: 37ft (11.28m)

Complicated Connections

Another early cross-country service began in 1849, linking Liverpool and Hull, but it was only in the 1870s, with most companies now linked in to the Clearing House, that they began to

ABOVE One of the features of the LMS 'Duchess' 4-6-2s was a steam-powered coal pusher in the tender that brought the coal forwards to the fireman; a valuable aid on a long haul such as the 290 miles (466km) between Crewe and Perth with the Inverness-bound 'Royal Highlander' sleeper train.

LEFT In the bay platform at the former Midland station in Stamford, an ex-Midland 0-4-4T, LMS No. 1416, is ready to leave with a full head of steam on the one-coach 8.50 a.m. service to Seaton, via Ketton and Luffenham, on 25 August 1947. Stamford was also the terminus of two Great Northern branches.

LOCOMOTIVE DESIGNERS

SIR NIGEL GRESLEY (1876–1941)

Though deeply identified with the 'East Coast' LNER, Gresley's career in fact began with the LNWR at Crewe, where he was a premium apprentice; then he went to the Lancashire & Yorkshire, before becoming carriage and wagon superintendent of the Great Northern Railway in 1905. The son of a Derbyshire country parson, he always retained something of the country gentleman's tweedy image among his fellow engineers. But there was no doubt about his commitment or ability in his chosen calling. Although his later fame as a locomotive designer overshadowed his work on carriage design, he was a pioneer of articulated carriages and designed the handsome elliptical-roofed carriages (the metal sides given a grained paint finish to resemble wood) of the East Coast Joint Stock in 1905. In 1911 he was appointed chief mechanical engineer of the Great Northern, and was appointed to the same post on the formation of the London & North Eastern Railway in 1923. Just before then he had introduced his first 'Pacific', the A1 class. Like many of his other classes, this was a three-cylinder engine, with simple expansion (apart from his experimental high-pressure 4-6-4, Gresley, like other British designers, did not favour compounding), and with a form of conjugated gear enabling the external Walschaerts valve gear to operate the inside cylinder also. It took some years before problems with the conjugated gear were resolved, and Gresley was felt to have been slow in dealing with the difficulties. With the introduction of the A3 'Super-Pacifics' in 1928, his reputation as 'speeder-up' of British railways began to rise. Unlike most other CMEs, Gresley did not pursue a policy of standardisation, partly because of lack of funds; but he also believed in 'horses for courses', with locomotives built for specific routes. This led to the design of Britain's first 3-cylinder 4-4-0s, named after counties and hunts, in 1928, and intended for lightweight expresses and cross-country trains, as well as the large P2 2-8-2s in 1934, for heavy expresses between Edinburgh and Aberdeen. Always an enthusiast and innovator, Gresley experimented with a super-high pressure locomotive (see main text) but also tried out many potential improvements to the basic steam locomotive, from boosters on his P1 freight 2-8-2s of 1925 to poppet valves on a number of types. He was the prime advocate of a modern British locomotive testing plant, similar to the French one at Vitry-sur-Seine, though it was not set up until after his death. The climax of his career came with the introduction of the streamlined A4 'Pacifics' of 1935. From the mid-1930s, he was increasingly troubled by heart problems, but insisted on maintaining a heavy workload. At the time of his sudden death, he had just completed a new three-cylinder 2-6-2 class, the V4, a lighter version of the excellent V2s introduced in 1936. His successor as CME, Edward Thompson, abruptly reversed the LNER's design policy, favouring two-cylinder engines and standardisation of locomotive types. Gresley's engines were undoubtedly difficult to service and repair, but they were intended to be high-quality machines.

Gresley received a knighthood in 1936, for services to engineering in general as well as for his railway work. An engaging detail of his life, in view of the fast-flying bird names of the A4s, is that at his successive country homes he maintained sanctuaries for wild ducks and other waterfowl.

develop. They took two forms, the cross-country train, and the through carriage. Cross-country trains included the Birmingham–Bath–Bournemouth service from 1874, and a Birmingham–Rugby–Peterborough–Harwich service from 1880. Once the Great Western had gone over to standard gauge, there were west-to-north services from Plymouth and Exeter to Manchester. But the nature of the system, with its radial focus on London, and the frequency of disputes and hostility between the companies, restricted the growth of an effective cross-country service. Companies preferred to obtain, or to try to obtain, 'running powers' over other lines in order to convey passengers in their own trains, hauled by their own engines. Passengers were generally resigned to the need to change trains several times on such journeys. Matters improved at holiday times, when trains would be laid on from the large inland cities to coastal resorts. A famous example was the Birmingham–Brighton 'Sunny South Express'. In its heyday this was a daily train, passing across west London by means of the West London and West London Extension Railways, from Willesden through Addison Road. Through carriages or connecting trains brought passengers from as far as Liverpool, Sheffield and Manchester, and the train had different portions for Eastbourne, Hastings and the North Kent coast, as well as Brighton. There were many others, linking the industrial districts to Skegness and Mablethorpe, Cleethorpes, the Norfolk coast, the Kent and North Wales resorts, Blackpool and Morecambe. Stations at these holiday towns normally had extra platforms,

ABOVE Sir Nigel Gresley with the new 'A4' that bore his name, No. 4498, at Doncaster in 1937. It was the 100th 'Pacific' built.

BELOW A 'Britannia' class 4-6-2, No. 70004 *William Shakespeare*, passes Wandsworth Road with the in-bound 'Golden Arrow', in September 1957.

Ex-LNER A1 4-6-2 No. 60161 *North British* leaves Edinburgh Waverley with the southbound 'Queen of Scots' Pullman. Designed by A.H. Peppercorn and built in 1948, this was a modern locomotive despite its traditional Gresleyan appearance, and it gave excellent service until dieselization brought about its premature end. The last was retired in July 1966.

THE
QUEEN OF SCOTS
60161

unroofed and exposed, used only to accommodate the extra trains of peak holiday times.

ABOVE Passenger direction sign at Ashchurch, on the Midland's Gloucester–Birmingham line.

A Full Day's Travel

Through carriages were more frequent than through trains. These were detached from one train and coupled to another in order to enable passengers to make cross-country journeys without changing trains. Here too the railway companies were somewhat ambivalent about the service. The shunting and re-marshalling of through carriages at junctions took up time and added to congestion. On the other hand, it enabled them to economise on trains and locomotives, to combine trains that would otherwise have been lightly loaded, and to offer a wider choice of destinations. A single Great Northern train in 1860 advertised through carriages from King's Cross to Manchester, Liverpool, Huddersfield, Leeds, Bradford and Newcastle. When the Midland Railway had completed its line to Carlisle, it offered through carriages to Dundee, Aberdeen and Inverness on its Glasgow and Edinburgh trains. The Midland also ran a through carriage from Birmingham to Southampton, by way of the Midland & South West Junction Railway via Cheltenham and Andover; and others from Bristol to York and from Leeds to Torquay and Kingswear. The longest through carriage route was that from Aberdeen to Penzance. Operating in the summer season only, this carriage left Aberdeen at 10.20 on an Edinburgh express. At 14.05 it left Edinburgh attached to a London train, and was detached from this at York, at 18.14. At 18.30 it left York on a train for Sheffield, which also carried a Glasgow–Swindon through carriage

BELOW Preserved Southern locomotives at work on a simulated 'Man of Kent'. 'King Arthur'-class 4-6-0 No. 30777 Sir Lamiel and rebuilt 'West Country' 4-6-2 class No. 34039 *Boscastle* make a powerful double-header passing through the Great Central station at Quorn.

from York. Its route went from Sheffield through Nottingham, Leicester, Rugby, Woodford and Banbury. Up to this point it had been on LNER metals all the way, using the former Great Central line south of Sheffield. Now on Great Western track, it was attached to a Banbury–Oxford train. From Oxford it went via Didcot to Swindon, arriving at 23.32. Here it was attached to the Penzance train, which had left Paddington at 21.50. Travelling through the night at an unhurried pace, it reached the Cornish terminus at 7.45 next morning, having run 794 miles (1277km) in 21 hours and 25 minutes, at an average speed of 37 mph (61km/h). One wonders what proportion of its passengers did the complete journey. At minor country

ABOVE The actual 'Cornish Riviera Express': 'King' class 4-6-0 No. 6002 King William IV hammers through Reading (West) with the down train in summer 1938. It will work as far as Plymouth, where a 'Castle' will take over the train.

Jocular greetings are exchanged as the Penzance–Wolverhampton express climbs past Dainton signal box. The locomotive is GWR 'County' class 4-6-0 No. 1019, *County of Merioneth*.

junctions, the detaching and re-attaching of carriages was done by a train engine, but larger stations invariably had a 'station pilot': a shunting tank locomotive, to do such work. These small engines were often given a special paint finish, and usually kept in a highly polished state, rather as if they were pets or mascots.

ABOVE 'Where's that train?' In this late 1950s scene, passengers seem impatient or resigned at Challow, on the Great Western main line between Didcot and Swindon, as they wait for a delayed local service to arrive.

A variant on the through carriage was the slip coach. A specially fitted carriage with its own brakeman and brake apparatus, it could be uncoupled from the moving train as it approached a station, and then come coasting in, while the express raced on without losing time. This was a uniquely British device, started in 1858, and unused elsewhere, but very popular with certain companies. In 1914, the main user, the GWR, offered seventy slip coach services; the London Brighton & South Coast had 21, and the Midland had 18. Special safety precautions were observed. The slip carriages were normally used only on outward journeys from London, and there was no equivalent means of attaching them on the run to a moving 'up' train. Slipping was abandoned during 1939–45, but the Western Region of British Railways resuscitated the practice in 1950, and used it for ten years. The last slip carriage was detached from a Paddington–Birmingham express at Bicester, in 1960.

Some services were a combination of the cross-country train and the through carriage. By 1926, the Birmingham–Bournemouth train had its point of origin moved back to Manchester. Known to its staff as 'The Diner' (it was formally named the 'Pines Express' in 1927) it left Manchester at 9 a.m. with five coaches, including

4-4-0 SCHOOLS
SOUTHERN RAILWAY 1930

Tractive effort: 25,130lb (11,396kg)
Axle load: 23,520lb (10.6 tonnes)
Cylinders: three 16½x26in (419x660mm)
Driving wheels: 79in (200.5cm)
Heating surface: 1604sq ft (149m^2)
Superheater: 280sq ft (26m^2)
Steam pressure: 220psi (15.5kg/cm^2)
Grate area: 28.3sq ft (2.6 m^2)
Fuel: Coal – 11,200lb (5 tonnes)
Water: 4000gall (4804 US) (183m^3)
Total weight: 150,080lb (68 tonnes)
Overall length: 25ft 6in (7.77m)

BELOW The Southern Railway's three-cylinder 'Schools' class 4-4-0 of 1930 was the most up-to-date and powerful of its kind in Europe. It was so successful that the original 30 was doubled, and they did express work on the Wessex route, as well as the Kent and Sussex lines.

THE CALEDONIAN RAILWAY

No one could ever accuse the Caledonian of not having, in the Scottish phrase, 'a good conceit of itself'. It began as a trunk line, the Scottish end of the London–Glasgow route, receiving its Act of Parliament in 31 July 1845. This was nine years after the original proposals, due to a long wrangle over the best route northwards from Carlisle. By this time a number of local railways had been built in the Glasgow area, and the new line came in over the Wishaw & Coltness, and the Glasgow, Garnkirk & Coatbridge Railways. Purchase of these, and price wars with the Edinburgh–Glasgow and North British Railways, brought the Caledonian to the brink of bankruptcy in 1849. However, it survived with a new board of directors and its network gradually extended to its northernmost point, Aberdeen, by acquisition of the Scottish Central, the Scottish Midland Junction and the Aberdeen Railway, a process complete by 1866. The original idea behind the Caledonian was that it should be the only rail link between Scotland and England, dividing at Carstairs to serve both Glasgow and Edinburgh, but the North British completed the Newcastle–Edinburgh line before the Caledonian opened, beginning many years of rivalry. The original terminus was at Buchanan Street in central Glasgow;

On a snowy day in the Vale of Strathmore, a Caledonian Railway Glasgow–Aberdeen express storms past a stopping train at a wayside station. The scene dates from around 1910.

COMPANY PROFILE

This illustration, dated around 1905, shows the 2 p.m. 'Corridor' express passing Beattock Summit between Glasgow and Carlisle.

later stations south of the Clyde were also used, until finally in 1879 Glasgow Central was built, on a site just north of the river. Buchanan Street continued as a station for the Caledonian's services to the north. Unlike the imposing Central and the G&SW's St Enoch, which impressed travellers arriving from England, it remained a collection of wooden sheds until it was pulled down in the 1960s. This was surprising, as the Caledonian otherwise had a reputation for building fine stations, of which Wemyss Bay and Stirling remain among the best examples. Its first Edinburgh terminus, Lothian Road, was relocated and renamed as Princes Street, fronted by a large hotel, though not so imposing as the North British establishment half a mile away. Between 1899 and 1906 Glasgow Central was greatly enlarged into the form it still has today.

Rivalry with the North British was the spur for much Caledonian activity, though despite its efforts it always remained the second largest of the Scottish railway companies. The competition between the two reached a point of absurdity when each built a line to serve the small and remote hamlet of Dolphinton, south of the Pentland Hills. In the Glasgow area, however, the rivalry led to many very smart commuter services linked to the Clyde steamers. The Caledonian also operated the trains on the independent Callander & Oban Railway, completed in 1880, which made end-on connection at Callander with the Caledonian branch from Dunblane. It built another scenic but uneconomic line between Crieff and Balquidder Junction. By 1923 it possessed just over 1000 miles (1600km) of route.

The real basis of the business was in freight operations, with the lion's share of traffic created by the Lanarkshire coalfield, the iron and steel industries of central Scotland and the Clyde docks and shipyards. But the company also worked hard to promote tourist routes and services, with the golfing hotel at Gleneagles as its flagship.

CALEDONIAN HEIGHTS

The Caledonian locomotive works were set up at St Rollox in Glasgow in 1854. The high point of Caledonian locomotive design was reached in the reign of J.F. McIntosh as chief mechanical engineer. His 'big boiler' policy, developed through a series of increasingly buxom 4-4-0 and 4-6-0 engines between 1895 and 1906, was highly influential at a time when all railways were looking for more power to haul heavier trains. The Caledonian colour scheme, a deep rich blue sometimes described as 'Prussian', was striking. Few of its locomotives were named; *Cardean*, first of the 903 class of 4-6-0, built in 1906, is remembered as an exception. For many years it ran the 'Corridor', the 2 p.m. Glasgow–Euston service, between Glasgow Central and Carlisle.

When the Grouping was being planned, the intention was to combine the Scottish companies into a single group. However, for various reasons, this was not pursued, and the Caledonian, along with the Glasgow & South Western and Highland Railways, became part of the LMS from 1 January 1923.

LEFT South Eastern & Chatham 'D' class 4-4-0 No. 145 with the 'Hastings Car Train' from Charing Cross, around 1905. The loading gauge on this line required specially narrow coaching stock.

the dining car. At Crewe it picked up another four coaches from Liverpool. It then ran south via Birmingham to Cheltenham, where two of the Liverpool coaches were detached. These were to be added to a Southampton-bound train running over the Midland & South Western Junction to Andover and from there on the London & South Western's Test Valley line through Stockbridge to Southampton. The 'Diner' carried on to Bath and the heavy slog over the Mendips on the former Somerset & Dorset Joint line to the Wiltshire Downs and at last the pine-clad dunes of Bournemouth. In East Anglia, the 10.15 p.m. from Norwich to Liverpool Street was formed from the stock of three trains that had started from Lowestoft, Yarmouth,

LEFT GWR 0-6-0 pannier tank No. 7443 stands at Blaenau Ffestiniog Central with the 11.15 a.m. mixed train for Trawsfynnydd, on 27 June 1956. The slate quarries are in the background.

ABOVE Rebuilt with a Belpaire firebox, ex-LNWR 'George V' 4-4-0 No. 5335 of the LMS scoops up water as it races over Whitmore Troughs, between Stafford and Crewe, with a down express on 7 June 1930. Express workings for this class were by then becoming rarer, as 'Royal Scots' took over.

and Sheringham. It did not take the more direct line through Ipswich, but ran via Wymondham and Thetford to Ely, where it changed engines. At Cambridge, two parcel vans were added before it left for Liverpool Street, arriving at 2.55 in the morning.

HOLIDAY TRAVEL

Excursion trains, offering day trips at special low prices, were extremely popular. By the later nineteenth century, Thomas Cook's modest outing of 1841 was left far behind in every way. It was quite usual for whole towns to virtually empty themselves for 'Wakes Weeks' when all the factories closed down at the same time, and the workers headed for the coast. There were also individual works outings and bank holiday excursions. The railway works themselves naturally led the way. On September 7, 1899, fourteen special trains, each comprising eighteen six-wheel coaches, took the employees and their families of the Caledonian Railway's St Rollox Works in Glasgow on a day trip to Carlisle. This was quite typical of such outings, featuring a colossal picnic. The trains were despatched at ten-minute intervals, and the whole exercise of moving almost ten thousand people was accomplished like a military operation. But the railways were well accustomed to coping with seasonal movements, of people as well as of farm produce.

GREEN ARROW
4771

LEFT No. 4771 runs past the rugged ruins on Conwy Castle, North Wales, on the former LNWR line from Chester to Holyhead, with a special excursion train. This route is at the other side of the country from the engine's 'East Coast' origins.

Each September there was an exodus of hop-pickers from London to the Kentish Weald, and, on a lesser scale, from Birmingham and its environs to Worcestershire and Herefordshire. The first hop-pickers' specials ran in 1856 from Bricklayers Arms station in south London, on the South Eastern Railway. They were an annual event after that. Invariably composed of the most ancient carriages available, and with vans for the passengers' baggage, the hop-pickers' trains were notorious for wild and noisy behaviour. Many of the passengers were camp followers rather than workers. The last such service ran in 1960. A more sedate crowd of seasonal passengers were the Scottish fisher-girls, who came south in large numbers to Yarmouth and Lowestoft for the herring-fishing season, to work as herring-gutters. Special trains were laid on from and to the Great North of Scotland Railway's termini at Fraserburgh and Peterhead. The little Derwent Valley Railway at York, which preserved a fragile independence for some years after the Grouping, ran September 'Blackberry Specials' into the countryside for berry pickers. Right up to the 1960s it was common practice to hire a special train for club outings and Sunday school picnic trips. From hop-pickers and Sunday school outings to the grand express trains seems a great step, but the railways applied the same professionalism to every service, though the accommodation and ambiance were very different.

ABOVE On the troughs: a 'Royal Scot' 4-6-0 in original form scoops up water at speed from Tebay troughs as it crosses the River Lune before climbing to Shap summit with the 'Royal Scot' London–Glasgow express. The sixth car is a clerestoried diner.

RIGHT Paddington night scene: a GWR four-cylinder 'Star' 4-6-0 express engine, No. 4022 *Belgian Monarch*, on the 10.15 p.m. Weymouth train.

ABOVE Pacifics returned to British rails in late 1922 when the Great Northern and North Eastern Railways both brought out 4-6-2 classes. The illustration shows the most famous, No. 4472 *Flying Scotsman*.

The railways invented the vocabulary of social class distinction. In 1830 the Liverpool & Manchester Railway used 'First Class' to describe its fastest service. As this was also the most expensive, its implied hierarchy soon extended to designating other services as second and third, and on some lines, fourth, class. The passengers were identified in the same way. Express trains took their name from the older use of such terms as 'express messenger', meaning messenger with one specific message. The original expresses conveyed passengers to a specific town – Brighton being the first in 1844 – and from this stemmed the connotation of speed,

LEFT One of Dugald Drummond's LSWR 'T9' class, on the up fast line near Surbiton with the Plymouth–London express, around 1902.

OPPOSITE, BOTTOM The LNER had two 4-4-0 engine types named after Sir Walter Scott's characters. One was an ex-Great Central design, class D11/2. No. 62674 *Flora McIvor* leaves Melrose, in the Scottish Borders, with a Hawick-Edinburgh train, in April 1952.

which soon eclipsed the old meaning. At first supplementary fares were charged for express trains, which aroused the ire of passengers who had already paid the high first-class fare. Most lines gave up the practice, though it was revived for the 'Coronation' and similar high-speed trains in the 1930s. Until the Midland's reforms of 1875, the contrast between the bare boards of Third and the luxury of First was great. In *The Beauty of Old Trains*, the railway historian Hamilton Ellis commented on the Great Eastern's carriages at this time, 'the shiny grimness of its third class, the red-plush stodge of its seconds, and the leathern pomposity of its firsts.' In first-class compartments, passengers sat three abreast, with armrests and deep cushions, linen antimacassars on the seatbacks, and ample leg-room. In third class, passengers might be up to seven abreast, without armrests and with knees almost touching those of the occupants of the facing bench.

The 1870s were the great decade of innovation as far as carriages were concerned, with the introduction – first on the narrow-gauge Festiniog Railway – of the eight-wheel bogie coach that has been standard ever since, the beginning of the abolition of second class and the introduction of regular restaurant-car services. These were made possible by interconnecting gangways between the carriages. Lavatories were also introduced. These improvements heralded an end of the luncheon basket and the long stop for refreshments at intermediate stations, though some lines, like the West Highland at Crianlarich (Upper), maintained the tradition well into the twentieth century. Although 'bed-cars' had been known from the 1830s, the North British Railway introduced the modern sleeping car in 1873, on its overnight Glasgow–London service. In the same decade the Midland built Pullman sleepers from parts imported

BELOW The other 'Scott' class, D30, was from the former North British Railway. No. 62436 *Lord Glenvarloch* stands at Thornton Junction with a Dunfermline train.

from the US. Hamilton Ellis glowingly described the Pullman sleeping car: 'The full exuberance of American decorative art of the President Grant era blossoms inside and out… She scintillates with silverplate and gilding, her handsome bronze kerosene lamps gleam in a coloured clerestory, shedding a warm radiance over rich panels and sleek plush.' In the 1890s both the East Coast and West Coast companies introduced new trains of 'Joint Stock' to run between London, Edinburgh and Glasgow, though some joint stock coaches found their way as far north as Inverness on through carriage services during the tourist season.

ABOVE LMS 2-6-2T No. 41287 at Llandudno Junction with 'The Welsh Dragon', in August 1951.

By Land and Sea

Boat trains, whose part in early speed exploits is described in a previous chapter, could be another test of the railways' capacity for getting large numbers of people on the move within a very short time. Regular boat trains ran to regular timetables to the Channel ports: Dover, Folkestone, Newhaven and Harwich; to Fishguard, Holyhead and Stranraer with Irish traffic; to Weymouth for the Channel Islands and to Heysham for the Isle of Man. But, from the 1890s to the 1960s, before the era of the wide-bodied jet, ocean liners were the primary means of transport across the Atlantic and further oceans. Up to one thousand or more passengers might be taken on board or disembarked on arrival. The two main passenger ports, Southampton and Liverpool, had their own dockside stations, Ocean Terminal and Riverside respectively, used only for boat trains. Trains were arranged, sometimes

65447

ABOVE Former LNWR 2-4-2T, now LMS No. 6757, on a Wellington train at the branch terminus, Coalport, Shropshire, in the 1920s. The leading coach is rebuilt from two old LNWR six-wheel carriages.

at short notice, to coincide with the departures and arrivals of the liners, and it was the task of the controllers to fit their paths into those of busy main lines to terminals in London. When liners like the *Queen Elizabeth, Cape Town Castle* and the *United States* left Southampton on the same afternoon, up to ten special trains were needed to run from Waterloo to Southampton.

Train Names

Naming of trains was always more selective than the naming of locomotives. The first official name was strictly descriptive: the Irish Mail, from Euston to Holyhead, was known as such from 1848; but there were no others. Railwaymen created nicknames for their own various fast services. These usually came from famous racehorses, like Beeswing and Flying Dutchman (hence 'Dutchman', the apparently bizarre name given to the 10.00 Paddington–Exeter train from 1849). Such in-house names continued. The staff always referred to the main London–Glasgow express as 'the Corridor', a name that commemorated its new corridor carriages of 1893. The most famous express name, 'The Flying Scotsman', for the morning trains between Edinburgh Waverley and London King's Cross, was also long current among the operating staff before it was given official

OPPOSITE The Mid-Suffolk Light Railway ran through deeply rural country from Haughley to Laxfield. On 26 June 1952, LNER class J15 0-6-0 No. 65447 (ex-Great Eastern class Y15) leaves Mendlesham.

blessing in 1923. With the growth of competing services, and a new skill in publicity, the companies perceived the value of giving a whole train its own identity. One of the first was the 'Cornish Riviera Express' in 1904. But the great era of train naming was in the 1920s. Some of these trains have already been noted: the 'Atlantic Coast Express' (1926), the 'Royal Scot' (1927) as the West Coast's answer to the 'Flying Scotsman' and the 'Golden Arrow' (1929). Such names were promotional, not factual or descriptive. The hope was that they would add a touch of glamour to the mundane experience of travelling by train. Naming was widely extended during the early 1930s. It is questionable, however, whether the travellers on the latter stages of the 'Cambrian Coast Express' or on the 'Lewisman', calling at the numerous wayside stations on the way to Pwllheli or Kyle of Lochalsh, had their spirits greatly uplifted by the fact that their trains had names. New train names were still being created in the 1950s on such services as the Carmarthen–London 'Red Dragon', the Glasgow–Aberdeen 'Granite City' and 'Saint Mungo' expresses.

ABOVE Southern Railway 'Schools' class 4-4-0 30909 *St Paul's*, with the 'Kentish Belle' Pullman, the 11.35 a.m. Victoria–Ramsgate, pauses at Herne Bay, on Sunday 1 September 1957.

THE NEED FOR SPEED

As the pace of express competition heated up in the later 1920s, both the East Coast and the West Coast routes had ambitions to run the 400-plus miles (644km) from London to Glasgow and Edinburgh non-stop each way, once a day. They were confident of enough passengers to make the trains pay; but the work involved was far beyond a single fireman's capacity. Nine tons of coal had to be shovelled into the firebox in the course of the journey. The LMS carried two crews on the footplate, but the LNER scored a definite *coup* in building the world's first corridor tender, in with a narrow passage along one side leading to a rear gangway which was connected to the leading coach. This enabled the relief, and the relieved, crew each to sit in comfort for half the journey. Using the new class A3 'Super-Pacific' engines, the 'Flying Scotsman's' regular non-stop runs began on May 1, 1928. The average speed, 47.6 mph (76.6km/h), was hardly of racing calibre, but the railway services gained much useful publicity. Even a classic instance of 'spoiling', when the LMS ran a non-stop 'Royal Scot' to both Edinburgh and Glasgow on the previous day, though only as one-off happenings, helped to promote the high-speed reputation.

BELOW LEFT GWR 4-6-0 No. 7803 *Barcote Manor*, at Machynlleth with the down 'Cambrian Coast Express' from Paddington to Aberystwyth and Pwllheli, on 25 September 1961.

BELOW An ex-LNWR Class 2665 4-6-2T of 1910, as No. 6987 of the LMS, passes Keeper's Cottage in the Staffordshire countryside with the 9.52 from Rugeley (Trent Valley) to Walsall, on 18 June 1936.

46478

8 • Special Locomotives

From early days, designers made improvements to the efficiency and effectiveness of the steam locomotive, but, despite some remarkable attempts, they found it very hard to replace the basic Stephenson model. The combination of firebox, tubular boiler, cylinders, smoke-box and blast-pipe, remains standard until the end of steam traction.

LEFT Picture of concentration: this shot of Driver Brown, at the regulator of the Southern Railway 'West Country' 4-6-2 *Templecombe*, was taken on 26 June 1958. The locomotive, on the 'Man of Kent' express, was travelling at 80mph (128km/h) at the time.

OPPOSITE The lofty Belah Viaduct, on the North Eastern line from Tebay to Darlington, was a more successful work of Sir Thomas Bouch, who also designed the first Tay Bridge. A lightweight Kirkby Stephen–Barnard Castle goods train is in the charge of BR Standard 2-6-0 No. 46478 and LNER J21 0-6-0 No. 65047, on 21 August 1952.

Few steam locomotive designers did not try, at one time or another, to improve on the basic set of constituents: blast pipe, cylinders, valve gear, tubular boiler and firebox. The three latter were the most usual sources for experiment. Even after British firebox design had been essentially confirmed by the work of Charles Markham and Matthew Kirtley on the Midland Railway between 1856 and 1859, attempts at improvement continued. Kirtley's aim was to obtain a firebox that would effectively burn coal, and it was achieved by the combination of the arch of fireproof brick built across the firebox, and the metal deflector plate above the fire door. The combined effect was to make a space that encouraged long flames, greater heat and more complete burning of the coal. It also moderated – somewhat – the smoke output, but by mid-nineteenth century, with thousands of factory chimneys belching smoke, it was more difficult to single out the locomotive as a source of

SIR WILLIAM STANIER (1876–1965)

Stanier was a child of the Great Western: his father was superintendent of stores at the Swindon works and he himself was apprenticed there at the age of 16. In 1920 he was appointed works manager, and became principal assistant to C.B. Collett in 1922 when the latter took over the top job from Churchward. In 1927 he accompanied the 'King' class locomotive *King George V* on its famous visit to the USA for the Baltimore & Ohio Railway's centennial celebrations. Collett was only five years older than Stanier, who thus had little hope of becoming CME at Swindon. But in any case he was 'poached' by Sir Josiah Stamp, chairman of the London Midland & Scottish Railway, in 1932. His appointment upset the 'Buggins's turn' principle previously used on the LMS, and was a disappointment to H.P.M. Beames, the internal heir-presumptive. Many years before, Churchward, Stanier's chief mentor, had remarked: 'When other railways wanted a good man they came to Swindon.' The new man found himself in charge of works at Derby, Crewe, Horwich and St Rollox (Glasgow), to name only the larger ones. After a series of changes of top-level staff, the company was in dire need of a confident and able locomotive chief, and Stanier fulfilled this admirably, damping down old internal rivalries and developing a strong team of subordinates. His 'hot line' to Stamp, his expertise as an engineer and his firm control restored the prestige of the locomotive engineering department, which had been previously pushed about somewhat by the locomotive running side. He was capable of keeping things going even during his two visits to India as a member of committees investigating management systems and locomotive accidents. Standardisation was his brief, and he set about producing standard locomotive classes to operate over the whole system, unashamedly importing Great Western ideas, and using standard parts as much as possible. The reduced revenues of the Slump years hindered the implementation of this policy, summarised as 'scrap and build', but by 1939 the LMS was in vastly better shape, in terms of its locomotive fleet, than it had been ten years previously. If Stanier's 'flagships' were the 'Princess' and 'Coronation' 4-6-2s, his far more numerous 4-6-0 and 2-8-0 workhorse engines were invaluable. A reticent man in public, he encouraged his senior subordinates to speak, and, to a greater degree than his contemporary Sir Nigel Gresley, he was capable of admitting and adjusting error. Stanier, the first locomotive engineer since Robert Stephenson to become a Fellow of the Royal Society (1944), always took a scientific approach, and in 1942 was seconded to government work, as scientific adviser to the Ministry of Production. He was knighted in 1943 and retired from railway service in 1944, though he continued to take an interest in railway matters. The principles, and, indeed the basic designs, of LMS locomotives established in his time were maintained by his successors, C.E. Fairburn and H.G. Ivatt, on the LMS and, with little change in the 2-6-0, 4-6-0 and tank engine classes, in the final steam designs of British Railways. If a problem in design or operation was found, he wanted to waste no time in getting to the bottom of it, and was certainly not above putting on overalls and exploring the insides of a locomotive himself, to the occasional surprise of the fitters at Crewe or Derby.

pollution, and the railways generally got away with what would not have been allowed twenty years earlier.

ABOVE The 'turbomotive', Sir William Stanier's turbine 'Pacific', LMS No. 6202.

ECONOMICAL DESIGNS

As locomotives grew bigger, economy of operation was the constant ambition of designers. Coal was much cheaper than coke but as soon as coal firing became the rule, efforts were made to get more steam from every pound of fuel. This meant either hotter steam – we are still in the era before super heaters here – or at least more steam, by dint of packing more pipes, and so more heating surface, into the boiler. Some designers brought water pipes right into the firebox, anticipating the thermic syphon used in such twentieth-century locomotives as Bulleid's Southern Railway 'Pacifics'. One of the earliest of these was Joseph Beattie, locomotive engineer of the London & South Western during the 1850s and 60s, who fitted a water tube within the combustion chamber (a forward extension of the firebox) of his 2-4-0 express locomotives in 1859. Much more extensive use of water-tube fireboxes and boilers was made by one of his successors on the South Western, Dugald Drummond, whose D15 and T9 4-4-0 classes had casings on each side of the firebox, giving access to the lateral water tubes. Drummond believed firmly in the virtues of the water-tube firebox; in a

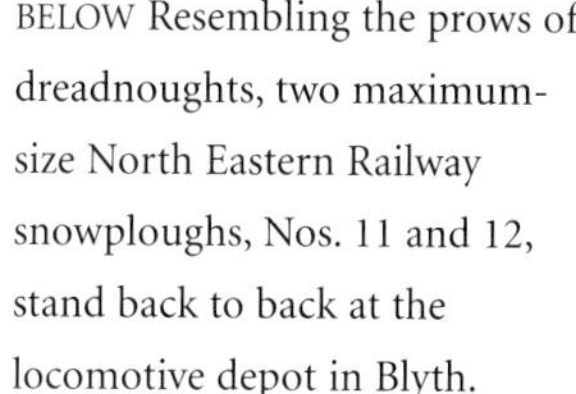
BELOW Resembling the prows of dreadnoughts, two maximum-size North Eastern Railway snowploughs, Nos. 11 and 12, stand back to back at the locomotive depot in Blyth.

6399

The official photograph of the LMS experimental high-pressure locomotive, 4-6-0 No. 6399 *Fury*, bears the signature of Sir Henry Fowler as the company's Chief Mechanical Engineer. It is standing outside the works of the North British Locomotive Company in Glasgow.

ABOVE Some engines in the late production batches of LMS 'Class Fives', built after 1945, embodied experimental features. No. 44687, photographed at Birmingham New Street, was fitted with Caprotti valve gear instead of the Walschaerts valve gear of the rest of the class, and also a double chimney and blast pipe.

4-6-0 5MT BLACK FIVE LMS 1934

Tractive effort: 26,000lb (11,790kg)
Axle load: 40,320lb (18.3 tonnes)
Cylinders: two 18½x28in (470x711mm)
Driving wheels: 72in (183cm)
Heating surface: 1460sq ft (135.6m^2)
Superheater: 359sq ft (33.3m^2)
Steam pressure: 225psi (15.8kg/cm^2)
Grate area: 28.7sq ft (2.6m^2)
Fuel: Coal – 20,160lb (9.1 tonnes)
Water: 4000gall (4804 US) (18m^2)
Total weight: 159,040lb (72.1 tonnes)
Overall length: 27ft 2in (8.28m)

quite typical way, his successor rebuilt most of his locomotives without them. Both Beattie and Drummond also favoured other kinds of secondary equipment. If the water fed into the boiler could be pre-heated, then it boiled more quickly into steam. Beattie's method diverted exhaust steam into a condenser, which heated water in two adjacent pipes, the whole assemblage being mounted in front of the chimney. A pump to force heated feedwater into the boiler was fitted on the left-hand running plate. The method had disadvantages – exhaust steam was mixed with oil and ashy material, not very good for readmission to the boiler, and any tapping of exhaust steam reduced the draught on the fire. But Beattie also offended against the general rule of Victorian British locomotive design: his engines, with their complex outside fittings (all Beattie's own patent devices) did not have the spare, unencumbered purity of line favoured by almost all other engineers.

Drummond, very much a traditionalist in this respect, hid his feedwater heater inside the side tanks of his M7 0-4-4 passenger tank engines and the tenders of his 4-4-0 engines, with the pumps also tucked away. But most designers simply did not trouble with such contraptions. The relatively tight British loading gauge made it difficult to add them on, and their consumption of either new or exhaust steam reduced the efficiency of what were already small boilers. Undoubtedly, however, a sense of the right appearance also played a part: British engineers frowned at French locomotives, with their pumps, feedwater heaters and air-brake cylinders all bolted on the outside. Only Churchward, on the Great Western, began to make regular use of limited feedwater heating with the top-feed system applied to new locomotives from 1913. The water, admitted through one-way 'clack' valves, was passed forward through a series of trays which both sieved out impurities and warmed it en route before it reached the

ABOVE The Midland Railway's one-off experimental eight-cylinder locomotive, No. 2209, built in 1908.

BELOW Almost a century of design lay between *Locomotion*, of 1825, seen here in replica, and *City of York*, one of the five 'Pacifics' built in 1922 for the North Eastern Railway.

THE NORTH EASTERN RAILWAY

Although its headquarters were at York, the Tyneside conurbation was the real source of the North Eastern's wealth and power. The company came into being in 1854, following the partial amalgamation of the York Newcastle & Berwick, the York & North Midland and the Leeds Northern. Over the next thirty years it gradually absorbed the other companies in its region, including the Stockton & Darlington (1863) and the Newcastle & Carlisle (1865). The NER stretched from Carlisle and Berwick south to Leeds, Hull and Doncaster. Its main line was the north–south East Coast Main Line but it also operated two cross-country lines, from Darlington to Penrith and Tebay on the LNWR, and from Northallerton to Hawes on the Midland's Settle & Carlisle line, in addition to the Newcastle & Carlisle. Substantial coal and iron-ore traffic was carried on these lines. The NER's monopoly was not to the liking of the city of Hull, which promoted a competing link to the Yorkshire coalfield, the Hull & Barnsley Railway, which was built despite fierce NER opposition in 1885.

MANAGEMENT STYLES

The strengths and weaknesses of individual managers could make a big difference to a railway company. While Huish and Moon hammered the LNWR into a single empire, the NER in its first decades was more like a cluster of associated railways, retaining much of their own systems and practices. In 1871 the general manager, William O'Brien, was sacked after a number of accidents had revealed deficiencies in the way the company was run. He was replaced by the company's accountant, Henry Tennant, during whose tenure a number of improvements were made, including the rebuilding of York Station (1877). But it was not until the appointment of George (later Sir George) Gibb as general manager in 1891 that the NER began to be reformed into a modern railway. Gibb, like James Allport on the Midland, visited the USA and felt there was much to be learned from there. But a strong conservative tradition remained in the NER board, and Gibb was often frustrated. He resigned in 1906, though remaining a director until 1910.

Railway companies used horse-drawn steam and motor vans for delivery and collection from an early stage.

COMPANY PROFILE

The warning horn is a notable feature of this NER example.

AN AGREEABLE FELLOW

The locomotive superintendent, Edward Fletcher, typified the easy-going nature of the old NER. He was a worthy figure greatly beloved by his men and a reliable if unoriginal designer. O.S. Nock wrote in *Steam Locomotive* that: 'In cold print the policy he pursued over a period of thirty years appears haphazard, often illogical, and hopelessly uneconomic. In contrast to the standardisation of Crewe, Fletcher seemed at times to go deliberately in divergent directions.' The attempt of his successor Alexander McDonnell to introduce changes and a more disciplined approach in 1882 resulted in successful protests from the enginemen and his resignation in 1884. The NER had locomotive workshops at Shildon (the original Stockton & Darlington works), Gateshead, established by the York Berwick & Newcastle in 1854 and Darlington, opened in 1863. In the later nineteenth and early twentieth centuries, locomotive design on the NER was as advanced as anywhere in the country. Thomas William Worsdell, the chief mechanical engineer from 1888, introduced compounding on a large scale, building 270 two-cylinder compounds. His younger brother Wilson succeeded him in 1890 and built the first passenger 4-6-0 class in Britain in 1899. Vincent Raven, the company's last CME, was a pioneer of three-cylinder design – a practice picked up by Sir Nigel Gresley – and produced a class of five 'Pacifics' in 1922, just before the Grouping.

In the years before the 1914–18 war, the NER ran some very fast services, including what was known as 'the fastest train in the British Empire'. This was the 12.20 p.m. Newcastle–Sheffield express, which was allowed 43 minutes to cover the 44.5-mile (71.6-km) Darlington–York section, at an average speed of 61.6 mph (98.6km/h).

The NER was the largest owner of docks among British railway companies, with major installations at Blyth, and on the Tyne, the Tees, the Wear and Humber (where, after initial warfare, it collaborated with the Hull & Barnsley in the building of the King George V dock in 1914). Unlike other companies, it did not have its own fleet of ships. In its final form the NER had 1754 miles (2822km) of route. It became the largest constituent of the London & North Eastern Railway in 1923.

hottest point around the firebox. This system was perpetuated on the LMS and in the British Railways 'standard' locomotives.

STANDARDISATION OF DESIGN

Modifications such as these – of which the greatest and most significant was the super heater – did not however affect the basics. From quite early in the twentieth century, if not before, steam engineers were concerned about the efficiency of the classic Stephenson type of locomotive. At its most efficient, only about 13 per cent of the energy generated by a steam locomotive was applied in tractive power. Unless it was a compound, its steam was only used once, then exhausted. Heat radiation, internal frictions and leakages, steam and heat loss in the

BELOW Inside Crewe Works, No. 6100 *Royal Scot*, with the commemorative bell and name plate of its American tour, undergoes repairs in July 1934. The name-board on the smokebox door was fitted for its American tour.

pipes, use of steam for heating the train, all contributed to this sad statistic, which would in due course be seized upon by proponents of diesel traction. As long as good coal was available at low prices, this matter of thermal efficiency was not an operating problem, and a number of experts have pointed out that in terms of actual mechanical efficiency, the steam locomotive rates well. Another problem also became apparent. While the use of gearing could enable an internal combustion engine to develop high power at starting and low speeds, this was not possible with a steam locomotive. To get a train under way was comparable to a cyclist starting a pedal-bike in top gear, with consequent problems of wheel adhesion, especially on wet or greasy rails.

Revolutionary designs tended naturally to be 'one-offs', and remained so. In 1907 the Midland Railway's Derby Works produced a 2-6-2 type with outside frames and eight inside cylinders, set in two groups of four, and operating on the opposed principle, with the pistons entering one set as they withdrew from the other, giving a completely balanced motion. Numerous other novel aspects were incorporated in the design, which was not the work of R.M. Deeley, the CME, but of Cecil W. Paget, his former assistant, recently promoted to general superintendent of the line. Paget was also the son of the company's Chairman, but his ability was not in doubt. Deeley and Paget had never seen eye to eye. Given the running number of 2209, the locomotive never entered regular service. On a test run it was reputed to

ABOVE Some Great Eastern B12 4-6-0s were equipped with feed-water heating systems; their back-packs won them the nickname of 'hikers'.

BELOW This 15-ton break-down crane was built in 1890 for the Glasgow & South Western Railway. It was scrapped in 1963.

have reached 82mph (132km/h). Paget personally paid for the construction cost – but his investment failed to bring later dividends.

The conventional Stephenson boiler could withstand operating pressures of up to 300 psi (21.6kg/cm²), though few British locomotives worked at over 250 psi (17.6kg/cm²). Two one-off attempts were made to utilise a much higher pressure. On the LNER, H.N. Gresley worked with the Glasgow marine boilermakers, Yarrows, to produce a prototype high pressure (450 psi, 31.76kg/cm²) boiler which was fitted to a four-cylinder compound locomotive frame, with the two high-pressure cylinders inside, and twin sets of one-axle trucks, making it Britain's only 4-6-4. It was a water-tube boiler: the water being inside the tubes with heat applied from outside, the opposite of the normal arrangement. The long high-pressure steam drum was fed with steam from the tubes. Three air-intakes at the front passed air along the length of the boiler, being heated as it went, to the firebox to aid in combustion. Oddly, it became known as the 'Hush-hush' engine: something of such unusual bulk and shape could hardly be unobtrusive. Completed in late 1929, it was subjected to extensive testing. Its bulbous outer covering, with a front end designed to deflect smoke upwards, was striking, and it was given a special number, 10000. Although it did operate on scheduled services, it produced, as prototypes do, many problems and was unavailable for service for more than half the time prior to its eventual rebuilding in the same form as an A4 'Pacific', though it retained its unique wheel arrangement. Rebuilding took place in 1935, and it ran in main-line service until 1959.

ABOVE During the 1920s and 30s, modern scientific techniques were increasingly applied to steam design and construction. Two LNER technicians work with a model of the 4-6-4 No. 10000 during wind-tunnel tests on the locomotive's external design.

RIGHT Britain's most powerful 2-6-0 type was the LMS 'Crab' mixed-traffic engine of 1926, designed under the aegis of Sir Henry Fowler. On a typical duty, No. 42323 passes Stafford with a goods working.

The official photograph of the so-called 'hush-hush' engine, LNER No. 10000, with Sir Nigel Gresley's signature. Its streamlined and futuristic appearance was a considerable propaganda coup for the LNER.

LEFT A much-altered T9 4-4-0 of the LSWR, No. 118, standing at Salisbury shed in 1933. the T9s were among Dugald Drumond's best and most favoured designs. He would not have appreciated the altered smoke-box and the stovepipe chimney.

OPPOSITE The rebuilt 'Merchant Navy' Pacifics looked quite different (and were very different mechanically) from the original design, but remained imposing machines. Here, No. 35028 *Clan Line* transcends the unlovely surroundings of the coaling plant, as the fireman perches on the tender.

BELOW Old and new inside the former Midland Railway locomotive shed at Kentish Town, London, still gas-lit in 1933. The Class 1 0-4-4T dates from Kirtley's time. No. 5905 is a 'Baby Scot', rebuilt from a 'Claughton' 4-6-0.

High-Pressure Problems

Though it was a dead-end exercise, No 10000 was more fortunate than the LMS's almost-simultaneous project, a 4-6-0 locomotive using the frame and motion designed for the 'Royal Scot' class of 1928. Its triple-section boiler had a super high-pressure drum at up to 1800 psi (126.86kg/cm^2); the two preliminary stages were pressed to 950 psi (66.96kg/cm2) and 570 psi (40.1kg/cm^2) respectively. Fire-tube super heaters were attached to these two boilers. A traditional name from the old LNER, *Fury*, was given to the engine. Its first road test, on 10 February 1930, came to a disastrous end with a pipe burst in the firebox, which blasted fire and steam back into the cab, killing one of the four men on the footplate. Though further trials were made up to March 1934, recurrent problems brought an end to the tests and *Fury* was rebuilt as a taper-boilered 3-cylinder 'Royal Scot', and renamed *British Legion*. The unsuccessful British experience with high-pressure boilers was echoed in the other countries that tried them.

Another form of propulsion from sea transport was also tried out – the steam turbine drive. It dispensed entirely with the traditional motion of valves and pistons. Steam was raised in order to drive the vanes of a turbine wheel. The LMS was again the pioneer here, though under a new chief mechanical engineer, W.A. Stanier. As in the other experiments, the chosen vehicle was an express engine, perhaps a surprising choice, but like the high-pressure boilers, turbine power worked best with sustained steady running, most likely to be attained on passenger expresses. The frame of the third locomotive in Stanier's new 'Princess Royal' 4-6-2 class was used though the locomotive, No. 6202, was never named in its turbine form. Its 'works' were inside the frames or inside the long casing on the left-hand side that housed the main (forward) turbine mechanism and the shorter casing on the right housing the reverse turbine, giving it the appearance of an inside-cylinder engine, but of course it had no cylinders at all. Like the LNER No. 10000 it had a front-end air intake, in its case a single one that opened when the engine was moving, but this was to cool the oil that lubricated the turbines, not to add to the draught. The 'turbomotive' was put to work in 1935 on the London-Liverpool service, in which it spent its working life, though this was

4-6-2 MERCHANT NAVY SR 1943

Tractive effort: 38,000lb (17,233kg)
Axle load: 48,384lb (21.9 tonnes)
Cylinders: three 18x24in (457x609mm)
Driving wheels: 74in (188cm)
Heating surface: 2451sq ft (236m²)
Superheater: 822sq ft (76.3m²)
Steam pressure: 280psi (19.75kg/cm²)
Grate area: 48.5sq ft (4.5m²)
Fuel: Coal – 11,200lb (5.1 tonnes)
Water: 5000gall (6005 US) (22.75m³)
Total weight: 212,240lb (96.25 tonnes)
Overall length: 36ft 9in (11.2m)

LEFT The British railways 'standard' No. 75020 has been fitted with a double chimney in experiments to improve the steaming rate. It stands at Machynlleth with the Pwllheli portion of the 'Cambrian Coast Express' on 11 July 1962.

interrupted by long pauses for repair or modification. In tests against other LMS 'Pacifics', the turbine engine did not show an outstandingly better performance, though its tractive capacity seemed slightly greater, it did not offer any savings in coal consumption. However, from the crewmen's point of view, its stability and lack of vibration were a welcome change from the typical reciprocating locomotive, on which lurches, swings and heavy vibration were all too frequent at speed. Inevitable problems of uniqueness, including a lack of spare parts, meant that it spent longer in the workshops than its conventional sisters. In November 1949, after a turbine failure, it was finally taken off, and reappeared in rebuilt form in 1952 as a 4-cylinder simple expansion 'Pacific' on the lines of the later 'Coronation' class, and named *Princess Anne*. As such it came to an untimely end in the Harrow disaster of 8 October 1952, when three trains collided, following which it was scrapped.

What Might Have Been

It is impossible to judge new and ambitious design prototypes against the performance of established types. The 'post-Stephenson' designs of the 1920s and 1930s were not the brainchildren of irresponsible money-wasters, but serious attempts by eminent engineers to extend the frontiers of steam traction. It was unfortunate that they coincided with the era of the Great Depression, when railway business fell drastically. Even though the 'turbomotive' survived both the war and the years of austerity that followed, no plan was made for developments based on the thousands of miles of experience derived from its running. Its only successor was to be found in the USA, where in 1946, during the final throes of steam locomotive engineering, a mighty turbine-driven 6-8-6 was built by the Pennsylvania Railroad, inspired by the performance of No. 6202.

When the Railway Executive, in charge of the nationalised system from 1948, came to consider new locomotive designs, it opted unhesitatingly for the tried-and-true Stephenson model. At that time, a final fling in the direction of new-generation steam was being undertaken at Brighton Works on its Southern Region. Here, O.V.S. Bulleid, formerly chief mechanical engineer of the old Southern Railway, was superintending the building and testing of his 'Leader' class locomotive, a steam engine intended to replicate the performance levels and operational characteristics of a diesel, including a driving position at each end. In effect an 0-6-6-0T, it had two power bogies supporting a long girder frame. Even more unusual than his 'Pacific' design, it had six inside cylinders, three on each bogie, driving the central axles, which were chain-linked to the other two axles, using an enclosed oil-bath system. Five were laid down but only one, No. 36001, was completed, and though it was quite extensively tested between September 1949 and September 1950, with some successful runs demonstrating high speed and heavy haulage, the failures were far more frequent. In September 1950, by which time Bulleid had retired, it was decided to abandon the 'Leader' project: all work was stopped and the prototype and the part-built engines were cut up for scrap.

BELOW Gresley's two P1 2-8-2 freight locomotives were built in 1925. No. 2393 was also fitted with a steam booster to the rear trailing wheels. The steam pipe and 'engine' for this can be seen beneath the cab.

No 39

9 • State Occasions

With the advent of the railway, royal progress about the country is greatly eased and speeded up. Prince Albert shows the way in the 1840s, and Queen Victoria follows, at a sedate pace. With decorated engines, sumptuous carriages, and special operating arrangements, the railways rise splendidly to the challenge of state occasions.

LEFT The velvet, plush and gilt interior of Queen Victoria's day saloon on the London & North Western Railway. From around 1844 the Queen was a regular user of the Royal Train, and this saloon was built in 1861. A dressing room, toilet, and attendants' room were included.

OPPOSITE LB&SC Class B4 4-4-0 No. 39, named *Le Président*, decorated to pull the French President Loubet's train on his state visit to London, to celebrate the entente cordiale, in 1903. This locomotive was used on several occasions to pull royal trains.

The only time when a locomotive bore the full array of headcode lamps, three on the buffer beam and one (often surmounted by a small crown) above the smoke-box door, was when it was chosen to pull the Royal Train. Often, on such occasions, the lamps were hardly visible among the decorative crowns, coats of arms, union flags and floral sprays with which the engine's front was bedecked. Royal trains were particularly special, and the railway companies, who made this distinction, played up to it fully. Some had more to do with royalty than others did. The most frequently travelled lines were on the Great Western, from Windsor to Paddington; the Great Eastern line to Wolferton, north of Kings Lynn, for Sandringham and the Great North of Scotland's Deeside branch to Ballater, for Balmoral. In Queen Victoria's years, the London & South Western's Gosport line, connecting to the Isle of Wight and Osborne House, was also well used. For these companies, and the locomotive sheds that supplied the engines, the demands for trains for royal use was a matter of regular occurrence. But the very existence of railways made it possible for the monarch to travel the country more speedily and widely than ever before. The train accommodation could provide an overnight home, instead of having to find a suitably aristocratic residence for the night's stay, with all the attendant formalities and domestic disruptions.

Prince Albert and the Dowager Queen Adelaide, using the Great Western station at Slough, made the first royal train journeys. The first rail journey of a reigning monarch was Queen Victoria's from Slough (Windsor had no station at the time) to Paddington on 13 June 1842. By this time railways were an established part of national life, though still a novelty to many people. She was only 23, and appears to have been favourably impressed, but even then she felt it went too fast. The royal official in charge of the journey was the Master of the Queen's Horse and the royal coachman is said to have ridden on the footplate of the steam-powered rival to his team of greys. After that, travel by train became an accepted part of the royal family's life. Although they were a civilian service, the railways of the 1840s and 50s had a strong sense of being a disciplined force. The large number of former naval and army officers at different levels of management helped to give this impression, as did the uniforms of the staff, and of course

BELOW A set of borrowed Pullman cars forms the royal train, seen here in 1935 leaving Portsmouth's South Railway Jetty with the Prince of Wales on board, after the naming ceremony of HMS *Duke of Gloucester*. The engine is an ex-LSWR class T9 4-4-0, No 729 of the Southern Railway.

LEFT Signs of horse-drawn coachbuilding are visible in this early carriage built by the London & Birmingham Railway in 1842 for Queen Adelaide, widow of William IV. The 'boot' extension at one end is to enable to Queen's bed to be fully extended for a night journey.

the timetables and the whole apparatus – though still far from perfected – of signalling and safety checking. Managing the important ceremonial aspect of royal transport also came naturally to such men. This sense of service and efficient control undoubtedly contributed to easing Queen Victoria's sense of anxiety when travelling by train.

BELOW Interesting features of this LNWR saloon, built for the Prince of Wales in the 1880s, include electric light and electric fan. A thermometer is also apparent, to ensure that the heating is correctly adjusted.

Socially Acceptable Transport

From the start, the railway companies treated royal trains differently. Soon they were being used for occasions of state as well as the royal family's personal convenience. The first was a visit to Great Britain by Louis Philippe, king of France, in October 1844. He landed at Portsmouth, which did not then have a station but Gosport did. From there he was conveyed by the LSWR to Farnborough and the journey to Windsor was then completed by road. There was prestige to be gained from such service, but it was also good for business. Once the queen had become a patron of the railway, no one could consider it socially unacceptable to go by train. Conveyance of royal personages was also, of course, a great responsibility. If anything should go slightly wrong, there would be embarrassment, internal enquiries and reprimands. If anything should go seriously wrong, the consequences were unthinkable. The rules for royal train operation were quite different to the normal working instructions, and were designed to obviate problems of any kind. Once a route, date and time had

OLIVER BULLEID (1882–1970)

He is remembered as the great radical designer from the last years of steam, yet Bulleid's career went back to the early 1900s, when he was apprenticed at the Doncaster works of the Great Northern Railway. Born to expatriate parents in Invercargill, New Zealand, he was brought to Britain by his mother in 1889 after the death of his father. Between 1896 and 1901 he attended Accrington Technical College. In 1908 he married the daughter of his boss, the CME H.A. Ivatt, and left the GNR for a time from 1910 to 1912 to work for the Board of Trade at international exhibitions in Brussels and Turin. During World War I he was in the Royal Engineers, and became an expert on welding techniques. Back with the GNR in 1919, for two decades he lived in the shadow of Sir Nigel Gresley, acting as the latter's assistant from 1923 to 1937. In 1934 he accompanied the new 'Mikado' *Cock of the North* to France for testing on the Vitry rig and on French tracks. Gresley's innovative approach and his flair for publicity appealed to Bulleid. Following his appointment as CME on the Southern Railway, in 1937, his awareness of French practice brought about improvements in draughting of the Southern's 'Lord Nelson' and 'School' classes, with multiple blast-pipes and wide Lemaître chimneys. He himself fully emerged in the public eye when, four years after joining the Southern he introduced his 'Merchant Navy' 4-6-2 and Q1 0-6-0 locomotives. Their distinctive styling, and the numerous unique aspects of the 'Merchant Navy' design, aroused great interest.

It was ironic that Britain's most electrified system should harbour an out-and-out steam man like Bulleid, yet perhaps it was partly the Southern's sense of modernity that allowed him to produce such novel locomotives. Among their up-to-date features was electric lighting, hitherto unknown on British locomotives; in other ways too, like power-operated fire doors and reversing gear, Bulleid paid unusual attention to ease of operation for the engine crews. It says much for his confidence, and perhaps his powers of persuasion, that plans were made for the construction of thirty 'Merchant Navy' engines although the design was quite untried. Despite the many problems, particularly with the chain-driven valve gear, 109 of the similar but lighter 'West Country' class were also built from 1945. In the later 1940s, Bulleid went on to develop his 'Leader' 0-6-6-0 design, which was even more advanced. An attempt to build a steam engine with the operating characteristics of a diesel, the 'Leader' was dogged by design troubles. Only a single prototype was completed, but it never got beyond the test phase. With a driving cab at each end, and a torrid space for the fireman in the middle, it was mounted on two articulated six-wheel bogies, each driven by a 3-cylinder engine on the centre axle, with steam distribution through sleeve valves. All the motion and cranks were encased and automatically lubricated, as in Bulleid's 'Pacifics'. Four thermic syphons were fitted in the firebox. At this time, plans were going ahead for the British Railway's 'standard' locomotives, and work on three part-built 'Leader' engines was abandoned at Brighton Works after 1949. By 1951, all were dismantled.

After his retirement from the Southern, Bulleid worked for a time as CME of the Irish Railways, CIE, where he built a prototype peat-fuelled engine similar in design to the 'Leader', but this too was not taken beyond the testing stage. Meanwhile the 'Merchant Navies' and sixty of the 'West Country' engines were being rebuilt with conventional valve gear. Bulleid died at his retirement home in Malta at the age of eighty-eight. His designs remain controversial, with both their critics and their fierce adherents.

been established, the system went into action. If it was on a double line, no moving train, other than mail trains, was allowed to pass the royal train in the opposite direction. Twenty minutes before the royal train, a pilot engine was despatched to run along the chosen route. Signalmen were forbidden to alter the setting of points and signals between the passage of the pilot and the royal train itself. The only line not to run a pilot engine was the Great North of Scotland. However, for the passage of royal trains it normally had men positioned along its entire Deeside line, within sight of one another. Its other arrangements, noted in Sir Malcolm Barclay-Harvey's history of the line, included, 'On the single part of the line no train was allowed for at least twenty minutes before the Royal Train was due to pass. On the double line, all trains meeting it had to slow up to ten miles an hour. Each section needed to be cleared for the train fifteen minutes before it was due and no one except the station staff was allowed on the platform of any station while it was passing. All facing points had to be clipped and padlocked twenty minutes before the train reached them, and all level crossing gates (of which there were many) also locked till it had passed.' A very senior official, normally the Superintendent of the Line, always travelled on the train, ready to take control if anything untoward should occur. On the LNWR, George Whale, while he was Locomotive Running Superintendent up to 1903, always drove the engine himself, though most railways gave the job, considered the top professional accolade, to a senior driver. The royal train often seemed surprisingly long to observers, especially when its only passengers

ABOVE In 1902 the LNWR built a completely new set of vehicles at Wolverton to form its royal train. This is the sleeping compartment of the King's twelve-wheeled saloon. At 65ft 6in (19.9m) long, this and the Queen's saloon were probably the longest passenger carriages in the country.

LEFT These twin saloons were built for Queen Victoria in 1869. Although a bellows vestibule joined them, she would only use it when the train was at a standstill. In 1895 they were rebuilt on a single frame mounted on two six-wheel bogies.

might be one elderly lady and a handful of attendants. But even when more courtiers and guests were not being carried, there was normally a substantial railway team on board. The team included telegraph men, fitters, electricians, painters and other skilled repair and maintenance men, under a Royal Train Foreman. They were able to carry out unobtrusive work when the train was stabled at its journey's end and so they too needed accommodation.

ABOVE This London & North Western postcard view from 1904, somewhat surprisingly shows the locomotive in undecorated state and with normal express headlights. It may be that the train was in 'private' use rather than for a state visit.

A Sense of Occasion

Disruption to normal services was inevitable, especially if the royal train should be delayed. This was particularly likely in Queen Victoria's time, as she had a life-long aversion to travelling at a speed greater than forty mph (64km/h). From the time of Edward VII on, it became normal for the royal train to travel at express train speed, though still with the full range of

LEFT Two Great North of Scotland engines, the train engine and the advance 'pilot', Class 'T' 4-4-0 No. 99 and Class 'A' 4-4-0 No. 68 respectively, beflagged and decked out in evergreens, at Kittybrewster shed before going on royal train duty in the early 1900s.

precautions. The change set in very early: various problems contributed to the delay in departure of the queen's funeral train bearing her coffin from Gosport to Victoria Station, London, on 2 February 1901. The new king, Edward VII, who was to meet the train at Victoria, was known to be a stickler for punctuality. The train, hauled over London Brighton & South Coast metals from Fareham, is believed to have reached speeds of around 80 miles an hour (128km/h), hustling the old queen's mortal remains in a manner that would have been unimaginable while she was alive. Eventually it arrived two minutes early. The LBSC 4-4-0 engine of class B4, named *Empress*, was decorated in funereal mode, with a gilt crown set on a crimson cushion above the smoke-box door, and swags of purple cloth along the boiler side. Whether the pageantry of the event was glad or sombre, one feels the railways entered into the spirit of the occasion and played their part with aplomb down to the smallest detail. It was important, for example, that the door of the royal saloon should be perfectly aligned with the inevitable red carpet when the train finally stopped at its destination. To help the driver, a flagman was stationed at exactly the spot where the locomotive would have to halt. A locomotive with an appropriate name was selected for the service, if possible. Otherwise a named locomotive might undergo a sudden change of identity to suit a royal duty. The Great Western 4-4-0 engine *Atbara*, which took the second stage of Queen Victoria's funeral train, from Paddington to Windsor, was given a new name, *Royal Sovereign*. On the occasion of the funeral of King George VI in February 1952, the name and number-plates of No. 4082 *Windsor Castle*, were transferred to another 'Castle' class locomotive, No. 7013 *Bristol Castle*, which worked the train. The Great Western's 'royal engine', *Windsor Castle*, had been driven by King George V on a visit to the Swindon works and had later hauled his funeral train. Some

BELOW A coloured view of the LB&SCR royal train, drawn by 4-4-2T No. 15, conveying King Edward VII from Victoria Station to the races at Epsom. Tank engines were unusual on royal trains, except on short trips like this one.

enthusiasts complained about the change of identity, but the Western Region management of the nationalised railways was unperturbed. Tradition had to be seen to be maintained.

STYLISH SALOONS

Several railway companies built special vehicles for royal service. The first was built by the Great Western, in 1840, followed by the London & Birmingham, which built two in 1842–43, one of them for Queen Adelaide, widow of William IV, the other for Queen Victoria. These still bore clear traces of the railway carriage's descent, in design terms, from the horse-drawn coach. The GW carriage was divided into three compartments, with the central one intended for the queen. Originally a four-wheeler, it was fitted by Brunel with eight wheels to improve its ride. Queen Adelaide's coach survives. This was a combined day and bed carriage of two and a half compartments. In the end compartment a bed could be set up. The design was similar to first-class carriages of the time. Its ride, on four wheels, without the benefit of close coupling and

BELOW King Edward VII and Queen Alexandra arrive at the specially-decorated Newcastle Central in July 1906, with civic dignitaries and notables lined up to greet them. The train is the London & North Western one. The occasion was the opening of the King Edward VII Bridge.

GREAT WESTERN RAILWAY.

THE TRAIN BY WHICH

Their Majesties

THE KING AND QUEEN

AND SUITE

WILL TRAVEL ON

Friday, March 7th, 1902,

WILL RUN AT THE FOLLOWING TIMES:—

PADDINGTON STATION -	depart 10 30 a.m.	KINGSWEAR STATION - -	depart 4 10 p.m.
KINGSWEAR do. -	arrive 2 55 p.m.	PLYMOUTH (NORTH ROAD) STATION -	arrive 5 30 p.m.

J. L. WILKINSON,
General Manager.

LEFT The cover of the GWR timetable for a royal journey to the Dartmouth Naval College. The Paddington–Kingswear leg was the Great Western's longest non-stop run to date: 228.5 miles (367.7 km) at an average speed of 51.7 mph (83.2 km/h).

BELOW Cushioned comfort marks Queen Alexandra's day compartment, in her carriage from the new LNWR royal train of 1902. The carriage also held an attendants' compartment, toilet, dressing room, sleeping compartment, and a further dressing room.

with slender leaf springs, cannot have been conducive to repose – but then, neither was the contemporary horse-drawn carriage. The London & Birmingham's carriage for Victoria and Albert was again a four-wheeler, with a single central compartment flanked by two very narrow end-vestibules, which did not communicate with the main chamber. It featured an early attempt at heating, with warm air entering through floor grilles. Underneath, an arrangement of water tank and oil heater circulated hot water through pipes. This remained unique and even in first-class carriages, nothing better than pre-heated foot-warmers were available for a long time after the 1840s. These were one-off vehicles, to which regular stock could be added if necessary. Like many other first-class passengers, the royal family would often take their horse-carriages with them for use at the end of the rail journey, and often too, they travelled with a substantial entourage. The first railway to provide a full royal train was the London & South Western, which had a set of three saloons available from around 1850. The oldest of these, dating back to 1844, which was to survive for more than a century was decorated in typical style. As Hamilton Ellis describes it in *The South Western Railway*, 'In the saloon was a long cross-seat, at one end, and four fixed armchairs, upholstered in silk damask laced in crimson and white. The ceiling was quilted in white watered silk, embroidered with rose, thistle and

THE TAFF VALE RAILWAY

Numerous railways were established to carry South Welsh coal from the pit heads to the sea. The Taff Vale, authorised in 1836, was the first, and remained the largest. Its first engineer was I.K. Brunel, but here he used standard, not broad gauge, because of the confined space available. The original main line linked Merthyr Tydfil and Cardiff and was completed in 1841, with access to the Bute West Dock, which had opened in 1839. However, relations between the railway company and the dock owners were never cordial. The Bute Trustees helped to establish the Rhymney Railway from 1854, and in 1858 this line was granted running powers over the TVR's last six miles (9.6km) to the Bute West Dock. A battle ensued over the charges payable, and eventually the Rhymney built its own line into Cardiff. From 1859 to 1865 the TVR developed new docks at Penarth. At this time Cardiff was growing enormously to become the largest city in Wales. The TVR, with its lucrative coal traffic, became probably the most prosperous railway in Britain, with a regular dividend of 14.9% in the period 1880–88. But the volume of coal production and exporting was such that the facilities were constantly under stress. The Bute Trustees, who owned most of the Cardiff dockland, were slow to build a third dock. Coal owners, frustrated at delays and high charges, obtained authorisation for construction of the port of Barry and the connecting Barry railway (effectively duplicating the Taff Vale) to the coalfield in 1884. From 1889 it drew much of the coal trade away from the Cardiff bay docks and ports. Traffic on the TVR was hardly reduced, however, as South Wales coal production doubled between 1889 and 1913. In 1892 the TVR opened a line to Aberthaw, west of Barry, in an effort to siphon off some of the coal export business, but this failed to become a major coal line.

INDUSTRIOUS TIMES

The route mileage of the TVR never exceeded 124 miles (199km) but the intensity of traffic was enormous. In 1897 it carried 13,869,439 tons (14,091,350 tonnes) of coal and coke, hardly less than the entire Great Western system. In 1909, with a total of 384 miles (618km) of track, the railway achieved a total train mileage of 2,809,688 (4,520,788km): rarely can a system have been so intensively used. At its main junction, Pontypridd, around 500 trains were dealt with daily. It had a stock of 216 locomotives, almost entirely tank engines. The majority of the engines were 0-6-2T, but from 1888 it also possessed a stock of 4-4-2T inside-cylinder passenger engines. Painted red, these were handsome locomotives, and they too were well worked. With its access to the towns of Merthyr, Aberdare and the Rhondda Valley towns, the Taff Vale also ran an important passenger service, linking the valleys to Cardiff and the GWR main line. The historian E.L. Ahrons described its original Cardiff terminus as 'a moderately glorified fowl-house', but it opened a worthier one at Queen Street in 1887. The TVR's most distinctive locomotives were the three that operated on the

Taff Vale Passenger: Class 'A' 0-6-2T No. 373 approaches Troedyrhiw with the 4.35 p.m. Quaker's Yard (Low Level)–Merthyr, on 5 June 1957.

COMPANY PROFILE

redoubtable Pwllyrhebog incline on its Clydach branch. This mineral line had a maximum gradient of one in 13, and the engines had specially-designed sloping tops to the fireboxes, and sledge-brakes to press down on the rails as well as normal wheel brakes. They were cable-assisted on the steepest section, and worked from 1884 until 1951.

The Taff Vale Railway hit national headlines as the result of a strike in 1900. The general manager of the company, Ammon Beasley, was a patriarchal Victorian who did not recognise trade unions. Many of his men however were members of the Amalgamated Society of Railway Servants. On 19 August 1900, the signalmen went on unofficial strike, followed next day by the enginemen. The ASRS made the strike official. Beasley obtained an injunction against it and went on to sue the union for loss of revenue caused by the strike. He won his case; the union appealed and it won on appeal. Beasley went to the House of Lords, which in July 1901 ruled in his favour. The substantial sum of £23,000 was paid to the TVR in damages and costs. Among some sections of the community, Beasley became a hero; among others he was reviled. The Taff Vale case played a large part in the return of a Liberal government in 1905 and the consequent amendment of trade union law so that such a situation could not occur again. Beasley's reign continued until 1917, when he became deputy-chairman of the company. With the Grouping, the TVR, like all its rivals, became part of the Great Western, but by then the great days of Welsh coal exports were rapidly receding.

LEFT The twelve-wheeled coach built from Queen Victoria's two six-wheelers, its twin bogies providing a much smoother ride than its rigid-framed predecessors. It was last used by her in travelling from Ballater to Windsor on 6-7 November, 1900. It is preserved at the National Railway Museum, York.

shamrock in velvet and silver thread. The curtains were of peach-coloured silk with silver tassels… Externally the body was very grandiose, with moulded cartouches bearing the royal arms and the insignia of the highest orders of chivalry.'

Around the same time, the GWR built a new saloon for the queen, one of the first railway carriages to include a water closet. It also had enlarged windows, giving the queen a fine view, but also enabling her to be seen by people on the line-side. This carriage ran on eight wheels. In 1869 the London & North Western built a pair of six-wheel coaches, joined by a bellows connection, the first of its kind in Great Britain, though the queen would only use it when the train was stopped. The two carriages were separately furnished for day and night use respectively. They were elaborately furnished and decorated as a matter of course, and a toilet compartment was included; but there was no heating and only oil lighting. The latter was a sign of the queen's conservatism. Even when gas or electric lighting was possible, she insisted on retaining oil lamps in her carriages. In 1895 the two saloons were rebuilt as one, running on two six-wheel bogies, and in this form it still survives at the National Railway Museum in York.

In the late nineteenth and early twentieth centuries, with the advent of improved signalling, and interlocking points and signals, the arrangements for running royal trains were slightly relaxed in order to cause less disruption to an increasingly busy system. But still, with the advent of block working, at least two blocks had to be clear ahead of and behind a royal train, to reduce the risk of collision or delay effectively to zero. The use of the pilot engine was increasingly dispensed with. But the attention to detail did not alter in the least.

BELOW A side view of Queen Adelaide's saloon and a portrait of its royal occupant. It was modelled on the standard 'two-and-a-half-compartment' first-class carriage of the time, though the internal arrangements, most notably the seat that folded out into a bed, were unique in 1842.

LUXURY CARRIAGES

By the early twentieth century, many railway companies had at least one royal vehicle. In 1923 the 'Big Four' inherited a somewhat miscellaneous collection of fine, if often of rather antique construction, coach building. Royal trains had a varied appearance, with coaches of different heights and lengths, some clerestoried, some elliptical-roofed, on six wheels or on bogies. None of them built new vehicles until 1941 when the LMS built three carriages with armour plating for the use of King George VI in travelling during the Second World War. The GWR abandoned its antiquated royal stock in the 1930s and came to an arrangement with the LMS about borrowing carriages when necessary. The Southern used what was basically the South Eastern & Chatham set, which had been frequently employed to carry royalty and state visitors between Dover and London. The LNER maintained its own royal train, with carriages built in the first decade of twentieth century by the Great Northern and North Eastern Railways. The royal carriages of the Edwardian years represent the peak of luxury railway coach building in Britain. Luckily, several of these handsome vehicles, with their clerestory roofs, six-wheel bogies, magnificent woodwork and opulent interiors, survive in preservation. The wartime LMS carriages were intended to provide protection against incendiary bombs and shrapnel; their combination of armour plating and an early form of air conditioning made them the heaviest passenger vehicles to run on British rails,

BELOW Royalty on the footplate: on 28 April 1924, King George V and Queen Mary visited Swindon Works and the King drove No. 4082 *Windsor Castle* for a short distance. This locomotive was to haul the King's funeral train from London to Windsor, on 28 January 1936.

ABOVE One of the Southern Railway's handsome 'L' class 4-4-0s, No. 1776, at Ashford, Kent, on stand-by duty as royal train engine, with discs in place of lamps, in July 1938.

weighing about 56 tons each. One of the three was a 'power car', equipped with a diesel-powered generator, which supplied light and power to the rest of the train. This was a useful feature when the train, with passengers, was stabled for the night on some quiet siding in the course of a several-day royal tour whose stopping-points were necessarily classified as top-secret. Telephone lines were set up so that the king could communicate with the government from wherever the train was stabled. As for other types of train, the railways had code names to identify royal trains. During the Second World War these names, intended for telegraphic use, had the additional advantage of secrecy. One was 'Grove', which signified a complete royal train with the king on board. Another was 'Deepdene', which could signify either a royal train, which did not have the king on board, or a train in normal service, which had a royal saloon attached. This latter practice was rare in wartime but increasingly common in the post-war years. With the introduction of locomotive headcodes, royal trains were denoted by IX, with the numbers 00 to 03, depending on whether they were empty stock, or hauling royal passengers.

After the war the Great Western restored its own royal train, using vehicles that had been built as special saloons for its own directors and VIP guests. In the first years of her reign, with the railways under state ownership, Queen Elizabeth II had three royal trains at her disposal: the former LMS and LNER trains and the GWR one. The Southern royal train no longer

LEFT The external appearance of Queen Alexandra's handsome twelve-wheeled carriage of 1902 (see page 251). The double doors, to permit stately entrances and exits, can clearly be seen.

existed, though the Southern Region of British Railways had a stock of Pullman cars it sometimes drew on for a royal occasion. The last royal vehicles to be built while steam locomotives still ran were two saloon carriages built in the mid-1950s for the then royal children, Prince Charles and Princess Anne.

NOT FOR PROFIT

Steam locomotives pulled the Royal train regularly until the end of main-line steam traction in December 1968. Some steam-operated lines still had royal visitors after that, including the Isle of Man Steam Railway, where the 2-4-0 tank engine *Kissack* was used for the Queen's visit in August 1972; and the narrow-gauge Romney Hythe & Dymchurch Railway's 4-8-2 *Samson* was lent to the Liverpool International Garden Festival in May 1984, when the Queen and the Duke of Edinburgh travelled behind it to tour the grounds. Even after 1968, steam locomotives were occasionally brought into main-line use for relevant events, as when the preserved LNER No. 4472 *Flying Scotsman* drew the Queen Mother's train to the opening of the North Woolwich Old Station Museum on 20 November 1984. More recently, the preserved LMS 'Pacific' No. 46233 *Duchess of Sutherland* was used on the Royal Train in North Wales in the Golden Jubilee year of Queen Elizabeth's accession, 2002.

Although built for the exclusive use of the royal family, and sometimes for that of individual members, who were consulted as to the décor and the layout of the carriages, the trains were not in royal or government ownership, but belonged to the railway companies. Nor did royalty travel free: the numbers of those travelling, including dogs, were noted and charged for at the first-class rate, plus a special train supplement. Nevertheless, the railways certainly did not make a profit on their royal services.

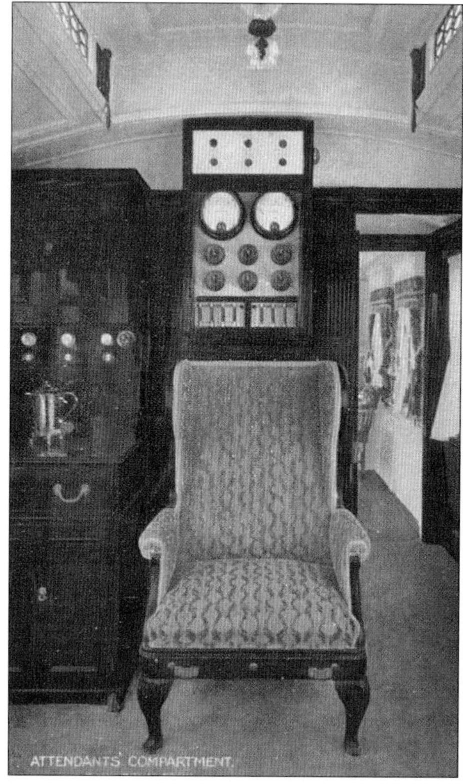

BELOW Dominating the attendant's quarters in the royal saloon is the electric bell system for summoning staff to different parts of the carriage. King Edward VII used to summon a footman to light his cigars, despite the provision of electric cigar lighters in his smoking compartment.

D
5085

10 • The Steam Railway at War

From the 1850s onwards, wars are won by locomotives as much as by soldiers or armaments. In two World Wars, the British railway companies play a vital strategic role in supplying the home front and in backing the military effort. But, especially between 1939 and 1945, they pay a heavy price in public estimation through the inevitable delays and overcrowding.

LEFT The railway companies spent much of their advertising budget on explaining to passengers why the war effort so often caused delays. In this joint campaign, the expression 'British Railways' was used for the first time as a generic way of referring to the whole railway system. Artwork by Leslie Carr.

OPPOSITE Early in the war a GWR driver shows the correct wearing of a tin hat and an anti-gas respirator. The locomotive, 'Castle' class No. 5085 *Evesham Abbey*, is a rebuild of a 'Star' 4-6-0, No. 4085, of the same name. The cab has not yet been fitted with black-out materials.

Britain's involvement in the two World Wars of the twentieth century meant a crucial role for the railways in each period of conflict, 1914–18 and 1939–45. From an early stage the strategic value of the railways had been recognised. In 1842 the government had imposed on the railway companies the duty of carrying troops in emergency. A War Railway Council, composed of railway officials and military and naval staff, had been in existence since 1865. In 1912 a Railway Executive Committee formed of the general managers of nine of the largest companies replaced the Council, smoothly assuming control in August 1914. The railways' role in the First World War has already been touched on. The main aims were to ensure the supply of men and munitions to the Channel ports, and the efficient use of resources in moving goods and people, military and civilian, about the country. General mobilisation required 1408 special trains, in all parts of the country, with a further 689 to

LEFT Verse – of a sort – was pressed into service to communicate the 'Travel only when you must' message. Undeterred, the public continued to travel when it felt like doing so.

convey the British Expeditionary Force to the Channel ports. For the first time, the Ministry of Munitions selected a specific locomotive type for building as a 'war engine' for use in overseas military operations. This was the Great Central's two-cylinder 2-8-0 freight locomotive, designed by J.G. Robinson in 1910. A robust design, it was relatively easy to service and maintain – 521 were built to government order. But many other locomotives, mostly 0-6-0s, were requisitioned by the Ministry for the Railway Operating Department (R.O.D.) of the War Office and used behind the lines in France and Belgium.

Demanding Times

The Second World War was a much sterner test for the railways because of the far greater destruction caused by air raids, the need to observe a 'black-out' and the much greater tonnage of equipment to be moved. Once again, state control was imposed, and women workers reappeared in large numbers. No woman ever drove a steam locomotive professionally. The task of a fireman, the unavoidable preliminary to driving, was considered far too onerous. On a long-distance express, the

BELOW Wartime freight: an ex-Great Central 2-8-0 of World War I vintage hauls a long mixed goods train near Bishopton, Warwickshire, on 4 August, 1940. The cattle trucks are vacuum-braked.

fireman had to shovel coal into the firebox at the rate of a ton an hour. Likewise, the job of a guard or shunter, who required both muscle and expertise to operate the long-poled coupling hook which attached and detached wagons on the move, remained an exclusively male preserve. But the railways also had certain advantages in 1939 that had not been there in 1914. One was the number of new locomotives designed and built in the 1930s, providing a more standardised and efficient stud of motive power. Though many pre-1914 engines were still running, a good proportion had been fitted with superheaters, improving their steaming and economy. There were now some 40 'Pacifics' on the LMS and over one hundred on the LNER,

ABOVE Women track workers clean and oil pointwork – normally a man's job – in the shunting yards at Reading, GWR, in March 1943. From 26,000 women employed on the railways before the war, the number rose to 114,000 during the war.

and powerful 4-6-0s, both express and mixed-traffic types, on all main lines. There was also the advantage of centralised traffic control. This had been pioneered by the Midland before World War One, with a control office at Derby monitoring and ordering train movements throughout the entire company system. Following the Grouping of 1923, this method was extended over the whole LMS network, with main regional centres at Crewe and Derby, and district control offices as far north as Inverness. Each 'control' was in constant touch by telephone with train movements and events in its area, and the regional offices also kept a record of the locations of all locomotives and rolling stock, so that no piece of equipment was unaccounted for. By 1939, all the Big Four had adopted the centralised control system. In wartime, it was even more vital and effective than in peacetime. Hour by hour, minute by minute, the effect of air raids and air raid warnings could be minimised. Paths could be found

OPPOSITE The LNER class B1 4-6-0s were sometimes known as 'Antelopes', as a few had acquired zoological names including *Antelope* and *Springbok*.

BELOW A railway policeman helps evacuee children board a train at an un-named city station on 14 December 1939.

for troop train movements, for anti-aircraft gun patrols on the rails, and for emergency engineering trains. It was all the more necessary as, from August 1940, air raids were frequent and on a large scale. Apart from bombs, fighter planes shot up many trains, especially on the Southern. The worst single effect of enemy bombing was not the destruction of locomotives (only eight were written off, with 484 damaged and repaired), but damage to control centres. On one occasion, both the Manchester area control and its emergency replacement were both put out of action by bombs. But a booklet entitled *It Can Now Be Revealed*, published by the 'British Railways Press Office' in 1945, described some aspects of the railways in wartime. The booklet states that, 'of the trains serving Ministry of Supply ordnance depots, for instance, less than 1% ever arrived more than ten minutes late' – a remarkable achievement.

Railway workers were often in the front line. The story of how Driver George Gimbert GC and Fireman Nightall, whose George Cross was posthumous, saved the town of Soham by detaching a burning wagon from an ammunition train on the night of 2 June 1944 is deservedly well-known, but there were many other instances of heroism. One midnight in the summer of 1940, bombs began to fall

BELOW 'V' signs scrawled on the smokebox door and boiler of LMS 'Jubilee' 4-6-0 *Kolhapur* mark VE Day on 8 May 1945. The train is at Shilton, Warwickshire.

THE GREAT CENTRAL RAILWAY

Great Central trans-Pennine expresses entering and leaving the Woodhead Tunnel.

The name proclaimed a desire to be seen on the same terms as the other 'Great' railways, and its adoption in 1897 coincided with its construction of the last main line into London before the Channel Tunnel rail link of the early 2000s. But the origins of the GCR go back to 1845, when the Sheffield Ashton-under-Lyne and Manchester Railway was proposed, to link the two growing terminal cities. Its Woodhead Tunnel was a three-mile (5-km) endurance test for crews and passengers. In 1847 it was renamed the Manchester Sheffield & Lincolnshire Railway, after amalgamation with three other lines and the Grimsby Docks Company. Absorption of the South Yorkshire Railway in 1863 gave it access to the coalfields of that area, though also setting up a long rivalry with the Great Northern. From 1854 to 1862 Edward (later Sir Edward) Watkin, a shrewd and not wholly scrupulous businessman who was chairman from 1864 until 1894, managed it. Adept at railway politics, Watkin may be given credit for keeping the MS&L alive and modestly profitable, but he always had great ideas for it. The vision of a new trunk line from Yorkshire to London was his, and was linked to the grander concept of a Channel Tunnel.

The new line was built from Annesley in Nottinghamshire, through Nottingham, Leicester and Rugby, threading its way between and across the Midland and LNWR main lines, to Quainton Road in Buckinghamshire, from where a joint line with the Metropolitan Railway ran via Aylesbury to a new London terminus at Marylebone. The company's new name was a clever one, emphasising both greatness and centrality, implying that here was a more direct route through the heart of England. But it was a duplication of existing facilities, and though the Great Central ran excellent, fast and comfortable trains between Manchester, Sheffield and London, they could only prise away a share of the other companies' traffic. While the humble MS&L had always paid a dividend, the lordly Great Central was sometimes unable to pay any dividend on its ordinary shares.

Under Watkin's successors, Alexander Henderson (later Lord Faringdon) and Sir Sam Fay, the company also paid attention to developing its freight business, always the principal source of its revenues, with the building of the giant

COMPANY PROFILE

Wath marshalling yard and the development of the dock complex at Immingham. The GCR also operated its own ships on the Immingham–continental service. An alternative way into London from Aylesbury, via Princes Risborough and High Wycombe, built jointly with the Great Western, was opened in 1906.

DESIGN CLASSICS

In J.G. Robinson, the GCR had a notable chief mechanical engineer, joining in 1900 and given the top job two years later. The locomotive works were at Gorton, Manchester; opened originally by the MSL in 1848. Robinson catered well both for the passenger and freight needs of the company, and his engines showed a care for design and finish that was exceptional even in the spacious years before 1914. For the Wath Yard he designed some very large 0-8-4 shunting tank engines, with three cylinders. His 4-4-2 express engines of 1903, the 'Jersey Lilies', were widely held to be among the most handsome 'Atlantics' ever built. Four were built as compounds but, like most designers, with the advent of super heating Robinson lost interest in compounding. He also built 4-6-0s, but his 4-4-0 'Directors', introduced in 1915, of which one survives, are nowadays perhaps the best known of his designs, along with the 2-8-0 'war engine', also preserved. In the Grouping, the Great Central was folded into the London & North Eastern Railway, at last joining the Great Northern, with which it had carried on a mixture of flirtation, desertion, co-operation and hostile rivalry for more than fifty years, under the same corporate umbrella. The enlarged company's independent existence, never less than precarious despite its high-quality services and heavy investment in new facilities, lasted just over a quarter of a century, to the last day of 1922.

The Great Central provided 'En Route' stationery for passengers on its best trains. This message was written from the Yarmouth train in 1904.

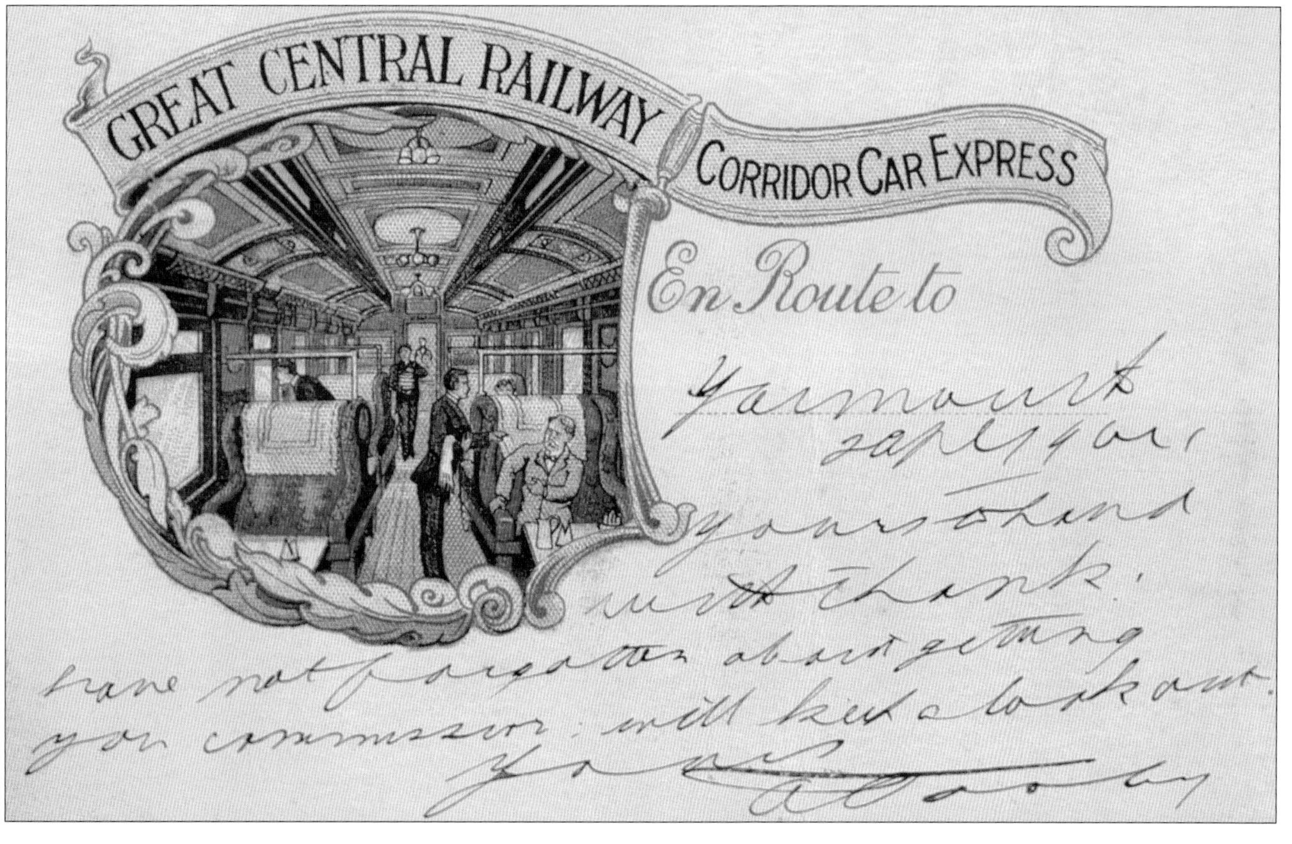

LEFT The window-plate and rolled-up tarpaulin screen for night-time blackout can be seen on LMS 'Patriot' class 4-6-0 No. 5522 *Prestatyn*, photographed at Rugby station in 1942.

OPPOSITE These women are not cleaning, but blackening, the panes of the gas lamps outside the L&Y works at Horwich, as a precaution against air raids in 1917.

on and around Cannon Street Station, London, just as the locomotive of the 12.53 a.m. train to Dartford was being attached to its train. As the station began to burn, it hauled the empty carriages out on to the bridge over the Thames, but all the signal lights were out. The carriages caught fire, and the driver and fireman, after unsuccessful efforts to put the fire out with buckets of water, uncoupled their engine and ran it forward, then stayed with it on the bridge waiting for daylight, while bombs exploded, gunfire crackled, searchlight beams laced the smoky sky, and fires blazed all around.

Special Services

The demands of the war economy alone, once it got fully under way, would have been enough to keep the railways fully occupied, especially as much freight was diverted from coastal shipping to the railways. But it was in the nature of a modern war to create the need for a huge number of special services, all of which had to be integrated with the normal working timetable. The first of these exceptional tasks came with the declaration of war. Fear of urban devastation from the air had been strong in the 1930s, and a massive programme of evacuation of children had been planned and was put into action from 1 September 1939. In four days, 607,635 people, mostly children, were moved out of London to destinations in the countryside. Large outer

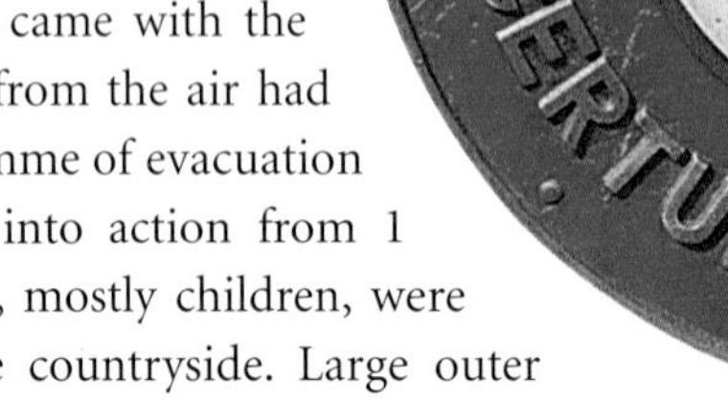

BELOW Name plate of a 'Merchant Navy' 4-6-2. The motto means 'Seek a sure end'.

ABOVE 'The London Midland Scottish express being bombed, October 1940' – this oil painting by Norman Wilkinson from the 'LMS at War' series shows a train on the four-track main line near Bletchley, under attack from the air.

suburban stations were used as the starting points: Bowes Park, Ealing Broadway, Watford Junction and Wimbledon. Similar evacuations were made from other large cities, and in all, 1,334,358 people were involved in the process. Even smaller, but specially vulnerable towns were catered for; Rosyth, close to the Forth Bridge and a large naval base, sent off two train-loads of children, by comparison with Glasgow's 322 and Liverpool's 382. As it happened, the alarm was premature: the months of the so-called 'phoney war' were beginning. But quite soon matters became real enough, as June 1940 brought first the evacuation of the British Expeditionary Force, plus many French troops, from Dunkirk, 319,056 in all. The brunt of this fell upon the Southern, but trains were supplied by the Great Western, LMS and LNER also, and brought to the Ashford yards or the nearest available sidings. In all 186 ten-coach trains were marshalled and used, including ambulance trains. Redhill, where westbound trains had to reverse direction in the north–south aligned station, was the centre of co-ordination and control. Soon afterwards, the blitz prompted a new rush of evacuees from London and large cities. Though the severest burdens fell on the Southern, all railways, under the control of the Executive, became accustomed to treating the exceptional as normal. They ensured that enormous sudden movements of people, baggage and war materials were accomplished with as much speed and as little disruption as possible, often by working greatly extended shifts and accepting conditions which in peacetime would have had the union convener hammering at the management's door.

Dangerous Conditions

Operating a railway in blackout conditions created new problems, as well as hazards for staff working on platforms and in the yards. A steam locomotive working hard at night with a heavy load was difficult to conceal – each time the fire door was opened, a glare of red light rose up. And most engines still had open cabs. Tarpaulins and blackout sheets were draped around, but the enginemen still had to be able to look out for signals and landmarks. Big stations had their glass roofs taken out, and trains came and went in twilight dimness. The needs of warfare meant curtailment of many services, and delays were accepted as part

BELOW Damaged beyond repair following a heavy bombing raid on the locomotive sheds at York, A4 'Pacific' *Sir Ralph Wedgwood* lies amid the wreckage. Before the LNER began re-naming A4s after its directors, this engine carried the name *Herring Gull*.

More than fifty women cleaners pose on and by a Lancashire & Yorkshire 'Atlantic' in this World War I view taken in 1917 at Horwich.

1406
CASHIRE & YORKSHIRE

of everyday life. Long-distance trains were often twice as long and heavy as they had been in peacetime, and a single locomotive hauled twenty or more carriages. Even large stations could not accommodate such trains and it was quite usual for a train to stop, allow passengers from the first ten or so coaches to get on and off, then draw forwards to let the rear passengers do likewise. Schedules reflected the heavy loads and the likelihood of delays – the racing days were over. Locomotives like the first LNER A4 *Silver Link* now had to show their prowess by load hauling rather than high speed with lightweight trains, but many fine performances were recorded. The writer O.S. Nock noted one such occasion with this engine in *Britain's Railways at War*. He wrote, 'On April 5, 1940, the first coach of the 1 p.m. [King's Cross–Newcastle express] was in the tunnel – in fact no fewer than *nine* coaches were beyond the platform end… it was not surprising that some difficulty was experienced in getting this vast train under way… The 2.6 miles to Finsbury Park, indeed, took 16 minutes. After that, however, some remarkably fine work was done covering the ensuing 103 miles (166km) to Grantham stop in 123 minutes, an average speed of 50.25 mph (81km/h) with a gross load of 840 tons (853 tonnes) behind the tender.' The packed twenty-five-coach train was well over three times the weight of the pre-war 'Silver Jubilee' express.

BELOW The black-out was a frequent cause of personal accidents, especially when very long trains stretched beyond platform limits. Warning notices were posted inside carriages.

Wagon Watching

One of the trickiest tasks for control centres was to monitor the use of wagons and ensure that they were in the right places at the right times. Apart from the railway companies' own wagon stocks, numbering around 652,000 in 1939, there were almost as many privately owned wagons, some 585,000. The vast majority of these were coal and mineral trucks, though some were tank cars or other kinds of specialised vehicle. While the railway-owned wagons were used as intensively as possible, to avoid empty running, the private wagons normally ran loaded one-way only, from supply point to destination, returning empty. A special national office was set up in March 1941, the Inter-Company Freight Rolling Stock Control, based at Amersham. Its function was to ensure that the entire national stock of wagons was deployed among the Big Four according to the operating needs of each day. The Control supervised the wagons as well as the tarpaulins and ropes needed to cover the loads in open trucks. Daily reports from all stations were collated and combined, under two main headings: 'coal and coke' and 'general traffic'. The Amersham office played a vital part in industry and the war effort, and it in turn had to work with a whole range of government and military departments. The Food Ministry was responsible for food supply and distribution. The Ministry of Supply was concerned with coal and iron ore, the War Office with military supply and the RAF Bomber and Fighter Commands for aviation fuel. The Amersham staff had to form joint committees with all these and many others, satisfy all demands and keep the traffic flowing. The end of 1941 showed their success: empty wagon miles had fallen compared with 1939, while loaded

OPPOSITE Edward Thompson's wartime mixed traffic design for the LNER. Class B1 4-6-0 No. 1281 stands at Grantham on 17 June 1941.

BELOW The great train shed at St Pancras took a direct hit during the Blitz of 1940 but its structure survived, relatively unscathed. Trains were running again in two days.

LEFT It is May 1940 and in a month or so the Battle of Britain will rage overhead. But at Smeeth, between Ashford and Folkestone, all is yet peace and the signalman has time to pose for his photograph.

wagon miles had increased by almost one-quarter. The heaviest and bulkiest single loads were two stators – the frames for giant generators – transported from Newcastle to Coleshill, near Birmingham, in May/June 1941. Thirteen feet 1.5 inches (354.4cm) wide, they were carried on girders supported by five special wagons, and the girders were mounted on rails so that they could be moved laterally by about one foot (27cm) in either direction to avoid obstacles. Travelling only on Sundays, and needing occupancy of both tracks, each stator took five weeks to make its journey.

A Concentrated Effort

The way in which all main lines focused on London was a grave disadvantage to military traffic. Much of this was routed north–south or west–east, and had no need to go anywhere near the capital, whose lines were heavily congested in any case. As a result, certain cross-country lines, lightly used in pre-war years, suddenly became of great strategic importance. One of these was the now-closed line from Didcot via Newbury to Winchester, where it met the London–Southampton main line. It formed a vital north–south link and was completely closed to all but military traffic for much of the war. Other rural byways, like the Meon Valley line linking Aldershot and Southampton, were unnaturally busy. The huge drive in 1942 to build airfields in eastern England brought a vast amount of construction traffic to east–west lines running into East Anglia from the Midlands. This affected the Midland and Great Northern Joint railway and the former Great Northern and Great Eastern lines in Lincolnshire, Norfolk and Suffolk. Between November 1942 and April 1943, 750,000 tons (762,000 tonnes) of rubble from blitzed London streets were shifted by train to form the foundations of runways and hangars, over lines more accustomed to seasonal trainloads of potatoes and holidaymakers. From July to September in 1943, 240,000 tons (243,840 tonnes) of tarmac and slag were transported from the Midlands to the new airfields. Once these were in use,

BELOW Again war seems far away as the former LB&SC Class D3 0-4-4-T No. 2363 reaches journey's end at New Romney with the 1.30 p.m. from Ashford, on 23 March 1940. The station name-board, just out of the picture, has not yet been removed.

LOCOMOTIVE DESIGNERS

ROBERT RIDDLES (1892–1983)

Riddles was Britain's last chief mechanical engineer to design and build steam engines, standing at the end of a long tradition that had begun with Hackworth in 1825. His career demonstrates the many changes in railway management during the twentieth century. In 1909 he joined the LNWR Crewe works as an apprentice. By 1920, after war service with the Royal Engineers, he was an assistant to the works manager. He played a leading part in the modernisation of workshop practice at both Crewe and Derby between 1923 and 1931. In 1933 he was appointed Locomotive Assistant to W.A. Stanier, the new CME of the London Midland & Scottish Railway, and two years later was promoted to Principal Assistant. In 1937 he was moved to Glasgow as Mechanical and Electrical Engineer for the LMS's Scottish division. With the outbreak of war in 1939 he was seconded to government service and became Deputy Director General, Royal Engineer Equipment. The LMS reclaimed him in 1943, first as Chief Stores Superintendent, and then as Vice-President, Engineering – a board role that made him senior to the chief mechanical engineer, H.G. Ivatt. When the railways were nationalised in 1948, he was a member of the controlling Executive, in charge of mechanical and electrical engineering. It was under Riddles' supervision and direction that the British Railways 'standard' classes were designed and built in the early 1950s.

Riddles was responsible for such successful designs as the wartime 'Austerity' 2-8-0 and 2-10-0 classes, and the British Railways 2-10-0 which succeeded them. But perhaps the most exciting point of his career was his close involvement in the design and introduction of the LMS 'Pacifics' of the 1930s. O.S. Nock has left a graphic picture of Riddles on a record-breaking 1936 non-stop London–Glasgow test run of No. 6201 *Princess Elizabeth*: 'Riddles stood behind the driver. He had a chart showing the speed required for timekeeping over every mile of the journey. The chart was displayed on a tray, which Riddles carried pedlar-fashion from his neck, and as the journey progressed the turning of a screw wound the graph from a roll at one side of the tray…' He was also one of the four men on the footplate in the celebrated test run of the 'Coronation Scot' on 29 June 1937 when the speed record of 114 mph (183.4km/h) was attained at a point perilously close to Crewe Station, with its many cross-overs. He wrote a lively account of the event later. On his appointment to the Railway Executive, Riddles was old enough to remember the difficulties of integration of old companies into the LMS, and, though his aim was always to introduce new types, he used tact and diplomacy in co-ordinating the functions of his many new subordinates and workshops. The inter-regional comparative tests of 1948 were really part of this exercise. Design of various elements of the new standard types was split among several depots, and was surprisingly successful. Riddles felt that electrification was the real future of the railways and that steam should last until that was accomplished. This was not to be how things turned out, however: his locomotives were to be retired long before their potential working lives were over. Riddles retired in 1953, just two years before the British Railways Modernisation Plan announced the phasing-out of steam traction in favour of diesel-powered engines. He died in 1983.

CARPETS

LEFT The free buffet for soldiers and sailors in transit was a feature of main stations in both World Wars. With patriotic symbols on display, women volunteers stand behind the counter at Paddington Station, London, during the First World War.

ABOVE LMS 2-6-0 No. 2971 waits for its train at Coventry station in 1940. Introduced in 1934, its domeless boiler shows Stanier's earlier practice on the LMS; it also has a narrow Fowler-type tender.

GWR·LMS·1923-1944·LNER·SR

21ST BIRTHDAY

ON this, the 21st anniversary of the formation of the four main-line railways, we send our congratulations to the Managers and Staff..
We are grateful to all railway servants, of every grade, for the way in which they have responded to the calls made upon them. They will certainly have the satisfaction of knowing, when the final triumph of our cause is achieved, that they have played a proud and praiseworthy part in the victory of the United Nations.

FIRST LORD OF THE ADMIRALTY

SECRETARY OF STATE FOR WAR

SECRETARY OF STATE FOR AIR

1ST JANUARY 1944

LEFT January 1944 – time for an encouraging message to the staff of the 'Big Four'.

railways conveyed the trainloads of fuel and bombs needed. To get a thousand-bomber raid off the ground, 28 trainloads of fuel-tank wagons, with a total of 2,600,000 gallons (11,585,600 litres) of fuel and eight 40-wagon trainloads of bombs were needed. In 1944 an even more concentrated effort was mounted in order to make 'Operation Overlord', the invasion of German-occupied Europe, possible. Inevitably this focused on the Southern network, where entire new holding yards were set up. In the two months between March and May 1944, 24,459 special trains were run to move troops, ammunition and equipment to prepared positions ready for the invasion. A peak was reached in the three weeks prior to 6 June 1944, when 9679 special trains were run. Among the many 'specials' were two military headquarters trains, for Generals Eisenhower, supreme allied commander, and Montgomery, commander in chief of the British land forces. First used in Britain, and later in Europe, they were code-named ALIVE and RAPIER respectively. The ALIVE, prepared by the GWR Swindon works, consisted of:

Two carriage vans for baggage and staff motorcars
Power van with boiler and generator
Corridor brake van
Corridor third, armour plated, for personnel
Restaurant car
Saloon or conference car
Two sleeping cars for officers
Corridor brake third
First-class sleeping car with saloon
Third-class sleeping car
Six vans for baggage and cars.

The rail network was far denser in the 1940s than it is today, making it easier for Control offices to choose between alternative routes for special services, for example between Perth and Aberdeen, or Swansea and Liverpool, or Leeds and Hull. However, there were a number of places where converging mainlines formed bottlenecks that not only limited the passage of trains but were also vulnerable to attack. At a number of these locations, new tracks were laid.

BELOW Victoria Station. London, during World War II. Heavy tarpaulins are placed to prevent glass dropping from the roofs in the event of an attack, and the giant plan shows routes to the nearest air raid shelters.

The double track between Cheltenham and Gloucester, a funnel for Midlands–South West and Wales traffic, was quadrupled in the winter of 1941. Similar exercises were carried out north of Carlisle, where a new bridge was built over the River Eden to improve access to Kingmoor Yard and locomotive sheds; and in South Wales between Newport and Severn Tunnel Junction. On the LNER, the partially quadrupled track between York and Northallerton was fully quadrupled. At hundreds of other locations, new crossing loops, sidings and sorting yards were built. To serve new factories like the vast munitions plant near Bridgend in South Wales, large new stations and yards were built, in that particular case involving 24 miles (38.6km) of railway lines and sidings and a four-platform station. By the end of the war, its staff of 37,000, working three shifts a day, needed 58 daily trains to bring them to and from the nearby towns.

New Designs

Such intensive use of the railways naturally caused a massive and consistent demand for motive power. Many engines that would otherwise have been scrapped were retained to work through the war. Although once again company workshops were used for many other purposes, from building tanks to rafts, aircraft parts and guns, intensive building continued, especially of the

BELOW It is August 1939 and the world is on the brink of war. Among the uncountable scenes of destruction will be this great arched roof over Cannon Street Station, London.

OPPOSITE, TOP War engine – thirteen 0-6-0 tanks of the US Army Transport Corps were acquired by the Southern Railway. In post-war British Railways livery, No. 30068 works in Southampton Docks.

LEFT The Southern Railway launched its light 'Pacifics' after the war had ended, but in austere times, they still had to be publicised as mixed traffic engines, though not at all suited to the British type of goods train. The 'Battle of Britain' and 'West Country' locomotives were identical.

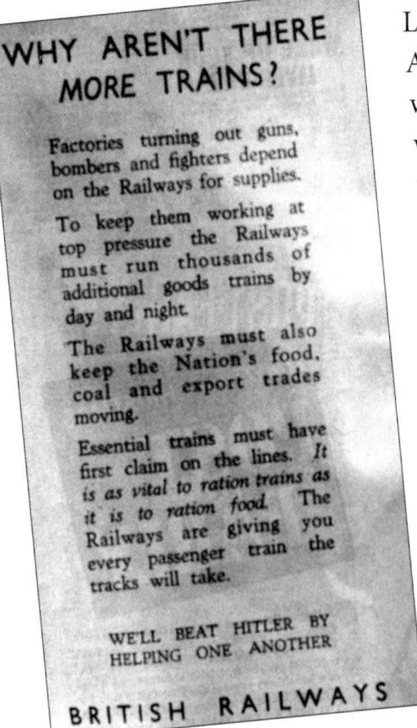

WHY AREN'T THERE MORE TRAINS?

Factories turning out guns, bombers and fighters depend on the Railways for supplies.

To keep them working at top pressure the Railways must run thousands of additional goods trains by day and night.

The Railways must also keep the Nation's food, coal and export trades moving.

Essential trains must have first claim on the lines. *It is as vital to ration trains as it is to ration food.* The Railways are giving you every passenger train the tracks will take.

WE'LL BEAT HITLER BY HELPING ONE ANOTHER

BRITISH RAILWAYS

TOP LEFT The railways ran a series of small ads in national newspapers in the hope of reminding the public that delays and congestion in passenger train services were an inevitable result of the war effort rather than of incompetent management.

OPPOSITE War damage at York Station. Platforms 1, 2 and 3 are piled with debris from the shattered roof following one of the Luftwaffe's 'Baedeker' raids on historic cities. As at other bombed stations, services were restored with remarkable speed.

LMS Class 5 4-6-0, the Class 8F 2-8-0 and the LNER V2 2-6-2. A new LNER mixed-traffic class, the two-cylinder B1 4-6-0, was introduced in 1942 and 442 were built. The LMS 2-8-0 was designated as a 'war engine' for overseas use and many were built for this purpose before the new 'Austerity' designs replaced it. Austerity was evident in other ways. The streamlined 'Coronation Pacifics' lost their outer casing. But home production of locomotives was not enough to satisfy the need. In late 1942, American-built 2-8-0s began to arrive and brought a distinctively transatlantic look with them. The former Great Western workshops at Ebbw Junction, near Newport, became the British headquarters of the United States Army Transportation Corps, and hundreds of locomotives were prepared here for work in North Africa and Europe. From early 1943, the Ministry of Supply was producing the 'war engines', a 2-8-0 and (from 1944) a 2-10-0 designed for speedy construction, with many welded parts, and with a light axle-weight, intended to operate over lightweight or temporary tracks. The 2-8-0 was based on the LMS 2-8-0 but, pared of all inessential details and with working parts made as accessible as possible, it had a somewhat gaunt look compared to its predecessor, and a rather American air. The 2-10-0 was the first British class of that configuration. Both it and the 2-8-0 were very successful designs, which also proved durable in the post-war years.

The most striking wartime designs emerged on the Southern Railway, where O.V.S. Bulleid had become chief mechanical engineer in 1937. First came the Q1 0-6-0 of 1941, intended for mixed-traffic work. Its resemblance to a gigantic clockwork toy caused Sir William Stanier to ask 'Where's the key?' Britain's most powerful 0-6-0, it proved a most useful engine. Unlike most tender engines, it could go as well in reverse as in forward gear. Running tender-first, with its designer sitting on the rear of the tender, it achieved a speed of 75 mph (120km/h). Despite its odd looks it was a conventional inside-cylinder locomotive, but the 'Pacific' that also first emerged in 1941 was far from being such. To avoid accusations of waste in constructing a new express passenger locomotive in the middle of a world war, it was officially classed as a mixed-traffic type. Bulleid had been Gresley's assistant on the LNER, but the new design owed little, beyond perhaps its three cylinders, to the Doncaster tradition. The boiler, with a pressure of 280 psi (19.76kg/cm^2), was hidden beneath a

LEFT This Helen McKie cartoon of June 1942 shows a porter in Southern Railway uniform looking as elegant as the WRAC officer whose luggage she is pushing.

ABOVE It was hard to conceal the activity of blast furnaces at night. . . But the message here is that the railways too worked unceasingly, twenty-four hours a day, to help towards ultimate victory. Artwork by Frank Henry Mason.

smooth-sided box-shaped casing; it had solid wheels resembling the American 'Boxpok' design and a new internal valve gear, chain driven and encased in a bath of lubricating oil. There were many other original features. This was the 'Merchant Navy' class, followed at the end of the war by the lighter-weight 'West Country' 'Pacifics'.

Thinking Ahead

In the summer of 1939, the companies and the government, both sides remembering the acrimony that followed the 1914–18 war, worked to produce a financial agreement between the railways – which, though under government control, remained joint-stock companies owned by their shareholders – and the Treasury. Mutual suspicion was not absent: there was a fear on the government side that the companies would make excessive profits from their unprecedented activity, and on the railway side that they would be the government's handmaid for an insufficient recompense. The original agreement was that the railways would be guaranteed a minimum annual payment of £40,000,000, shared out on a basis of their average revenues for the years 1935–37. Any excess up to £56,000,000 was to be shared between the

LEFT Unashamedly American, lacking only headlamp, bell and cowcatcher, and regarded with horror by purist British locomotive enthusiasts, the USATC 2-8-0 war engine of 1942 was an immensely useful 'go anywhere' locomotive. Hundreds passed through Britain, and many remained in service after the war.

companies and the Exchequer. Revenue beyond that figure went solely to the coffers of government. In 1940 this system was amended to provide a fixed annual sum of £43,000,000 to be shared among the companies, irrespective of the total revenue earned. Everything above that sum was retained by the government, which also assumed responsibility for fixing the level of fares and freight charges. *The Railway Gazette* commented on the terms in October 1941: 'At best it ensures a very meagre return upon the capital which has been invested in the undertakings and without which, allied to the patience which, perforce, has been exercised by a long-suffering body of stockholders, the railways of this country could not have reached their present high standard of efficiency, which has contributed so greatly to the successful prosecution of the war.' By 1943, the railway companies were retaining less than half of what they were earning. Between 1941 and 1944, the Big Four, plus the London Passenger Transport Board, earned a total of £350,075,000, with fares controlled by the government. They retained a little under half of this amount, at £173,876,000.

Inevitably, during six years of maximum strain and effort, the railways gradually became run-down and decrepit. Restaurant cars were taken off for the duration of the war, though as in 1914–18, free buffets for troops in transit were set up in all major stations. Sleeper services were much reduced and restricted to first-class only, provoking some resentment. Questions were asked in parliament about the 'Ghost Train', restricted to government officials and services' staff, which ran a nightly service each way between London Euston and Glasgow St Enoch. There were frequent official attempts to discourage travel by the general public: 'Is your journey really necessary?' asked disapproving posters. But, war or no war, people wanted to lead as much of a normal life as possible. With petrol tightly rationed, and the blacked-out roads dangerous to use, trains were the only feasible means of longer-distance travel, and this added to the general overcrowding. Travel by train in wartime was frequently an unpleasant experience, and the railways suffered in public perception for discomforts, difficulties and delays for which they were not directly responsible.

BELOW The first LMS woman guard in London, 22-year old Sally Knox, from Glasgow, gives the 'Right Away!' on a suburban service on 9 March 1940.

80104

11 • The Last Years of Steam

After achieving triumphs of speed and contributing admirably to the war effort, the steam locomotive enters decline in the second half of the twentieth century. Political changes bring an end to the Big Four, while economic and environmental concerns prompt the swift abandonment of steam traction.

LEFT Night train scene on the Gloucestershire & Warwickshire Railway: the tank engine and its one-coach train wait at the empty platform of a country station. Re-enacted for 'atmosphere', this was the actual state of things all too often in the last years of steam traction.

OPPOSITE Preserved British Railways standard 4MT 2-6-4T No. 80104 drains off the cylinder cocks as it begins to reverse into the station at Swanage. Its descent from the LMS 2-6-4 type is clear, but the design is more fluid – and it is a two-cylinder engine. Built in 1955, it is one of Britain's last production steam locomotives.

The postwar General Election of 1945 brought in a Labour government, part of the programme of which was to bring the country's railways under state ownership. The Transport Act of 1947 set up a central Railway Executive, and the nationalized system took effect from 1 January 1948. The Big Four companies were replaced by six regions: Eastern, London Midland, North Eastern, Western, Scottish and Southern.

Despite their imminent demise, the old companies did not wholly mark time. The Southern continued to expand the stud of 'Merchant Navy' Pacifics and their lighter companions, now also known as the 'Battle of Britain' class and named after RAF squadrons, rather than West Country towns. Bulleid also built an experimental locomotive which he hoped would rival the performance of the new diesel-electric engines being tested by the LMS; however, his bogie-mounted 'Leader' never got past the prototype stage. The LMS, at which H.G. Ivatt had succeeded Sir William Stanier, was rebuilding the 'Royal Scots' and their lighter counterparts, the 'Patriots', and greatly improving their performance; 'Black Fives', sometimes with experimental modifications such as Caprotti valve gear, continued to appear.

There were controversial developments on the LNER. During the war, Gresley's successor, Edward Thompson, had rebuilt the P2 2-8-2s as rather ungainly-looking 4-6-2s, classed A2/2, to a howl of protest from Gresley's admirers. Thompson, however, was a standardization man. He provided the LNER with a much-needed good 'utility' 4-6-0, the B1 class, using the 'Sandringham'-class boiler, the K2-class cylinders and other standard parts, so avoiding the costs of new patterns and tools. He went on to produce a new Pacific, the three-cylinder A2/1, in 1944. Further acrimony was kindled by his drastic rebuild of the very first Gresley Pacific, *Great Northern*. Rightly or wrongly, it was seen as a deliberate slur on his distinguished predecessor. Just before his retirement in 1946, Thompson brought out his most successful Pacific design, classed A2/3. Fifteen were built.

His successor, A.H. Peppercorn, produced a further two Pacific designs. The first was classed as A2 (former classification of the by now scrapped Raven Pacifics) and 64 were built, nearly

OPPOSITE A GWR 'King' 4-6-0 class on the 'Cornish Riviera Express' emerges at speed from the tunnel at Dawlish Warren, where the Exeter–Plymouth line hugs the coast. The '130' on the smoke-box door is the train's identifying number.

BELOW The LNER Pacifics were often seen on secondary services as dieselization progressed in the early 1960s. Edward Thompson's A2 60521 *Watling Street* is seen here on a parcels train.

all of them under the nationalized British Railways. His A1 followed in mid-1948, and 49 of these were built. The reclassification of LNER Pacifics in the 1940s can be confusing. The rebuilt *Great Northern* was reclassified first as A1 and later as A1/1. Including rebuilds, the LNER managed to produce six Pacific designs between 1943 and 1948, adding to the four bequeathed by Gresley, whose A1s became A10s.

HIGH ENGINEERING STANDARDS

The company that showed the least degree of innovation was the Great Western. 'Kings' and 'Castles' still ran its express services, but they were acquiring a rather old-fashioned air. The Churchward-Collett tradition remained very much in force. F.W. Hawksworth succeeded the latter in 1941 and produced the two-cylinder 'County' 4-6-0 in 1945, the ultimate descendant of the 'Saints'. Like the 'Merchant Navy' class, it was rated as a mixed-traffic engine, with 75in (190.5cm) coupled wheels, though the intention was for express passenger work. The GWR was still building 0-6-0 pannier tanks, little different from those of earlier generations, in 1948.

What Swindon did have, and other centres lacked (until the establishment of the Locomotive Testing Plant at Rugby

BELOW The rebuilt and preserved Southern Railway 'West Country' 4-6-2 No. 34039 *Boscastle* bears the nameplate of the 'Atlantic Coast Express', which it might well have hauled when in service. Here it is on an exhibition run.

in 1948), was a testing plant where the performance of an engine could be assessed in the workshops. GW engineering was still working to a higher standard of precision than any other company's. When it became the Western Region, though, it was a Darlington-trained mechanical engineer, Alfred Smeddle, who took over at Swindon; he completely regenerated the 'Kings' by fitting them with double blast-pipe chimneys and a number of other modifications which gave them a new lease of life as high-performance engines. Reciprocally, a Swindon man, K.J. Cook, went to Doncaster on Peppercorn's retirement and introduced a degree of fine tuning with optical instruments that markedly improved performance.

But the Railway Executive, whose locomotive specialist member was R.A. Riddles, a former senior LMS engineer, was pressing towards a single national standard of locomotive design, with a set of basic types which should fulfil all service needs. Particularly on the Southern, a

ABOVE Channel Island steamers at Weymouth berthed alongside the harbour station; a tank engine drew the train, at walking pace, along the pier to join the main line, where more substantial motive power was waiting to make the swift run to London.

OPPOSITE British Railways standard 'Britannia' class 4-6-2 No. 70032 *Tennyson* with an Eastern Region Norwich express. Fifty-five of this class were built between 1951 and 1953. Their impact on the London–Norwich service was dramatic, with a 20 per cent improvement on the previous best timings.

LEFT The ill-assorted protuberances on the boiler top, the high running plate, tall chimney and boxy tender combine to give the LMS Ivatt 2-6-0 a somewhat foreign look. American and Continental influences are visible in the design. All too often in the past, however, British designers had been too insular in their attitudes.

70032
TENNYSON

great deal of electrification had taken place using the third-rail system, and the heavily used Sheffield–Manchester freight route via the Woodhead Tunnel was being equipped with overhead electrification, completed in 1954. At this time, though, it was hardly questioned that steam should continue to be the principal source of motive power.

There were historic and economic reasons for this. Railways and the coal industry had been intimately linked for 150 years. The mines, also brought into public ownership in 1948, were the railways' biggest customer; the railways were the mines' third-largest customer, after the gas and electricity industries. In the immediate postwar years, as a peacetime economy struggled to become established, there was no capital available for large-scale conversion to electrified traction (something that had been contemplated for the East Coast main line since the 1930s). It was easiest to press on with coal-fired steam traction in its most efficient forms.

BELOW The most successful of all the BR standard types designed under the auspices of R.A. Riddles was the 9F 2-10-0. In this 1965 photograph, No. 92234 heads south over Rowington troughs on a Birmingham Washwood Heath–Eastleigh vacuum-brake fitted freight. To the right of the engine is the troughs' water tank.

ABOVE In line with official philosophy, the 'Britannias' were two-cylinder, simple-expansion engines, free of gadgetry and intended to be easy to drive and maintain, with the working parts as get-at-able as possible. No. 70013 *Oliver Cromwell* is shown on the traverser at Crewe works, in 1967, when it was the last steam engine to be repaired there for British Railways.

4-6-2 BRITANNIA BR 1951

Tractive effort: 32,000lb (14,512kg)
Axle load: 46,144lb (20.9 tonnes)
Cylinders: two 20x28in (508x711mm)
Driving wheels: 74in (188cm)
Heating surface: 1950sq ft (181.2m^2)
Superheater: 530.6sq ft (49.2m^2)
Steam pressure: 250psi (17.6kg/cm^2)
Grate area: 42sq ft (3.9m^2)
Fuel: Coal – 15,680lb (7.1 tonnes)
Water: 4200gall (5044 US) (19m^3)
Total weight: 210,560lb (95.5 tonnes)
Overall length: 36ft 6in (11.12m)

Many observers felt that such forms already existed among the more recent locomotive types inherited by British Railways. There were plenty to choose from. The rebuilt 'Merchant Navy' and 'West Country' Pacifics of the Southern were reliable and powerful, apart from a propensity to wheel-slipping. In the interregional locomotive tests of 1948, a 'West Country' put in some remarkable work on the Highland main line between Perth and Inverness. The Peppercorn A1 Pacifics scored very high for reliability, although they could be rough riders (in an average lifetime of about 15 years, the class members fitted with roller bearings ran over a million miles [1,609,300km] apiece). The LMS 'Black Five' was an established staple. The GW 'Kings', fitted with double-blast chimneys from 1953, excelled even on their previous merits. And in fact all these types, and very many more, survived in service until the end of the steam era (it was assumed that the useful life of a locomotive was anywhere from 30 to 50 years). Perhaps it was such variety, combined with the jealous, old-established company loyalties behind each, that made Riddles and his team opt for a completely new set.

New-Look Engines

The new engines, sharing a distinct family look, began to be unveiled from 1951 onwards, starting with a new Pacific, the 'Britannia', classed as 7MT and intended for fast freight as well as passenger duties. It was followed by two 4-6-0 mixed-traffic types, 5MT and 4MT (one with a lighter axle-loading than the other), and two tank types, a 2-6-4T classed as 4P and a 2-6-2T classed as 3P. Later, three types of 2-6-0 and a lightweight 2-6-2T were also added to the range. A lighter Pacific, the 6P 'Clan', was built in small numbers. The final product was a 9F 2-10-0 goods engine. Surprisingly perhaps, there was no 2-8-0 among the standard types: this wheel arrangement had been the principal mainline freight engine of all of the Big Four. But more than 700 of the 'Austerity' 2-8-0s were in service.

The BR 'standards' attracted mixed opinions on all counts. Their design was intended to make maintenance as straightforward as possible, and the high running-plates and exposed

ABOVE The finely drawn lines of the BR standard 2-6-4T No. 80098, picked out by the paint lining of tanks and bunker, are apparent in this view, as it approaches Swanwick station, at the Midland Railway Centre.

2-6-4T BRITISH RAILWAYS 1951

Tractive effort: 25,500lb (11,564kg)
Axle load: 43,792lb (19.8 tonnes)
Cylinders: two 18x28in (457x711mm)
Driving wheels: 68in (17.75cm)
Heating surface: 1366sq ft (126.9m^2)
Superheater: 245sq ft (22.7m^2)
Steam pressure: 225psi (15.8kg/cm^2)
Grate area: 26.7sq ft (2.5m^2)
Fuel: Coal – 7840lb (3.5 tonnes)
Water: 2000gall (2400 US) (9m^3)
Total weight: 194,880lb (88.4 tonnes)
Overall length: 38ft 6in (11.74m)

piping offended some purists. In service, they did not exceed the performance of comparable types, and the 'Britannias' were criticized by enginemen for hot, noisy cabs compared with the Gresley and Stanier Pacifics. The 'Clans' were undistinguished in performance. The 4-6-0 was hardly more than a revamp of the 'Black Five'. A single prototype of an express passenger type, rated 8P, No. 71000 *Duke of Gloucester*, was built. Unfortunately it proved to have serious problems with its boiler and consequently was little used. Rescued from scrap in 1973 and extensively rebuilt, its restored form suggests that the type could have been a true Super-Pacific.

The undoubted star of the BR range was the 2-10-0, which proved capable of very fast running – up to 90mph (145km/h) at least – and it was used on summer passenger trains on the hilly Somerset & Dorset line. In Britain, high speed had always been identified with big driving wheels, a legacy of the old nineteenth-century single-drivers; however, the 9F's coupled wheels were only 60in (152cm) in diameter. Some were built with a Crosti boiler, intended to preheat the water and so speed up steam production. It was suggested that they could be used to haul expresses on the Highland main line (train-heating equipment would have had to be installed), but this never happened.

Standardization was embarked upon in other ways too. New standard coaching stock was introduced from 1951, and the problem of standardizing and modernizing a vast range of different wagon types was beginning to be tackled.

From 1952 onwards, however, the shades began to close in on the steam-powered railway. In the postwar world of light industry and 'clean' power, the steam locomotive began to seem a

OPPOSITE The scene at Ropley shed on the Mid-Hants railway, in 1997, conveys something of the old-time steam depot, although the traditional architecture of sooty brick and arched doorways and windows is lacking. The engines on shed are appropriately of Southern Railway origin, although mostly in BR livery.

smoky relic of a bygone time. It was more and more difficult to find staff prepared to undertake the gruelling task of the fireman and the grubby job of the engine cleaner. A society increasingly sensitive to pollution looked askance at the pall of smoke that hung over any large locomotive depot. The national railway system, still employing nearly 600,000 people, was losing money. The 1947 Transport Act had envisaged a coordinated national policy for inland transport, with rail, canal and road all combined in an integrated system. Political changes in the 1950s, allowing 'free enterprise' on the roads, put a stop to that, and soon road haulage was carrying more freight than the railways. The need for economy and cost-saving resulted in lower standards of maintenance and cleanliness.

ABOVE In 1948, F.W. Hawksworth produced a new variant on the 0-6-0T theme for the Western Region of BR, in this powerful side-tank engine with outside cylinders and Walschaerts valve gear. No. 1501 of the class is seen here at Kidderminster on the Severn Valley Railway.

Effects of Modernization

In January 1955, a new modernization plan for the railways was unveiled by Sir Brian Robertson, chairman of the British Transport Commission. An investment of £1200 million was to be made in new facilities. 'Modernization' became the key word of railway managers, and modernization meant, above all, two things. One was a much reduced network. The other was the abandonment of steam traction. The plan noted that 'many factors combine to indicate that the end of the steam era is at hand. These include the growing shortage of large coal suitable for

locomotives; the insistent demand for a reduction in air pollution by locomotives and far greater cleanliness in trains and railway stations; and the need for better acceleration.'

2-8-0 8F LMS 1935

Tractive effort: 33,000lb (14,965kg)
Axle load: 34,720lb (15.75 tonnes)
Cylinders: two 18½x28in (470x711mm)
Driving wheels: 56½in (143.5cm)
Heating surface: 1463sq ft (136m^2)
Superheater: 235.25sq ft (21.8m^2)
Steam pressure: 225psi (15.8kg/cm^2)
Grate area: 28.7sq ft (2.6m^2)
Fuel: Coal – 20,160lb (9.1 tonnes)
Water: 4000gall (4804 US) (18m^3)
Total weight: 159,040lb (72.1 tonnes)
Overall length: 26ft (7.93m)

Riddles was not wedded to steam, but considered that, in the conditions of the time, it provided 'the most tractive effort per pound sterling'; he had been building new steam locomotives with the expectation of their lasting until large-scale electrification took place, a period of perhaps 20 years. The policy of general introduction of diesel-powered engines immediately altered that. This sentence of death for steam locomotives, even if set for the future, had an immediate impact. Care and maintenance could not be entirely stopped, as the traffic schedules had to be maintained, but a run-down in standards began and became progressively more noticeable. Research and development came to a halt. As more and more diesel multiple-unit

OPPOSITE Prestige trains of the 1950s: LNER class A4 4-6-2 No. 60033 *Seagull* leaves King's Cross and approaches Copenhagen Tunnel with the down 'Tees-Tyne Pullman', while A3 No. 60044 *Melton* backs towards the terminus to attach the 'Yorkshire Pullman', the nameplate already fitted above the smoke-box door.

BELOW An LMS 8F 2-8-0, No. 48399, approaches the highest station in England, Dent on the Settle–Carlisle line, with a lengthy mixed goods train.

trains and diesel-electric locomotives appeared, so the declining stock of steam engines became ever more grimy, decrepit and unreliable.

There were a few exceptions to this. Gresley's A4s, finally displaced from the East Coast main line, spent a few years from 1960 to 1964 hauling fast, lightweight Edinburgh–Aberdeen expresses, cherished by Haymarket Shed in Edinburgh just as when they had been the pride of British land transport.

THE END IN SIGHT

In the last years of steam, there were occasional moments when drivers, often with their own retirement at hand, and perhaps more aware than anyone of the approaching end of an era, allowed themselves a 'last fling' when the locomotive was up to it. On one of those occasions, in 1964, a rebuilt 'Merchant Navy', No. 35005, topped 100mph (161km/h) between Basingstoke and Winchester on the 21.20 Waterloo–Southampton. On a similar occasion, the double-chimneyed *King Richard III* reached 102mph (164km/h) while hauling

BELOW The Bulleid 'West Country' class Pacific 21C23, in original Southern malachite green paintwork.

ABOVE The preserved Southern U class 2-6-0 as British Railways No. 31625 at Ropley, on the Mid-Hants line. It was one of a 50-strong class of mixed-traffic engines, designed by Richard Maunsell and built in 1931.

the down 'Bristolian'. Such feats were often encouraged by amateur enthusiasts, keen to log a performance never likely to be repeated.

In 1962, the railways were finally relieved of their responsibility as a common carrier to accept any freight. The number of goods trains and depots fell drastically and with it the number of goods locomotives. The reduction in the steam stud was further accelerated from 1964 by the implementation of the 1963 Beeching Report, 'The Reshaping of British Railways'.

LEFT The non-stop King's Cross–Edinburgh 'Elizabethan' passes Welwyn Garden City in 1956, hauled by one of the last LNER A4 4-6-2s, No. 60007 *Sir Nigel Gresley*, named after its designer. Engines for the non-stop service were fitted with corridor tenders to allow a change of engine crew.

The consequent closure of many branch and secondary main lines – and of some main lines, such as Dumfries–Stranraer, that might have been regarded as of strategic importance – sent thousands of locomotives to the scrapyards. As electrification and dieselization proceeded, the territory occupied by steam locomotives grew smaller. A yellow stripe across the cabside number indicated 'Not to Work South of Crewe'. Passengers became familiar with long lines of condemned engines standing at former locomotive depots. Barry Island, in South Wales, was the largest but by no means the only engine-breaking yard.

In these latter years, only the 9F 2-10-0 remained in production. One of these, No. 92250, was the last steam engine to be built at Crewe Works, in 1958. The very last, No. 92220, was completed at Swindon in March 1960, and, uniquely in the class, given a name – *Evening Star*.

In 1952, British Railways had 19,276 route miles (31,021km), 8212 stations (passenger or goods) and 956 marshalling yards (mostly small). In 1968, the last year of steam traction, the route mileage of British Rail (renamed thus in 1964) was 12,447 (20,031km), the number of stations and depots was 3155 and the number of marshalling yards was 184. Over the same 16-year period, 20,000 steam locomotives, many of them with up to 30 years of potential active life ahead of them, were scrapped. As the last representatives of famous locomotive types were withdrawn, the call for preservation of at least one example was invariably made, although not always successfully.

BELOW The preserved A4 No. 60009 *Union of South Africa* is one of the members of the class fitted with a double chimney and blast pipe, which improved an already exceptional performance. The characteristic chime whistle of the A4 can be seen in front of the chimney.

45428

12 • Little Lines

At the end of the steam era, a wonderful, and sometimes weird, collection of minor lines could be found across the country, often preserving antique equipment. Run and lovingly maintained by dedicated enthusiasts, a surprising number of them still exist today, introducing a whole new generation to the joys of steam.

LEFT Engines often did seem to spend a certain amount of time standing around doing nothing...

OPPOSITE One of 15 preserved LMS 'Black Fives', No. 45248 brings a passenger train round a curve on the Keighley and Worth Valley Railway. This was by far the most widely distributed locomotive class. It was stationed throughtout the system, from Wick to Bournemouth, undertaking every kind of work from fast passenger trains to local goods services.

Some European countries developed a cross-country network of light railways, mostly narrow-gauge, complementary to both the mainline system and its secondary cross-country lines. This never happened in England or Scotland. The Light Railways Act of 1896 was designed to encourage the building of rural lines to an easier specification than main lines and did result in the building of numerous standard-gauge branches, although most of the lines built under the Act were short-lived. They were normally operated by the 'one engine in steam' principle, which meant that only one engine ran on the line, simplifying operations considerably. Goods and passengers were usually conveyed in one mixed train.

In the years before 1914, there emerged the distinctive figure of Colonel Holman Fred Stephens, a determined advocate of light railways, who assembled under his ownership or management an amazingly varied set of lines. The largest unit was the Kent & East Sussex

Railway, but he also had the East Kent, the Weston, Clevedon & Portishead, and the Shropshire & Montgomery railways. Stephens brought the latter back from the dead, but his lines rarely paid their way. They became famous for the antique and heterogeneous locomotives and rolling stock likely to be found on them, referred to by one writer as 'an animated railway museum'. Although the K&ESR was run with relatively up-to-date stock, at the Shropshire & Montgomery's little depot at Kinnerley Junction he had such items as a Bury engine, *Severn*, dating back to 1840, and a tiny 0-4-2T, *Gazelle*, coupled to a former horse-drawn tramcar of the London County Council. Also in use was the ex-LSWR Royal saloon of 1844, as the Colonel's inspection vehicle.

ABOVE Preserved ex-LMS 2-6-4T, British Railways No. 42085, running in sylvan surroundings on the Lakeside & Haverthwaite railway in Cumbria. This type of engine was built for heavy passenger suburban services, and there were several LMS classes from around 1930. This one, designed by C.E. Fairburn, was built in 1951.

LEFT Locomotive No. 4 of the Talyllyn Railway, the 0-4-2 saddle-tank *Edward Thomas*, nearing Rhydronen on the downhill run from Abergynolwyn to Towyn. Built originally for the closed Corris Railway, it was acquired by Talyllyn in 1951.

Colonel Stephens was also involved, at different times, with various narrow-gauge lines. Narrow-gauge lines were rare in England. The Light Railways Act had prompted the building of two, the 2ft 6in (76.2cm) gauge Leek & Manifold line in North Staffordshire, which ran between 1904 and 1934, and the 23½in (60cm) Lynton & Barnstaple, in North Devon (1898–1935). Among the few other English narrow-gauge lines were the Southwold Railway in East Anglia (3ft/91.4cm gauge), linking the town to the GER at Halesworth, and closing down in 1929; and the 23½in (60cm) Ashover Railway in Derbyshire, built as a stone carrier, but, under Colonel Stephens's aegis, also running passenger services from 1924 to 1931. The latter closed completely in 1950. The Ravenglass & Eskdale Railway was originally a narrow-gauge minerals-hauling line, which closed in 1913 and reopened in 1915, rebuilt to a miniature gauge for visitor traffic. Also on a miniature gauge (15in/38cm) is the Romney Hythe & Dymchurch

BELOW There is no mistaking a steam locomotive's departure. A whistle blows hoarsely. Steam hisses forth, smoke rises and a determined noise, slow at first but rapidly increasing in frequency, can be heard. On the Swanage Railway, BR standard 2-6-4T No. 80104 shows it all on leaving the terminus with an empty stock train for Norden.

ABOVE This scene of slate quarry working demonstrates what lines such as the Ffestiniog and Talyllyn were all about, in the days when Wales exported thousands of tons of quarried and cut slate. Most of it was sent down to the coast by narrow-gauge railway, for onward shipment by sea.

Railway in Kent. Although built in 1926 as its rich owners' toy and a tourist attraction rather than as a serious railway, it performed useful service in World War II as a military supply line, with a unique miniature armoured train.

Scotland had only one steam-worked narrow-gauge railway, the 2ft 6in (76.2cm) Campbeltown & Machrihanish, running across the southern tip of the Kintyre Peninsula. Built after the Light Railways Act of 1906, and far from any other railway line, it lasted until 1932.

Welsh Narrow Gauge

In Wales, numerous narrow-gauge railways were built. Some of them, indeed, pre-dated steam and the standard gauge, using pony haulage. The usual reason for choosing narrow gauge was difficult terrain, and the usual reason for building such a line was the transport of mineral or stone traffic. Such lines were especially numerous in the mountainous districts of Wales. East and west of the Snowdon massif, several railways clung to, and tunnelled through, the mountainsides, in order to serve the vast slate quarries which were at a peak of activity between 1860 and 1903.

The oldest of these was the Ffestiniog Railway, established in 1836, though it did not acquire steam engines until 1863. Many pundits

LEFT Peckett 0-4-2 side-tank engine Karen, photographed on the Welsh Highland Railway. It was built in 1942 to haul chrome ore at the Selukwe Park Light Railway in Rhodesia (now Zimbabwe). Brought back to Britain in 1976, it was restored by 1983.

prophesied that its 23½in (60cm) gauge was too narrow to support a steam locomotive. The Ffestiniog triumphantly proved them wrong with its first engine, *Little Wonder*, a highly original double-ended locomotive designed by Robert Fairlie, effectively two boilers mounted on a single frame, each resting on a four-wheel bogie driven by outside cylinders, with a central firebox and cab. The Ffestiniog ran passenger services from 1865 and was the first British line to use an eight-wheel bogie carriage. Its inland terminal, the slate-mining town of Blaenau Ffestiniog, was also later tapped by two long standard-gauge branches, one from the LNWR main line at Llandudno Junction, the other from the Cambrian's cross-country line at Bala. Hit by the decline in slate usage, the Depression and World War II, the Ffestiniog line closed for passengers in September 1939, and for goods traffic in 1946. Since 1955, happily, it has been revived and restored by voluntary work and contributions.

To the west, the North Wales Narrow Gauge (later the Welsh Highland) opened in 1877, from Dinas Junction on the LNWR's Caernarvon–Afon Wen line, to Quellyn Lake and later to Beddgelert. It went into receivership in 1878, and its

0-4-4-0 FAIRLIE FFESTINIOG RLY 1872

Tractive effort: 7500lb (3400kg)
Axle load: 5600lb (2.54 tonnes)
Cylinders: four 8½x14in (216x355mm)
Driving wheels: 32in (81.25cm)
Heating surface: 713sq ft (66.2m^2)
Superheater: n/a
Steam pressure: 140psi (9.9kg/cm^2)
Grate area: 11.2sq ft (1m^2)
Fuel: Coal – 11,200lb (5 tonnes)
Water: 720gall (864 US) (3.3m^3)
Total weight: 44,912lb (20.4 tonnes)
Overall length: 18ft 8in (5.69m)

BELOW A Fairlie 'double-engine' from the Ffestiniog Railway, 0-4-4-0 *Earl of Merioneth*, earlier called *Taliesin*, and built at the line's own works in 1885. Another of the three *Ffestiniog* Fairlies was built in 1979, based on patents going back to 1864 for a 'double-bogie articulated locomotive'.

ABOVE The miniature gauge Ravenglass & Eskdale Railway has turntables at its termini, in order to have its locomotives working forwards. At first glance, this looks like a scene from a railway of much greater gauge.

OPPOSITE The romance of steam, of the night train and of the night mail are all captured together as ex-LNER inside-cylinder B12 4-6-0 No. 61572 stands at the canopied platform of Loughborough Central in this atmospheric re-enactment staged in 1998.

existence always remained precarious. Nevertheless, it completed the line from Beddgelert to Porthmadog in 1923, connecting with the Ffestiniog and forming with it the longest narrow-gauge line in Britain, at 34 miles (55km). The two lines were worked as one, under the management of the ubiquitous Colonel Stephens, until the Welsh Highland's closure in 1937.

Further south, the Corris Railway, of 2ft 3in (68.6cm) gauge, ran into the hills from Machynlleth from 1859, using locomotives from 1878; it was later owned by the GWR and survived briefly into national ownership, being shut down in August 1948. Some of its equipment survives on the Talyllyn line. Another victim of hard times was the Welshpool & Llanfair Railway, of 2ft 6in (76.2cm) gauge, which was opened in 1903 and acquired by the Cambrian; its passenger traffic was terminated by the GWR in 1931, though it ran goods trains until 1956. It has been resuscitated as a tourist line. One narrow-gauge line that never quite closed is the Talyllyn, 2ft 3in (68.5cm), running down from Abergynolwyn to the coast, and the Cambrian line, at Towyn; through the work of many volunteers, it survived the death of its patriarchal owner, Sir Haydn Jones, in 1950 and successfully converted from slate to tourist traffic. The Talyllyn venture became a model for many other preservation attempts.

The same success was achieved by the picturesque Vale of Rheidol line, opened in 1902, from Aberystwyth to Devil's Bridge. Acquired in 1913 by the Cambrian, it was notable at the end of 1968 as the only section of British Railways still to be operated by steam locomotives (it was privatized in 1989). Of purely touristic intention was the highest railway in Great Britain, the 2ft 7½in (80cm) Snowdon Mountain Railway, from Llanberis to the summit at 3540ft (1079m), opened on 6 April 1896. Worked as a rack railway on the Swiss Abt system, its one and only accident was on the very first day, when engine No 1, *Ladas*, jumped the tracks and went over the precipice.

The narrow-gauge steam scene in Wales remains buoyant in the twenty-first century, with work well in progress to restore the Welsh Highland's line between Porthmadog, Beddgelert and Dinas.

ISLAND RAILWAYS

Apart from Anglesey, which has carried a mainline railway since 1850, the only off-shore islands to have been provided with railways are the Isle of Man and the Isle of Wight. Plans to lay public light railways on Lewis and Skye never got beyond the discussion stage, though short narrow-gauge industrial/military tracks were laid in Orkney and Shetland. A short modern miniature steam line runs on Mull. The Isle of Wight lines were laid to standard gauge, beginning with the Cowes & Newport Railway in July 1862. By 1875, the island's network was complete, and two lines – the Isle of Wight and the Isle of Wight Central – were amalgamated with the LSWR in 1922; the remaining line joined them in the Southern Railway the following year. The Manx lines were built to a 3ft (91.4cm) gauge, like Irish narrow-gauge lines. The first were built by the Isle of Man Railway Company from Douglas to Peel and Douglas to Port Erin in 1873 and 1874, respectively. The Manx Northern joined Ramsey to the Peel–Douglas line via the west side of the island. The Isle of Man Railway was the first in the country to standardize electric lighting in its (admittedly small) stock of carriages. Steam-operated lines survive on both islands, although the original networks are considerably reduced, especially on the Isle of Wight.

ABOVE For a time the only part of British Railways still wedded to steam, the Vale of Rheidol line is now privately owned. This forward shot of one of its side-tank locos shows how much overhang a narrow-gauge train can have.

PRESERVATION VENTURES

The departure of steam and the closures of lines resulted in many private and voluntary ventures in preservation. The first successful reopening of a closed standard-gauge line was in the Severn Valley in 1959. Local councils, tourist boards and railway enthusiasts sometimes worked in harmony to maintain or re-lay branches that run through attractive countryside and to preserve buildings and equipment of the steam era. Some steam depots, such as Didcot, Tyseley (Birmingham), Carnforth, Barrow Hill at Chesterfield (the last working roundhouse) and

Southall, were preserved. A number of industrial lines have also been preserved or restored, one of them running through a still-operative steelworks at Scunthorpe. Not all such ventures flourished, but over 130 steam lines, centres and museums still exist in Britain. Heritage railways are quite a substantial industry in their own right. Even in the era of Railtrack and its successor, seasonal steam trains still run on the West Highland line between Fort William and Mallaig.

Some of the scrap merchants obligingly held off demolition while enthusiasts tried to assemble funds to buy a particular engine. Of the once vast steam stud, only a few dozen still survive, but they cover a considerable range of years and types. Among the real veterans,

ABOVE The preserved LNER J39 0-6-0, in British Rail paintwork as No. 65894, re-enacts a typical steam freight working, on the North Yorkshire Moors Railway, in 1996. The class dates from 1926, and most of the locomotives were built at Darlington Works.

LEFT O.V.S. Bulleid's class Q1 0-6-0 of the Southern Railway carried the wartime 'Austerity' look almost to the point of self-parody. On a crisp February morning in 2000, the preserved No. 33001 heads the 9.15 a.m. to Kingscote on the Bluebell Railway.

ABOVE Steaming bravely into a new dawn – ex-British Railways 9F 2-10-0 takes the first train of the day, year and century out of Loughborough Central for Leicester, Great Central Railway, on 1 January 2000.

remarkably, they include *Rocket* and the even earlier colliery engine *Puffing Billy* (1813) at London's Science Museum; and the equally old *Wylam Dilly* in the Museum of Scotland, Edinburgh. Kent's first engine, *Invicta*, survives at Canterbury. Two Stockton & Darlington engines are preserved, *Locomotion* and *Derwent*. The Liverpool & Manchester's *Lion* of 1838 survives, as does Crewe's first engine, *Columbine*, and a Bury 0-4-0, nicknamed *Coppernob*, of the Furness Railway. The record-breakers *City of Truro* and *Mallard* can still be seen, at the Swindon and York railway museums respectively. Engines which caught the public's imagination were most likely to be chosen, and several 'Castles' and A4s were preserved. Many other types survive in unique examples. No broad-gauge engine has survived, though the GWR retained two until 1905. Battles to preserve historic types go back to the 1930s at least, when public outcry saved the Caledonian single No. 123, the LNWR 'Jumbo' *Hardwicke* and the GWR *City of Truro* from the indifference or even hostility of railway officials. The LNER was the only one of the Big Four to have any proper care for its own heritage.

At one time it might have been thought that the urge to preserve steam trains would not survive the generation which had grown up with them. But the popularity of steam lines and steam centres is as strong as ever. Many have plans for extension of their lines and services. Increasingly, the visitors who come have never known the days when the steam locomotive was the most visible, exciting and essential feature of railway life.

Glossary

ATC: Automatic train control system.

Abt system: A rack-and-pinion track with two adjacent toothed racks between the rails, the teeth placed in staggered positions; used on the Snowdon Mountain Railway.

Adhesion: The ability of a locomotive to pull without slipping on the rails.

Atlantic: A 4-4-2 engine, so called from the Atlantic Coast Line in the USA, which first built them.

Axle load: The weight placed on the track by a pair of wheels with an axle between them.

Ballast: The materials, usually stone chips, on which the railway track is laid.

Baltic: A 4-6-4 tank locomotive.

Banking: The use of one or more engines to help push a train up a gradient, or 'bank'.

Bogie: A wheeled undercarriage for an engine or railway vehicle, pivoted to allow it to turn independently.

Boiler: The long metal barrel, filled with tubes for water, steam and fire exhaust, in which steam is generated by means of the firebox situated at one end.

Boiler pressure: The maximum pressure – expressed in pounds per square inch (psi) or kilogram per square centimetre (kg/cm^2) – of steam within the boiler before the safety valve opens to release excessive pressure.

Caprotti valve gear: A valve gear driven by a rotating shaft rather than by rods and levers.

Carrying wheels: The non-coupled wheels of a locomotive.

Clerestory: A central raised section of carriage roof, often with ventilators and window lights let into the side panels.

Composite carriage: A coach incorporating more than one class of accommodation; or a combined passenger coach and guard's van.

Connecting rod: The rod joining the driving axle crank to the piston rod via the cross-head.

Consolidation: A 2-8-0 locomotive; the term is rarely used in Britain.

Coupled wheels: Engine wheels joined by coupling rods.

Crank: An arm attached to an axle or rotating spindle, with a rod attached at right angles to the crank axle.

Crossover: A piece of track enabling trains to move from one line on to a parallel line.

Cut-off: 1) A term used to express the amount of steam admitted to the cylinder, in relation to the position of the piston. 2) A section of line built to bypass a station or circuitous length of route.

Cylinder: The part of the engine where the drive is generated; the power of steam is converted into motion by pushing the piston.

Dome: A feature of most but not all locomotives, normally holding the steam collection pipe controlled by the regulator.

Double chimney: A locomotive chimney with two exhaust blast-pipes inside; the form most common being the Kylchap double-blast exhaust.

Double heading: The use of two engines to pull a train.

Down: The direction leading away from the major terminus of the line; hence down line, down train, etc.

Driving wheels: Engine wheels driven from the cylinders.

Facing points: Points which a train meets when travelling forwards.

Footplate: The cab floor on which the enginemen stand, linking engine and tender.

Frame: 1) The structure of a locomotive, resting on the axles, that supports the boiler. It may be inside the wheels or outside them, or, in the case of a double fame, between them. 2) An interlocking set of tracks and signals, controlled by levers.

Gauge: The width between the rails.

Injector: A device for forcing water from the tank into the boiler; it can be driven by live steam or by exhaust steam that has already passed through the cylinders.

Limited: Used of trains, it means an express with limited accommodation, which should be booked in advance.

Mikado: A 2-8-2 locomotive.

Mixed train: A train with both passenger and goods vehicles.

Mogul: A 2-6-0 locomotive.

Off: A signal is 'off' when it indicates a clear road.

On: A signal is 'on' when it indicates stop.

Pacific: A 4-6-2 locomotive.

Pilot engine: Usually the front and smaller engine of a double-headed train; but on some lines, eg the West Highland, the pilot was the second engine.

Points: The system of movable rails, controlled by a points lever, enabling tracks to merge with each other.

Pony wheels: The trailing wheels of certain locomotive types, eg Atlantics.

Power classification: A notation devised by the LMS and used also by British Railways, with numerals broadly grading the power of locomotives from 1 up to 10; and letters specifying type of traffic: P (passenger), F (freight), MT (mixed traffic).

Prairie: A 2-6-2 locomotive; the term is rarely used in Britain.

Pullman: A luxury carriage built for and leased by the Pullman Car Company.

Rake: A line of coaches coupled together.

Regulator: The device controlling the flow of steam from the boiler to the cylinders; one of the key driving instruments.

Reverser: The device that sets the valve gear for forward or reverse motion.

Route availability: A code used by the LNER and other lines, sometimes painted on engine cab sides. Consisting of the letters RA and a numeral, it indicated the range of lines an engine was allowed to run on.

Running powers: The permission, for an agreed fee, to run trains on a track belonging to another company.

Safety valve: An automatic valve which opens to release steam if the boiler pressure exceeds the boiler's maximum operating pressure.

Sandwich frame: A type of locomotive frame in which wood (first oak, later teak) was used, with thin metal plates on each side.

Sleeper: 1) The transverse wooden or concrete slab supporting the track. 2) A carriage fitted with sleeping compartments, or a train of such carriages.

Slip coach: A carriage which could be detached from the rear of a moving train and, controlled by a brakeman, be allowed to coast to a halt in the station.

Tank engine: A locomotive carrying its coal and water supply within its own frame: no tender.

Tractive effort: Usually expressed in pounds (or kilograms) as 'nominal tractive effort', it is worked out by a mathematical formula to establish the theoretical backward push exerted on the rail by the driving wheels with the locomotive in full gear and with maximum boiler pressure, assuming no friction anywhere other than between wheels and rail.

Trailing wheels: Wheels of a locomotive positioned to the rear of the coupled wheels.

Up: The direction leading towards the major terminus of the line; hence up line, up train, etc.

Valve gear: The arrangement of rods and cranks controlling admission of steam to the cylinders.

Wheel arrangement: A standard notation for describing steam locomotives, known as Whyte's after its deviser, in which the number of driving or coupled wheels is placed in the centre, and that of leading and trailing wheels before and after respectively. Thus an engine with no leading wheels, six coupled wheels and two trailing wheels is an 0-6-2. If a tank engine, it is an 0-6-2T.

SELECT BIBLIOGRAPHY

Ahrons, E L, *British Steam Locomotives, 1825–1925.* London, 1927

Burton, Anthony, and Scott-Morgan, John, *Britain's Light Railways.* Ashbourne, 1985

Clay, John F (ed), *Essays in Steam.* Shepperton, 1970

Cooper, B K, *Great Western Railway Handbook.* London, 1986

Ellis, C H, *British Railway History* (2 vols). London, 1954–59

Ellis, C H, *Some Classic Locomotives.* London, 1949

Ferneyhough, Frank, *The History of Railways in Britain.* London, 1975

Fryer, Charles, *Experiments with Steam.* Wellingborough, 1990

Grinling, C H, *The Great Northern Railway.* London, 1898

Lloyd, Roger, *Railwaymen's Gallery.* London, 1953

Nock, O S, *British Steam Locomotives at Work.* London, 1967

Nock, O S, *Steam Locomotive* (2nd ed). London, 1968

Nock, O S, *Rail, Steam and Speed.* London, 1970

Reed, Brian, *Modern Locomotive Classes.* London, 1945

Richard, J, and MacKenzie, J M, *The Railway Station: A Social History.* Oxford, 1986

Simmons, Jack, *The Railway in Town and Country, 1830–1914.* Newton Abbot, 2000

Tuplin, W A, *British Steam Since 1900.* Newton Abbot, 1969

Westwood, J, *Railways at War.* London, 1980

'Black 5' No. 45474 takes on water at Achnashellach.

TIME LINE OF THE BRITISH STEAM RAILWAY

1804
Richard Trevithick successfully demonstrates a steam railway engine, for the first time in the world, at Penydarren, Wales, 22 February.

1813
William Hedley builds *Puffing Billy* and *Wylam Dilly* as colliery locomotives.

1815
George Stephenson invents the blast system, driving exhaust steam from the cylinders through the boiler to the chimney.

1825
Opening of Stockton & Darlington Railway, 27 September.

George Stephenson builds *Locomotion,* the first engine with coupled wheels.

1829
George Stephenson constructs the *Rocket* 0-2-2 locomotive.

Rainhill locomotive trials are held, 6–14 October. *Rocket* is the winner.

1830
The *Planet* 2-2-0 locomotive type is introduced, among the first to have inside cylinders beneath the smokebox.

1833
First British bogie engines (0-2-4) run on the Dundee & Newtyle Railway.

1840
First locomotive roundhouse is built at Derby (Midland Railway).

1843
The Grand Junction locomotive works are transferred from Edge Hill, Liverpool, to Crewe.

Swindon Works (GWR) opens on 2 January. The LSWR begins to build its own engines at Nine Elms.

1845
Crewe Works produces its first locomotive, *Columbine.*

1846
Gauge Commission reports against extension of the broad gauge.

Swindon's first engine, *Great Western,* is built.

1850
The brick-arch firebox, to facilitate coal burning, is developed on the Midland Railway between 1850 and 1859.

1851
J E McConnell introduces his 2-2-2 class (LNWR), known as the 'Bloomers'.

Stratford Works, Eastern Counties Railway, builds its first engine.

1853
The Great Northern sets up its locomotive works at Doncaster.

Stephenson's 0-2-2 Northumbrian of 1830.

1856
John Ramsbottom (LNWR) introduces his 'foolproof' safety valve and the screw reverser.

The Caledonian Railway opens its works at St Rollox, Glasgow.

1859
The steam injector is developed by the French engineer Henri Giffard and is rapidly taken up in Britain.

1860
First water troughs installed, by John Ramsbottom, on the LNWR Chester & Holyhead line.

Between 1860 and 1863 Alfred Jules Belpaire, Belgian engineer, develops his flat-topped firebox, used by many British locomotive designers.

1863
Steam engines replace horses on the Festiniog Railway (opened 1836).

1864
John Fowler's 'Metropolitan' 4-4-0T is introduced for underground running.

Robert Fairlie patents his double-bogie articulated locomotive design.

1866
William Stroudley develops three sizes of locomotive-mounted snowplough (HR).

1869
Fairlie double-ended engine first used, on the Festiniog line.

1870
The first of Patrick Stirling's 8ft (243.8cm) bogie singles, 4-2-2, is built, for the GNR.

1871
The first inside-cylinder, inside-frame 4-4-0 express type is built by Thomas Wheatley for the NBR.

1874
F W Webb's 'Jumbo' class 2-4-0 is introduced (LNWR); the first is called *Precedent.*
James Stirling introduces steam reversing gear (GSWR).

1876
Crewe Works builds its 2,000th locomotive.
First British use of the Walschaerts valve gear, developed in Belgium by Egide Walschaerts in 1844, is on an 0-6-6-0 Fairlie locomotive of the East & West Junction Railway.

Ex-LMS 'Jinty' class 3F 0-6-0T, at the Midland Railway Centre.

1878
The GER introduces the first British outside-cylinder 2-6-0 Mogul engines.

Corris narrow-gauge railway (opened 1859) acquires locomotives.

1880
F W Webb's 'Cauliflower' 0-6-0 class is introduced (LNWR).

1885
William Stroudley introduces the *Gladstone* 0-4-2 class (LBSCR).

1886
The Barry Railway introduces the first British 0-8-0 type, with outside cylinders.

1887
Crewe Works builds its 3,000th locomotive.

1888
'Races' from London to Edinburgh reduce journey time to 7 hours 45 minutes.

1892
All remaining broad-gauge lines are narrowed to standard between March and May; last broad-gauge passenger trains run on 20 May.

1894
David Jones introduces the 'Big Goods', first 4-6-0 to run in Britain (HR).

1895
'Races' from London to Aberdeen this summer reduce journey times to a minimum 8 hours 32 minutes (East Coast) and 8 hours 38 minutes (West Coast) on 22 August.

1896
J G McIntosh introduces the big-boilered 4-4-0 *Dunalastair* class.

1898
H A Ivatt builds Britain's first Atlantic type 4-4-2, *Henry Oakley* (GNR).

1899
Wilson Worsdell builds the first express 4-6-0 engines to run in Britain (NER).

Dugald Drummond introduces the T9 class 4-4-0, nicknamed 'Greyhounds' (LSWR).

Sir John Aspinall introduces his 'Highflyer' inside-cylinder 4-4-2 type (L&YR).

1900
'Claud Hamilton' 4-4-0 class introduced on the GER.

Wainwright/Surtees 'D' class 4-4-0 introduced on the SE&C.

1901
H A Ivatt builds his first large-boilered Atlantic, No. 251 (GNR), also the 'Long Tom' 0-8-0 for coal trains.

1902
The Midland Railway builds its first three-cylinder compound 4-4-0 for express passenger work.

Stratford Works, GER, builds the 'Decapod' 0-10-0 tank.

LNWR 'Jumbo' 2-4-0 *Charles Dickens* completes 2,000,000 miles (3,218,600km) of running since 1882.

1903
G J Churchward builds the first British 2-8-0 goods types (GWR) and introduces the 'City' class 4-4-0.

LBSC class B4 4-4-0 No. 70 establishes a steam-power record for Victoria–Brighton, 48 minutes 41 seconds, 26 July.

1904
102.3mph (164.6km/h) is claimed for 4-4-0 *City of Truro* (GWR) on the 'Ocean Mail', between Plymouth and Bristol, 9 May.

George Whale introduces the *Precursor* class 4-4-0 (LNWR).

1905
Deeley introduces his modification of the Johnson-Smith compound 4-4-0 with MR No. 1000.

Steam running in the London Underground tunnels is phased out.

1906
J F McIntosh introduces the *Cardean* class express 4-6-0 (CR).

W P Reid introduces his Atlantic class express 4-4-2 (NBR).

1907
G J Churchward introduces the four-cylinder 'Star' and two-cylinder 'Saint' class 4-6-0 types (GWR).

R M Deeley's first 4-4-0 compounds appear on the Midland.

A record non-stop run for Wales is made between Cardiff and Fishguard (GWR), 120 miles (193km), on 15 August.

1908
Churchward builds Britain's first Pacific, *The Great Bear,* the GWR's only 4-6-2 (later converted to 4-6-0).

D Earle Marsh applies the Schmidt superheater to express engines: the I.3 4-4-2 tank.

1909
The MR begins to extend centralized traffic control throughout its sytem.

1911
D Earle Marsh's superheated Atlantics are introduced on the LBSCR.

Sir Vincent Raven's Z-class Atlantics are introduced on the NER.

C J Bowen-Cooke's superheated 'Prince of Wales' 4-6-0s are introduced on the LNWR.

Dugald Drummond's 'Paddlebox' express 4-6-0s are introduced on the LSWR.

J G Robinson introduces his 2-8-0 goods engine (GCR); this will be the standard ROD military engine of the First World War.

1913
Bowen-Cooke introduces the 'Claughton' class 4-6-0 (LNWR).

R H Whitelegg builds the first British 4-6-4 express tank engines (London Tilbury & Southend Railway).

J G Robinson's 'Director' class express 4-4-0s are introduced on the Great Central.
W P Reid's 'Glen' 4-4-0 class is introduced (NBR).

British companies own 22,267 locomotives, of which 10,600 are 0-6-0 or 0-6-0T.

1914
First locomotives to be built in Germany for British use: 10 Borsig 4-4-0s to R E L Maunsell's design for the SE&CR.

1922
The first Gresley Pacific, Class A1 *Great Northern,* is constructed by the Great Northern.

1923
The first GWR 'Castle' four-cylinder 4-6-0, *Caerphilly Castle,* is built at Swindon.

The total number of steam locomotives in service reaches 23,963.

1924
Gresley's three-cylinder K3 express freight 2-6-0 is introduced: heaviest eight-wheeler British locomotive.

1925
Gresley's 'Garratt' type 2-8-0+0-8-2 is introduced for banking duties in the Yorkshire coalfield.

Maunsell's two-cylinder 'King Arthur' express 4-6-0s are introduced on the Southern.

1926
Maunsell introduces the four-cylinder 'Lord Nelson' class express 4-6-0 on the Southern.

1927
C B Collett introduces the 'King' class 4-6-0, *King George V,* claimed as most powerful express locomotive in the country (GWR).

The LMS introduces the 'Royal Scot' class 4-6-0; also a 2-6-0+0-6-2 'Garratt' type for heavy freight.

First British use of blinkers on locomotives to lift smoke away from the boiler, on the SR.

1928
Gresley introduces the A3 'Super-Pacific' on the LNER; also the corridor tender to enable non-stop running from London to Edinburgh, longest in the world; the first run is on 1 May with the 10 a.m. 'Flying Scotsman', drawn by A1 Pacific *Flying Scotsman.*

1930
Maunsell's 'Schools' class three-cylinder 4-4-0 is introduced on the Southern.

Restored GWR 4-4-0 City of Truro at Swindon.

The 'Patriot' or 'Baby Scot' lighter version of the 'Royal Scot' 4-6-0 is introduced on the LMS.

Gresley's experimental high-pressure 4-6-2 No. 10000 is built as a one-off.

1931
Launceston Castle on the 'Cheltenham Flyer' makes world record start-to-stop journey speed, 79.5mph (128km/h) from Swindon to Paddington, 16 September.

1932
Tregenna Castle improves on the 1931 record with an average speed of 81.7mph (131.4km/h).

1933
William Stanier builds the first LMS Pacific, *The Princess Royal.*

1934
First scientifically confirmed speed of over 100mph (160.9km/h) by a steam locomotive is attained by A1 Pacific 4472 *Flying Scotsman* (LNER) on 30 November.

Stanier introduces the 'Black Five' 4-6-0 mixed-traffic locomotive (LMS), also the 'Jubilee' express 4-6-0.

Gresley introduces the first P2 class 2-8-2 express locomotive for the Edinburgh–Aberdeen route, *Cock o' the North;* class later rebuilt as A2/2 Pacifics (LNER).

1935
Gresley's A4 class streamlined Pacific is introduced (LNER); the first is 2509 *Silver Link.*

Stanier's 'Coronation' class streamlined Pacific is introduced (LMS); the 'turbomotive' 4-6-2 No. 6202 is built as a one-off.

A3 Pacific No. 2750 *Papyrus* attains 108mph (173.8km/h) on a test run, LNER, 5 March.

A4 Pacific *Silver Link* twice attains 112.5mph (181km/h) on a demonstration run, LNER, 27 September.

The LNER runs the 'Silver Jubilee' London–Newcastle 4-hour express from 27 September.

1936
Gresley's V2 class express freight 2-6-2 is introduced on the LNER.

Last double-frame engines are built, the 4-4-0 'Dukedogs' of the GWR.

1937
The LMS reduces minimum London–Glasgow journey time from 7½ hours to 6½ with the *Coronation Scot.*

LMS streamlined Pacific No. 6230 *Coronation* reaches 114mph (183.4km/h) approaching Crewe, 29 June.

Stanier Pacific 46257 City of Salford at speed with the 'Caledonian'.

1938
LNER class A4 Pacific *Mallard* establishes world speed record for steam locomotives of 126mph (202.8km/h), 3 July.

Stanier's 'Duchess' Pacific class is introduced.

1939
LMS Pacific No. 6234 *Duchess of Abercorn* produces highest recorded power output for a British steam locomotive: 3,300 indicated horsepower.

1941
The first Bulleid air-smoothed 'Merchant Navy' Pacific is introduced.

1942
O V S Bulleid introduces the Q1 class 0-6-0 (SR).

1943
Edward Thompson's LNER B1 class 4-6-0 is introduced.

Rebuilding of the LMS 'Royal Scot' 4-6-0s begins, with improved performance resulting.

The LNER P2 2-8-2s are rebuilt as A2/2 Pacifics.

1944
Thompson's A2/1 Pacifics are introduced (LNER).

1945
A H Peppercorn introduces his A1 Pacific (LNER).

O V S Bulleid introduces the 'West Country' and 'Battle of Britain' light Pacifics (SR).

1946
Edward Thompson's final Pacific design, class A2, is introduced (LNER); the first is announced as Doncaster Works' 2,000th locomotive.

1947
A H Peppercorn's A2 Pacific is introduced (LNER).

O V S Bulleid begins work on the 'Leader' bogie-driven general-purpose tank locomotive (later abandoned).

British companies own 19,843 locomotives; 7,240 are 0-6-0 or 0-6-0T; 279 are Pacifics.

1948
Peppercorn's A1 Pacific is introduced (LNE Region).

Opening of the steam locomotive testing plant at Rugby, 19 October.

Interregional locomotive trials are staged.

1951
BR Standard 'Britannia' 4-6-2 locomotive introduced; also the class 4 mixed-traffic 4-6-0.

1954
Transport Modernization Plan envisages phasing-out of steam traction.

The class 9F 2-10-0 freight locomotive is introduced.

1955
A top speed of 107mph (172.2km/h) is claimed for 'King' class 4-6-0 6015 *King Richard III* (Western Region) near Lavington, September.

1956
The Clean Air Act requires the minimizing of smoke emission from railway engines.

1957
City of Truro is restored to main-line running order and achieves 84mph (135km/h) on a 280-ton (284.5-tonne) special working.

1958
The last Atlantic 4-4-2 in regular service (ex-LBSC) is withdrawn.

Construction at Crewe of its last main-line steam locomotive for Britain, Class 9F 2-10-0 No. 92250, the 7,331st engine built there.

British Railways owns 16,108 steam locomotives.

1960
BR's last steam engine, 9F 2-10-0 No. 92220, built at Swindon, is named *Evening Star.*

1961
Last steam service on the Metropolitan Line of London Transport, 9 September.

1963
A4 Pacific No. 60007 *Sir Nigel Gresley* on a special train reaches 103mph (165.8km/h) at Essendine.

British Railways ownership of steam locomotives is down to 7,050.

1964
'Merchant Navy' Pacific No. 35005 reaches 100mph (160.9km/h) near Winchester on the 21.20 Waterloo–Bournemouth, April 28.

A3 Pacific No. 60106 *Flying Fox* reaches 100mph (160.9km/h) at Essendine on a Gresley Society special, 2 May.

1965
Last regular steam service from Paddington ends, 27 November, pulled by *Clun Castle.*

1966
Steam services discontinued between Euston, Liverpool and Manchester.

1968
From 8 August, steam traction is withdrawn from British Rail.

By December, British Rail has only three steam locomotives in operation, on the Vale of Rheidol narrow-gauge line in Wales.

INDEX

Locomotive names and numbers are listed under the company that built them and are denoted in italics. Page numbers in *italics* refer to picture captions.

Picture Credits

Amber Books Ltd: 135 (t)

Campbell McCutcheon: 150, 229

Chrysalis Images: 17 (b), 62 (b), 113 (b), 118 (t), 199 (t), 207 (b), 215 (t)

David Ross: 242, 243, 244, 248 (t), 249, 254 (b)

G.M. Kitchenside: 251 (t)

Institution of Mechanical Engineers: 85 (t), 147 (b), 149 (t), 155, 158, 184, 200, 201 (t), 224, 225 (t), 226-7, 229 (t), 230, 231, 234, 236-7, 240-1, 246, 275

Millbrook House Picture Library (RAILPHOTOS): 13, 14 (t), 19, 20 (b), 21, 22 (b), 23, 24, 25 (both), 26 (both), 28 (t), 30 (both), 31 (t), 32 (both), 33, 34 (both), 35, 36 (t), 38 (t), 39, 41, 43, 44 (t), 47, 48 (t), 49 (t), 51, 54, 55 (b), 56 (b), 59 (t), 60 (t), 61, 63 (t), 64 (t), 65, 67 (t), 68, 69 (t), 70 (t), 71, 72-73, 81, 108 (b), 112, 113 (t), 115, 117 (b), 122 (t), 124 (both), 126-127, 132, 134, 136 (b), 138, 198, 217 (b), 202-203, 238 (t), 239, 288, 292, 297 (t), 315

National Railway Museum (Science & Society Picture Library): 250, 255, 258, 259, 260 (t), 261, 262, 267, 268, 269, 270-1, 272 (b), 273, 276-7, 278 (b), 279, 281, 282 (b), 283, 284, 285 (b)

Patrick Kingston: 249

Robert D. Turner: 104 (t)

Steam Archive: 260 (b), 263 (b), 266 (t), 272 (t), 278 (t)

Stephenson Locomotive Society: 7 (t) (W.A. Camwell), 9 (t) (W.A. Camwell), (b), 10 (E.E. Smith), 11 (b) (R.F. Roberts), 84 (both), 86 (both), (87) (R.F. Roberts), 88 (t), (b) (R.F. Roberts), 89 (W.A. Camwell), 90-91, 92 (W.A. Camwell), 93 (t), (b) (W.A. Camwell), 94-5, 96 (both) (W.A. Camwell), 97 (W.A. Camwell), 98, 99 (W.A. Camwell), 100 (both), 102-3 (W.A. Camwell), 101 (t), 102-103, 104 (b), 105 (both), 139 (R.F. Roberts), 140 (W.A. Camwell), 141 (both), 143 (b) (R.F. Roberts), 144-5, 146, 147 (t) R.F. Roberts), 148 (b), (R.F. Roberts), 149 (b), 151 (t), (R.F. Roberts), (b), 152-3 (Eric Treacy), 154 (t) (R.F. Roberts), (b), 156 (R.F. Roberts), 157 (t), (b) (R.F. Roberts), 159, 160 (t), (b) (W.A. Camwell), 161 (R.F. Roberts), 162, 164, 165 (t), (b) (R.F. Roberts), 166 (t) (R.F. Roberts), (b), 167 (both) (R.F. Roberts), 169 (R.F. Roberts), 170 (W.A. Camwell), 171 (t), 172 (b) (R.F. Roberts), 173 (R.F. Roberts), 174-5 (Fox Talbot), 176 (both), 178 (t) (R.F. Roberts), (b), 182 (t), (b) (R.F. Roberts), 183, 185 (t), 187 (t) (A.G. Ellis), (b) (W.L. Good), 188, 189 (b) (R.F. Roberts), 192, 193 (t) (W.A. Camwell), (b), 194 (R.F. Roberts), 195 (t) (A.B. Crompton), (b) (R.F. Roberts), 197, 199 (b) (W.A. Camwell), 201 (b) (R.F. Roberts), 204 (t), 208-209, 210 (both), 211 (W.L. Good), 215 (b) (R.F. Roberts), 216 (t), (b) (R.F. Roberts), 217 (t) (R.F. Roberts), (b), 218 (R.F. Roberts), 219 (W.A. Camwell), 220 (both) (R.F. Roberts), 221 (P.S. Kendrick), 222, 223 (C.W. Reed), 225 (b), 232 (W.L. Good), 228, 232, 233 (t) (R.F. Roberts), 233 (b) (P. Tatlow), 235, 238 (b), 240 (t) (R.F. Roberts), 245 (both), 247 (both), 248 (b), 251 (b), 252 (both), 254 (t), 256 (R.F. Roberts), 257 (both), 264-265, 274 (both) (R.F. Roberts), 280 (t), (b) (R.F. Roberts), 282 (t), 283 (t), 285 (t)

The News, Portsmouth: 244

TRH Pictures: 12 (Alan Barnes), 14 (b), 15, 16 (Alan Barnes), 17 (t), 18 (Paul Chancellor), 20 (t), 22 (t), 28 (b), 29, 31 (b), 36 (b), 38 (b), 40 (Alan Barnes), 42, 44 (b), 46 (Alan Barnes), 48 (b), 49 (b), 50 (both), 52, 53, 55 (t), 56 (t), 57 (both), 58, 59 (both), 60 (both), 62 (t), 63 (b), 64 (b), 66, 67 (b), 69 (b), 70 (b), 74, 75, 76 (both), 77, 78 (Paul Chancellor), 79 (both), 80 (both), 82 (Ian Loasby), 83, 85, 101 (b), 106 (Alan Barnes), 107 (Alan Barnes), 108 (t) (Alan Barnes), 109, 110, 111, 114 (t) (Alan Barnes), 114 (b), 116 (Alan Barnes), 117 (t) (Ian Loasby), 118 (b), 119 (Alan Barnes), 120 (Alan Barnes), 121 (t), 121 (b) (Alan Barnes), 122 (b), 125, 129 (t), 129 (b) (Paul Chancellor), 130 (Ian Loasby), 131 (both), 133 (t), 133 (b) (Alan Barnes), 135 (b) (Alan Barnes), 136 (t), 137 (t) (Ian Loasby), 137 (b), 143 (t) (Ian Loasby), 148 (t), 163, 168, 171, 177 (Ian Loasby), 179 (b), 180-181 (Ian Loasby), 185 (b) (Ian Loasby), 190-191, 196 (Alan Barnes), 204 (b) (Ian Loasby), 205, 206 (H.J. Ashman), 207 (t), 214, 228, 263 (t), 286 (Alan Barnes), 287 (Paul Chancellor), 289 (t), 289 (b) (Ian Loasby), 290 (b), 291, 293, 294 (Ian Loasby), 295 (t) (Ian Loasby), 295 (b) (Paul Chancellor), 296, 297 (b) (Alan Barnes), 298 (t) (Alan Barnes), 298 (b), 299 (K. Keanes), 300 (John Smith), 301 (Ian Loasby), 302 (both), 303 (Alan Barnes), 304 (both), 305, 306, 307 (b) (Ian Loasby), 308 (both) (Alan Barnes), 309 (Ian Loasby), 311, 312, 313 (Ian Loasby), 314

Maps by: Peter Harper